Technologies for Sustainable Green Environment

NIPA® GENX ELECTRONIC RESOURCES & SOLUTIONS P. LTD.
New Delhi-110 034

Technologies for Sustainable Green Environment

by

V. Davamani

Ms.M. Dhivya.

V. Punnuswami

E. Parameswari

R. Sankaranarayanan

Horticultural College and Research Institute

Tamil Nadu Agricultural University

Periyakulam – 625 604,Tamil Nadu (India)

NIPA® GENX ELECTRONIC RESOURCES & SOLUTIONS P. LTD.

New Delhi-110 034

NIPA® GENX ELECTRONIC
RESOURCES & SOLUTIONS P. LTD.

101,103, Vikas Surya Plaza, CU Block
L.S.C. Market, Pitam Pura, New Delhi-110 034
Ph : +91 11 27341616, 27341717, 27341718
E-mail: newindiapublishingagency@gmail.com
web: www.nipabooks.com

For customer assistance, please contact
Phone: + 91-11-27 34 17 17
Fax: + 91-11- 27 34 16 16
E-Mail: feedbacks@nipabooks.com

ISBN: 978-93-58870-59-6

Composed and Designed by NIPA®.

TAMIL NADU AGRICULTURAL UNIVERSITY

Dr. P. MURGESA BOOPATHI
Vice-Chancellor

COIMBATORE-641003
TAMIL NADU
INDIA.

Date :- 8.11.2011

FOREWORD

Climate change is a natural part of the Earth's dynamic system. The impact of global climate change is one of the hottest issues of the 21st century. However, there is very strong evidence that human activity, particularly the emission of greenhouse gases, is increasing the rate and degree of change. Climate change is already happening and the effects are easily observed and measured. In some cropping areas of Europe, average temperatures have increased by more then 1°C since 1988. In addition to simple temperature rises, there have been other observed changes such as decreases in snow cover, glacier melt, reductions in sea ice and clear changes in the timing of flowering and fruiting in plants. Consequently, it is necessary to change our existence to rely on green resources as "Go green and Live green" to shrink the green house gas emissions.

Green is the colour of the nature. It denots and symbolizes the preservation and conversation of natural resources which includes the Panchtatvas of universe (Soil, Water, Energy and Air). We thank for the sacrament and the divine inspiration of Mother Earth. Earth is the only Planet in the universe which has life including Biodiversity and Homo sapiens. It is our moral duty to loveable because it contributes to human society in more ways than we could even imagine. Nature has its own colours which symbolizes the greatness of the universe. When we Go Green we use only green house products that are healthy for the environment and include no toxins, recycle to help save and fills, and do everything possible to live healthy and reduce the impact on our earth. By living green and going green can reduce any negative impact on the planet in all possible ways. Many green products are packeged in recycled packaging, are biodegradable, and contain no phosphates, chlorine, artifical fragrances, or artificial colours. The main goal of green cleaning is to use eco-friendly cleaning solutions, recycle, using organic when possible, and promote methods that keep our environment healthy. Everyone should live in an eco friendly home. Many people are also finding that green building also reduces the impact on the environment and many businesses are now going green to reduce the impact on our earth. We ought to aware our message in conserving the beautiful Green Nature.

I congratulate the authours of this valuable publication entitled 'Technologies for Sustainable Green Environment and I sure, this will be incredibly handy for the scientists, teachers, students and everyone in the dwelling motherland. Let us raise Nature and feel its divinity.

(P. MURUGESA BOOPATHI) 8/11/11

PREFACE

We all hear a great deal these days about climate change and its potential problems. As long as we humans have existed on Earth, we have affected the environment around us. The more we produce and consume, the more we affect the environment around us. During the last 50 years, for the first time in history we have seen clear signs that human influence affects the environment of the entire planet; we are creating environmental problems that are not only *local but also global*. In the past, the major need of people in this world was arable land. Man did not have to think about animate things. However, now the adverse effects on environment through over-population and the development of various chemical elements in the atmosphere have led to irregular rainfall and global warming. One of these global environmental problems is the risk of *man-made climate change*, also known as *global warming*.

This global warming has brought changes in climate, including making perennial snow mountains melt, thereby adversely affecting not only human beings but also other living species. This dangerous situation is being taken very seriously by the world. Living beings and plant life on this planet also undergo change accordingly. Man's physical structure too changes from generation to generation along with the change in climatic conditions.

Because of the growth in the population, a large number of trees are cut for fuel, and to reclaim land for agricultural cultivation. This is not simply the destruction of trees but it also means harming what belongs to the earth. Similarly, the continuing decline in forests in many parts of the world, is adversely affecting the already changing global climate, thus upsetting the lives, not only of mankind, but also of all living beings.

There's a need for mitigating green house gas emissions through green energy, sustainable landscapes and gardens that seamlessly promote greenery and integrate the built environment with the natural. It makes sense and cents to apply conservation principles to landscape design whenever possible. Designing for outdoor living can spur inspiration and generate alternative ideas for functional outdoor spaces on home or commercial sites. And, people who work with greenery, landscape and urban trees have heard that can greatly reduce these problems by promoting greenery.

Similarly, the harmful effect on the atmosphere brought about by chemical emissions in industrialized countries is a very dangerous sign. Although this is a new thing for us, the world is paying a lot of attention to this problem. It is the responsibility of us, who speak of the welfare of all sentient beings, to contribute towards this. Since we have a responsibility in this matter, to work for the protection of the environment and to see that the present and future generations of mankind can make use of refreshing shade and fruits of trees.

- Authors

CONTENTS

Chapter–1

Green Energy

Energy is a measure of work done. Work done is karma. Good work done is good karma. It is green energy. Free-Energy is beyond karma and is discussed in the Vedas

Green Energy – An Overview

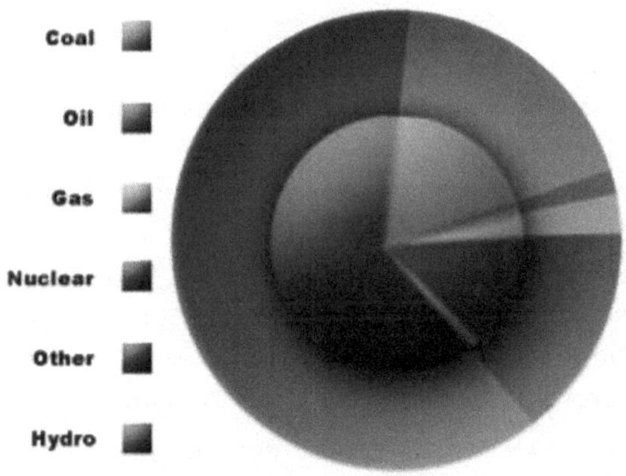

Green energy can be classified as any form of energy resource that results in zero greenhouse gas emissions and zero toxic byproducts. These constitute the alternate source of energy such as Solar, Bio, Hydrogen, Wind, Water etc. Renewable Energy is energy that is not depleted or expended. Previously the pressure to reduce CO_2 emissions dictated the energy sourcing. With recent findings from experimental evidence, global warming may not be attributable to CO_2 emissions in relation to other over-weighing causes. However the pressures to develop renewable sources continue since the cost of Oil is increasing in many countries. It is desirable and a necessity to develop renewable non-toxic energy resources. The global economy and welfare of all earth depends on it even if CO_2 is not the cause of global warming (GW). There are some factors not in the control of even the most technologically advanced society. These are solar activity such as sun spots which have huge and tremendous influence on the Earth's climate. However we should strive not to cause any undue imbalances in the proportion matter and composition of Earth's atmosphere. Although CO_2 is a small contributor to GW in comparison to H_2O, we still have responsibility to maintain the right balance of the gases in the atmosphere by not causing undue changes to the Carbon, Nitrogen and Oxygen cycles! We are far way off from a Oil-free technology. Most transportation is still petrol driven.

Electricity is a form of energy that is in use for both household and industrial purposes. However as such it does not entirely replace the use of fossil fuel in other forms of energy generation. The first law of Thermodynamics states energy can neither be created nor destroyed; Second: universal entropy never decreases; Third: absolute zero is unattainable. The implication of the first law is that Universal Energy is an absolute constant. However energy is expended when ever any work is done. This as experienced. However in reality one form of energy is transformed into another form. Still certain processes are irreversible. Entropy is a measure of the disorderliness. The quality of the energy is degraded when the usable form of energy becomes less available. When balancing energies involved in chemical reactions, the reversible reactions do not create entropy. Irreversible reactions do create entropy. Endothermic reactions extract heat energy from the surrounding and utilize to produce the end-product. Exothermic reactions on the other hand release energy in the form of heat which is dissipated (wasted and the entropy increases). To improve efficiency one must optimize the reaction in such a way that energy lost as heat is at a minimum.

'*Renewable energy*' is any energy that does not expend or deplete the available resource. In a thermodynamic open system an unlimited supply of energy from the environment feeds the system! Solar and wind energy are continuously pouring in! Even with small percentage conversion efficiencies, it has become worthwhile to tap into it. In that sense solar, wind, and water would classify as renewable resource since the depletion of these resources is not measurable within any measurable frame of reference. However over the last few centuries the world has seen measurable climatic changes to make even these resources less available for work. We see rapid increase in entropy of the planet earth as a unit of energy subset within the solar system.

There are some myths and misconceptions regarding concepts such as over-unity, perpetual machines and free-energy. Due to the very nature of this physical universe, it is not possible to do any work without a percentage energy wasted and dissipated as heat! However in a open system it is possible to achieve perpetual motion (apparently) by the clever use of the available natural energy! More of this in vacuum energy page... Even without over-unity we can achieve great energy sufficiency by continuing to develop renewable energy technology. We have long way to go. So far our achievements are only a scratch on the surface of a large body of knowledge!

The other resources which yield enormous energy in relation the amount of resource used is the nuclear fission energy as is the case in using ^{235}U. However it is to be remembered that the isotope needed is distributed on the planet as a limited resource and in that sense cannot be really considered as renewable. Besides enormous energy is spent in the extraction and concentration of the isotopes. The disposal of the radioactive waste products makes it non-green and a major problem requiring expenditure of energy. Hydrogen since water is available in abundance in the oceans of this planet. Bio-energy is also from limited resources of the world, however since only by-products from other productions are used here, it can be classified as renewable.

The main form of energy in present day use is from crude oil and coal. Both these are indeed in limited supply and therefore are non-renewable. The earth took several million years to convert plant and animal remains into what is referred to as fossil fuel. Our in-exhaustible demand for fuel for running our industries, motor vehicles, aircrafts have caused a serious shortage in the availability of this form of fuel. Hence the cost of travel, goods etc have sky rocketed. The immediate necessity to find alternate forms of energy to maintain life on earth means the need for serious focus on developing the alternate technologies.

Many countries, especially countries like UK, Holland, Denmark etc are already maximizing electricity generation through renewable sources such as wind, tidal and solar. Countries with abundant availability of coal and natural gas continue to depend on these for power generation.

'If I saw further than others, it is because I was standing on the shoulders of giants'

Isaac Newton

1.1. SOLAR ENERGY

Solar Energy is so fundamental to the creation and sustenance of life that there simply would be no life without the daily flows of the sun to the earth. Without solar energy the Earth's temperature would drop precipitously, becoming so cold and dark that the conditions that nourish life and humanity would be absent. It was been estimated that 1,000 times more energy reaches the earth's surface from the sun every single year than could be produced by burning all the fossil fuels mined and extracted during that same year

There are two different main technology streams that have been developed to trap solar energy. One is called solar thermal, which uses reflectors and piped water to collect the heat energy. The other is using materials that show photo-electric properties such as silicon and other semiconductors which absorb solar energy as light and generate electricity. These are called photovoltaic and photo-electrochemical devices The technology to harness this energy in a form that can be adapted for the current day requirements will require further development before it becomes cost effective. The current day installation of the solar panels for buildings has an average life time of 25 years. So it can be cost effective in the regions of regular and abundant sunshine to have roof top installation of solar panels. As it stands there are relatively cheap solar panels that can produce electricity for limited and special requirements. It is not uncommon to see the Solar panel decorated homes with part dependence on solar power for heating and lighting. These energy efficient homes are possible only in the developed countries where sufficient affordability is there for the initial cost of installation. However with greater public awareness and participation this can in fact be made more cost effective. In places of abundant Sunlight even simple traps such as solar light inlets and wind operated ventilators reduce the heating consumption from regular power supplies. These being cost effective, are increasingly used in modern buildings.

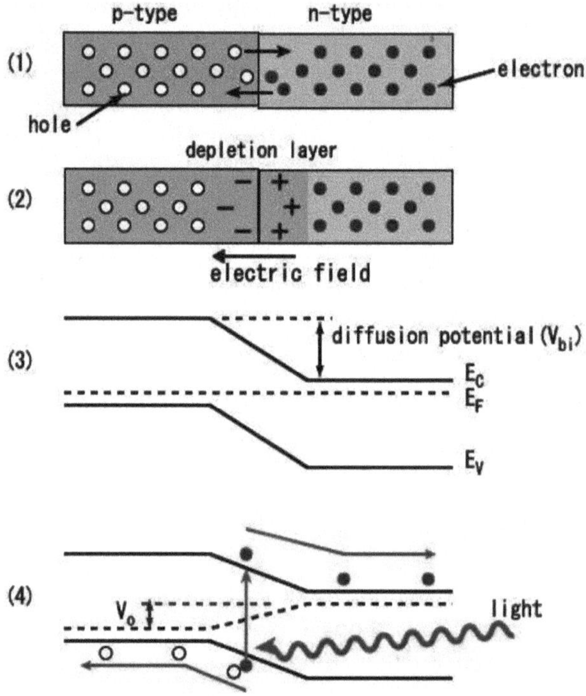

In general the panels convert the light to electricity by a simple mechanism of electron excitation by the absorbed photon. The overall mechanism is as illustrated generation of free conduction electron at p-n junction, i.e. at the junction of p-type and n-type semiconductor. A semiconductor such as Si having a band-gap which corresponds to the available energy level of the visible light spectrum can be used effectively. It would be most efficient to use single crystal Si. However it is more cost effective to use polycrystalline Si which are cheaper to manufacture. At the p-n junction due charge migration i.e., electrons from n migrate to fill the holes on the p side of the junction. Because of this a region of charge depletion is created at the junction. This causes shift in energy levels causing an overall effect called schottky barrier. The shift in the energy of the top of the valence band and the bottom of the conduction band due to p and n type impurities is called the fermi level. This is seen to be approximately at the middle of the bang-gap in the middle of the depletion region. Electron excitation from the fermi level to the conduction band happens at this junction. These electrons result in the observed photovoltaic current.

Although solar powered cars have been regularly showcased, for it to be practicable, the energy efficiency of the panels have to be much more to reduce cost and surface area outlay. The current day reported efficiency of photovoltaic panels does not warrant its use to totally power motor vehicles. However modern day innovators have not lost the enthusiasm to try the panels for not just road travel, but also for air travel. Panels on extended wings of airplane have been showcased for fuel efficiency and improvement in reduction of emissions. The most effective use of solar panels is on artificial satellites for powering sub-orbital flight.

India's current per capita energy consumption is among the lowest in the world. Its current generation capacity is 147 gigawatt. Based on growth estimates, India will need to add 280 GW by 2022. In some states, the supply shortage is over 20 percent. Based on these statistics, conventional energy resources will not be able to meet the demand and so alternate energy sources are needed. India is blessed with high solar insulation, over 300 clear, sunny days. We need to make the most of this opportunity. Our 2022 energy require-ments can be met by utilizing just 1 percent of the incident solar radiation. The Government will have to play its role in making India a leader in solar energy development at afford-able prices.

The major challenges with current solar technology are the poor efficiency of solar cells and their high manufacturing costs. To achieve widespread solar power generation in India, there is a need to (a) focus on both photovoltaic and solar thermal technologies; (b) innovate in three domains – effectively capturing sun's energy, effi-ciently converting it into useful forms, and economically storing it.

Technologists can focus on at least three areas of innovation—novel inexpensive mate-rials (beyond silicon), efficient energy con-version schemes, and improved storage mechanisms. Recent developments in nan-otechnology have the potential to enhance conversion efficiencies—use of novel mate-rials like nanocrystals that reduce heat loss or one-dimensional nanostructures like nanorods that improve charge transport. Pathways to improve storage include mimicking photosynthesis, using sunlight to power the hydrolysis of water and generating hydrogen fuel, using fuel cells, and phase change materials.

In order to meet the energy requirements, it is now mandatory to start using renewable resources. The exist-ing cost and possible electrical efficiency is still a challenge. Solar cells is a growing field for active research and must be grabbed by technologists, scientists, or academicians in India in near future.

Cost-effective photovoltaic (PV) technologies are the key for large-scale deployment of solar cells capable of produc-ing clean energy. Although conventional planar crystalline PV cells can provide good efficiencies, they are cost inten-sive. Solution to this problem can be addressed using a low-cost photostable material, namely TiO2 with the help of band structure engineering in order to increase the spec-tral absorption.

The Government of India already has a range of policies targeting solar energy: R&D on solar technologies; support for utilization of various kinds of solar-PV and solar-thermal systems for rural and urban applications; and feed-in tariffs for grid-interactive solar power gen-eration. While these programs have led to substantial progress in the demonstration and deployment of solar systems in India, we still have a long way to go. Just to take an example, worldwide solar-PV capacity was estimated to be more than 16,000 megawatts (MW) of which about 13,000 MW is grid-connected. In comparison, India's solar-PV capacity was estimated to be about 112 MW of which only about 2 MW is grid-connected. Thus, the enormous poten-tial of solar energy in the country, while alluring, remains relatively unrealized.

The Captive Solar Industry

It is a well known fact that India's electricity generation is insufficient relative to the demand the country has. In 2009-10, India's electricity deficit was approximately 10% (84 TWh) and the corresponding peak load deficit is 12.7% (over 15 GW). India's frequent electricity shortages are estimated to have cost the Indian economy 6% of gross domestic product (GDP) in financial year 2007–2008. To power the economic growth currently being targeted, it is estimated that India will need more than double its installed generating capacity to over 300 GW by 2017.

Another report states that there is an approximately 7% decrease in the turnovers of Indian companies due to power cuts. As a consequence, many factories, businesses, and private customers have set up their own power generation capacities in the form of captive power plants or diesel generators in order to ensure their power supply. This provides an attractive opportunity for renewable energy solutions; they compete not with power produced relatively cheaply by large coal plants but with much more expensive diesel back-up generators.

The reason why they compete more effectively with diesel generators is that while the cost of grid based power is in the range of Rs 4-5 per kWh, the cost of diesel based power generation is about Rs. 12 per kWh. With the levelized cost of electricity production from small scale, captive solar PV being about Rs 10 per kWh (including batteries, and after subsidies and incentives have been factored in, and including cost of capital in the calculations), it is easy to see why solar PV competes well against diesel but not against grid power.

Solar Power Vs Diesel Generator

1. Cost

People generally prefer diesel generators over solar powered ones due to the initial cost of installation. But if one can sit and think about the future expenses that would be in store, the individual would, without doubt, prefer solar generators. Diesel generators would need a constant supply of fuel – this would cause the investment to pay back itself, owing to the ever-increasing price of fuel. Add to that the amount of time each day or week spent making sure the generator does not run out of fuel, and additional savings can be realized

2. Pollution

The solar generator not only conserves power, but also reduces pollution. The diesel generator would produce continuous noise, whereas the solar generator doesn't.

3. Efficiency

When using a diesel generator, the device would go on and on, not considering the amount of power consumed. This can be avoided on a solar powered generator. And all you can do at that time is sit and look at all the energy being wasted.

The only drawback with the solar powered generator would be the amount of sunlight the locality receives. Though the system would run on charged batteries, once the sunny season sets away, there are chances of the batteries going dead.

4. Reliability

In warm/hot countries, solar generators are more reliable. But in countries where there is less sunshine and more rains and winds, solar energy doesn't come in handy. However, in Germany, solar energy is used at a much higher level than in North America. Hence, reliability is not an issue when it comes to solar powered gensets. Diesel generators, on the other hand, do not have this issue. But if there is a storm or any such disaster, the generators become useless. Thus, when looking at the investment point of view, solar generators win against the diesel generators.

Types of Solar Cells

Solar Cells are broadly classified into three types, as shown below:

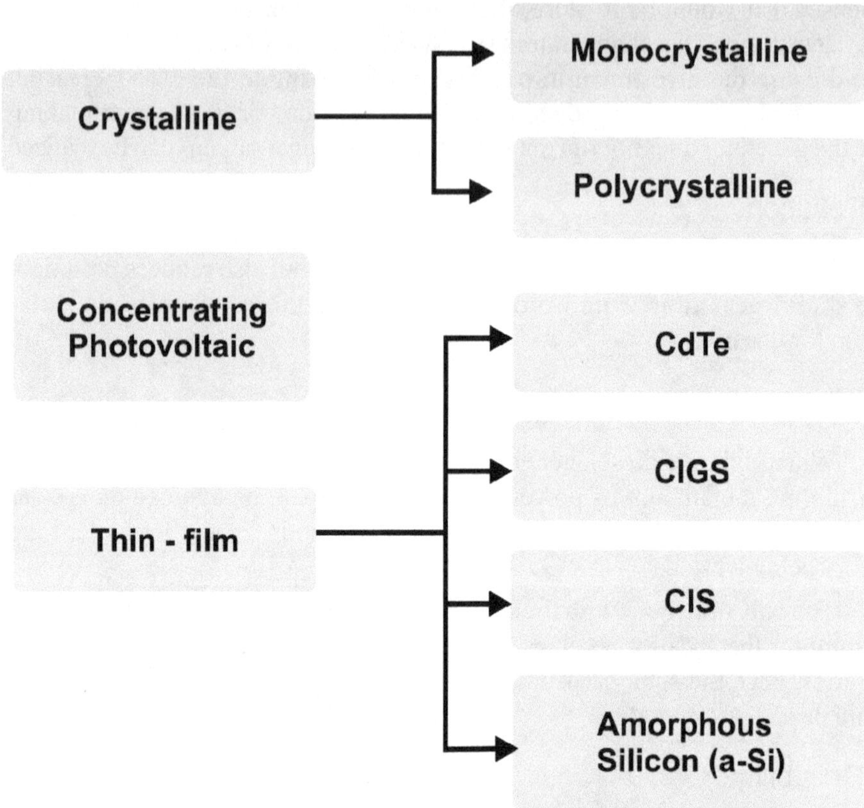

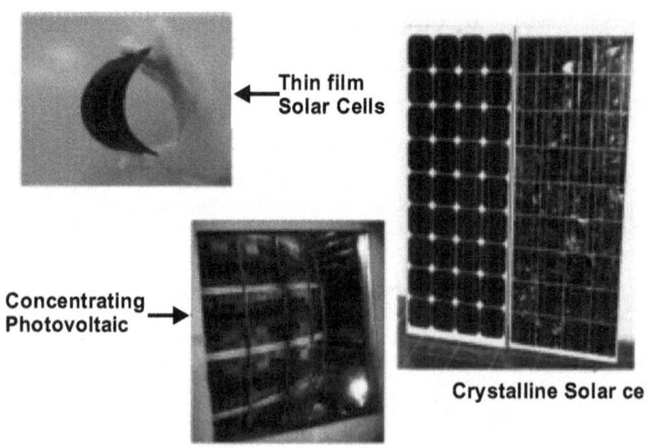

Crystalline Solar cells.

Crystalline Silicon – C-Si

The majority of PV cells produced today use crystalline silicon (c-Si) as it is a light absorbing semiconductor. The c-Si technology was originally developed for the semiconductor industry to produce PV cells for integrated circuits and microchips. These PV cells have energy conversion efficiencies between 11 percent and 16 percent. The energy conversion efficiency of a solar cell is the percentage of incident sunlight converted into electricity. While the efficiency of c-Si is high, it absorbs light poorly and requires many layers to perform efficiently in solar applications.

The two types of crystalline silicon technologies used to produce PV cells are mono and multi-crystalline (also called poly-crystalline).

Mono-crystalline technology uses thin wafers sliced from a single, pure crystal silicon ingot.

A polycrystalline cell is cut from a multifaceted silicon crystal. More surface area is required due to inherent flaws and these panels are less efficient in converting the sun's rays. However, a polycrystalline cell per watt is usually 15% cheaper than mono-crystalline cell.

Thin Film Solar Cells

The high demand for crystalline silicon PV cells has outstripped production, which has caused an increase in the prices of crystalline cells. As a result, a number of PV cell manufacturers have begun using less expensive semiconductor materials including amorphous silicon (a-Si), cadmium telluride (CdTe), copper indium diselenide (CIS) or copper indium gallium selenide (CIGS). These materials are good light absorbers and are fairly thin. Among these, CdTe is the most prominent technology being followed currently, followed by a-Si and CIGS.

They are known as thin-film because they are deposited in very thin layers on stainless steel, glass or a flexible substrate. The thickness of the film is less than 1 micron. Like c-Si, thin-film PV cells are combined into modules and laminated to protect them from the elements. They are less expensive than c-Si cells, but their demonstrated energy conversion efficiency is only around 8%. The advantage of thin-film technology is that it can be applied over large areas, providing more opportunity to generate electricity in cloudy conditions.

A Solar Thin Film

The production process of thin-film solar panels is different when compared to crystalline silicon panels. The most common thin-film manufacturing process is chemical vapor deposition. In the chemical vapor deposition process, gases react inside a chamber to form a condensate that settles uniformly onto a glass substrate. This method reduces the utilization of costly materials and energy as compared to conventional crystalline technologies, thereby dramatically reducing the total cost of PV modules.

Thermophotovoltaics (TPV)

MIT is developing a special type of solar cell that could generate electricity not from sunlight, but from the infrared radiation emitted by industrial waste heat. Called a thermophotovoltaic, or TPV, cell, the technology is unlike a conventional photovoltaic cell in that it is tuned to the infrared end of the light spectrum, which is invisible to the naked eye. Any warm object radiates infrared light, but some are warmer than others. Coke ovens used in steelmaking, for example, can reach temperatures up to 2,500 degrees F. As a result, such ovens can function as small suns for TPV cells — but providing radiation in the form of heat rather than light.

Solar Thermal

In places where the Sun light is abundant and is available all the year around, a simple trapping of the Solar energy as heat using simple heat transfer technology is used to generate steam which in turn is used to generate electricity by turning steam turbines. For instance, Siemens is providing steam turbines for Nevada Solar One, a solar-thermal plant whose collectors cover an area of one square kilometer. The collectors focus sunlight and reflect the concentrated energy onto steel pipes filled with heat-transfer oil, which is then used to heat water in a heat exchanger. The resulting steam drives a 64-MW Siemens turbine. When it goes on line this summer, the facility will supply about 40,000 households with electricity.

Nano-Technology

This is control at molecular level. This is whole new field of science where the semiconductors such as silicon are grown into nano sized rods or crystals. The promise of low cost photovoltaics with no sacrifice in efficiency in comparison to traditional single crystal semiconductors is the main motivation for development of these materials. The efficiency of absorption is enormous when compared to polished wafers. This is mainly because of great reduction in loss due to reflection and the significant increase in surface area. The ability to specifically attach molecules to the dangling bonds is a further advantage. With nano-fiber semiconductors, it is possible to architect the materials into flexible thin sheets and even integrate it to clothing. The status at present it is possible to have solar powered jackets with enough power for portable devices such as ipods. Even tents that power themselves. For the latest publications check out the news section.

Photo Electrochemical

Another way to trap sunlight is to use it in Photo-electrochemical devices where the sunlight excited Si electrode can effect important chemical reactions such as splitting of water to yield Hydrogen. These are yet to be commercialized in any significant way. Main limitations being low efficiency.

Biochemical

The natural biochemical traps such as chlorophylls have been subject of much research. Algae have been effectively used in the manufacture of many useful products. Of more recent interest are certain synthesized novel materials such as semiconductor polymers which are also effective traps of visible spectrum photons. i.e. they exhibit interesting electrical and chromatic activities upon interaction with the visible light. Composite materials such as polymer-fullerene blends are of great interest in achieving high efficiency low cost solar panels.

Major Obstacles in the Captive Solar Industry

Captive power generation is plagued with some issues. The main idea behind setting up solar based captive power plants was to get uninterrupted power supply and reduce the diesel cost. Industrial users who have the required resources to set up their own power plants for internal consumption can put up SPV captive power plant. But, there are certain issues in setting up solar based captive power plants.

Uncertainty in weather: The design of a solar power generation system involves either the use of historical weather data or weather forecast methods to predict the future temporal evolution of the solar energy system. Despite the use of such methods, the behavior of weather conditions always involves high uncertainty. Unless such uncertainty is accounted for during the system design, the performance of the solar-based system will only be optimum within the range of the considered weather conditions. Potentially unpredictable weather fluctuations will inevitably result to suboptimal system operation.

Solar irradiance: Solar irradiance is one of the most important factors in the operation of the PV systems and it can have a significant impact on the efficiency and power quality response of the whole system. The variable power flow due to the fluctuation of solar irradiance and temperature are some of the parameters that affect the power quality of photovoltaic systems. With high connection densities of photovoltaics in the distribution grid, low irradiance can lead to undesirable variations of power and supply quality (voltage and current) at the connection point which might even exceed acceptable limits. The system injects a highly distorted current (with respect to the fundamental frequency current) to the distribution network during low solar irradiance conditions. It has been found that low solar irradiance has a significant impact on the power quality of the output of the PV system.

Initial Cost: The high initial cost of solar PV systems is one of the most significant barriers to PV adoption. However, as the initial cost of PV system decreases and the cost of conventional fuel sources increases, these systems will become more economically competitive.

Surplus Power: In India, net metering system is currently not available and thus the surplus power generated from renewable energy sources cannot be sold to the utilities. When it is not connected to the grid, excess energy that is generated is not fed out to the utility to give you an energy credit (this can happen with **on-grid**systems). Off-grid systems must use the surplus or lose it.

Energy Storage: Offgrid PV systems typically use batteries for storing energy, and the use of batteries could increase the size, cost and complexity of the system.

Education: PV systems present a new and unfamiliar technology; few people understand value and feasibility. This lack of information slows market and technological growth.

Hottest Sectors in the Market That Use Solar Power

The basic off-grid applications have not changed, though new products that fit within these applications and sub-applications are and will continue to be introduced.Given below are the major market segments which are potentially utilizing the solar power to generate electricity for captive use:

- Large Industrial Facilities
- Large Commercial Buildings/Facilities
- Communication Sectors
- Water Pumping
- Warning Signals
- Lighting
- Refrigeration

In most of the above market segments, diesel displacement projects are the emerging area for solar. The Indian government is promoting the use of solar energy in place of diesel because about 70 per cent of the fuel is imported. About 15-20 per cent of India's diesel requirements are used for captive power generation applications; this is where solar provides most promising solutions for industries, commercial building, water pumping applications etc.

Setting up solar based captive power is cost competitive but, when the life cycle cost is taken in to account, it is cheaper than diesel. A 100 KVA diesel genset system, running for less than five hours a day, can be potentially replaced by a 100 KW rooftop system, and the economics works out in such a way that the payback period is about 6 years. The factor like escalation rate of fuel prices, accelerated depreciation and loan tenure of 7 years has been considered in arriving at the payback period.

Large Industrial Facilities That Use Captive Solar Power

Large industrial facilities have set up captive power generation (conventional) to mitigate the effect of frequent shortages of electricity from the national grid. 70% of electricity generated under captive power in the case of wind power was set up by large industrial facilities.

Industries that can set up captive power are:

- Textiles
- Cement
- Chemical
- Iron & Steel
- Light Engineering
- Ceramic industry
- Paper
- Sugar industry
- Dairy

Except for most of the textile industry, all other industries have set up fossil fuel based captive power plants. Wind based captive power plants have been set up by the textile sectors.

As a majority of the Indian industries are located at dry & hot areas with huge space, solar based captive power plants can be set up by the facilities which will be more profitable. Solar energy can be used for preheating boiler feed water in many plants. Industries can also use captive power plants on rooftops or in parks or other open spaces to meet factories' lighting loads and pumping water requirements.

Large Commercial Facilities That Use Captive Solar Power

Solar system, especially solar PV can be set up on commercial buildings for lighting, AC and other usage. This helps commercial business move away from relying solely on central power plants and dramatically reduce grid electricity use and electricity bills.

For most commercial and industrial buildings, rooftop solar technology is the clear choice as most other renewable energies aren't quite ready for prime time in the small-installation. They thrive in large megawatt-sized developments. Solar can be a solution almost everywhere.

There are other reasons why captive/rooftop solar systems make sense for these large facilities:

- Large, flat, relatively empty roofs top most industrial facilities, warehouses, and big-box retail stores, creating a solar-energy system's version of prime real estate. Low-slope commercial and industrial rooftops cover approximately 13-billion sq. yd. worldwide, enough to generate more than 800 gig watts of electricity. These flat and often easily accessible rooftops make solar-system installation and maintenance easy on roofers, solar photovoltaic integrators, and the building owners.
- Potential customers are likely to find companies that have gone green much more appealing. Solar installations are visible and one of the most recognizable symbols of clean energy and environmental consciousness. Whether it's the environmentally conscious consumer who would rather buy dinner ingredients in a solar-powered grocery store or a major industrial giant looking for positive press about their own green efforts, solar installations can make a difference to customers.
- The certain low cost of clean energy protects a company from volatile energy prices. The fuels that most of utilities rely on to produce electricity-coal and natural gas-fluctuate in price. While they may not vary as wildly as the price of gasoline, they historically have risen over time. In response, so do the rates electric companies charge, sometimes dramatically. Making the switch to generating power on-site from an eternally free source of energy-the sun-can bring certainty to operating costs for decades.
- Dozens of state and central tax rebate and credit opportunities are available for rooftop-solar systems.

Solar Power in the Communication Sector

Power system reliability is critical for most communications applications and availability must be near 100 percent. Most systems are in remote locations with limited access and often with extreme weather conditions part of the year. For these reasons, PV systems are increasingly being used to supply power for telecommunication applications.

Solar diesel hybrid systems can also be sometimes used to reduce initial cost, particularly if the peak power demand is much greater than the average demand. In these system setups battery is critical and deep-cycle lead-acid batteries or nickel-cadmium (NiCd) batteries are recommended for this application. Lightning is a common problem that must be considered while designing a system for communication towers.

Applications

- Two-Way Radio
- Radio Communications
- Telephone
- Mobile Radio Systems

Users

- Utilities
- Military
- Government Agencies
- Businesses

In India, more than a third of the PV capacity is devoted to the telecommunications sector. There is a vast potential for repeater stations for mobile phones powered by PV or PV/diesel hybrid systems.

Telecommunications companies are the prominent market segments looking toward renewable energy as they search for new solutions to power India's nearly 250,000 telecom towers. These towers consume 3-5 kilowatts power depending on the number of operators using the tower and about 2 billion litres (about 530 million gallons) of diesel are used every year.

Systems such as solar PV-based hybrid systems provide a less polluting alternative to diesel power, serve as a hedge against increasing diesel fuel prices, and help minimize the logistical challenges of transporting and storing diesel fuel at remote tower locations.

In addition, the government is planning to make it mandatory for mobile phone towers to be powered by solar energy, hoping to cut pollution and tamp down a key driver of diesel consumption in the country.

The telecom towers are also expected to scale up by another one lakh next year and it is important to note that the newer telephone towers are being installed based on a new technology that will consume less power and also do away with the air conditioning so critical to the telephone towers. Industry experts believe that for the older 3 lakh towers, grid power will be more economical than a solar powered tower. But for the newer towers, where air conditioning is not a requisite, it makes more sense to use solar power, especially where the EB electricity is not available for considerable duration.

Solar Power Generation to Pump Water

Pumping water is a universal need around the world and the use of photovoltaic power is increasing for this application. PV powered pumping systems offer simplicity, reliability, and low maintenance for a broad range of applications between hand pumps and large generator driven irrigation pumps.

The solar PV powered water-pumping system (DC Surface suction, DC floating, and DC or AC submersibles) can offer a veritable panacea to the problem of finding power to pump water for irrigation in India. Typical pump systems in India are of the DC surface suction type (approximately 86% of solar pumping systems installed in India), DC submersible type (2%), DC floating type (2%), and AC submersible (10%). The system for solar pumping depends on the nature of the well: deep well, bore well, open well etc.

Regardless of the type of pump used, water is usually stored in a tank or reservoir for use at other times. Most pumping systems do not include batteries for on-demand water. However, batteries are sometimes used in systems where pumping time must be controlled because of low water demand or low source capacity.

India has about 15 million grid-powered pump-sets and close to 7 million diesel-powered pumps. However, only about 7500 solar pumping systems have been installed for agricultural use in India.

The problems with the grid-powered pumping systems are:

- Demand for electrical energy far outstrips supply, and the gap continues to widen
- It is proving increasingly difficult for the government to continue subsidizing the rising costs of generation, transmission and distribution losses, pilferage, etc (to deliver 3600 kWh to a farmer to pump water, 7000 kWh is required to be generated, assuming a diversity factor 2). The loss of revenue to the government is colossal.
- The capital cost to the government to provide an electrical connection for a single pump-set of 3 hp capacity (sufficient for 2 hectares) is estimated at Rs 1.37 lakh by Andhra Pradesh Transco (2002 figures)
- The costs and tariffs of electricity continue to rise – the marginal farmer is unable to pay for the electricity)
- Grid power is unreliable and of poor quality, often leading to motor burnouts at the tail end.
- In a coal-fired thermal generating station, 1 kWh of electrical energy generated translates to 11.2 tonnes of carbon dioxide emission a year.

Applications

- Irrigation
- Village Water Supply
- Stock Watering

- Drinking water
- Agriculture related use
- Horticulture
- Animal Husbandry
- Poultry farming
- High value crops
- Orchard
- Farming

Users

- Farmers /Ranchers
- Villages

Solar Powered Warning Signals

Warning signals are used for public safety and their operational performance is often mandated by law. The warning signal must be located where the need is and using a photovoltaic power system offers the advantage of being able to place the system at the optimum location. System availability requirements are near 100 percent for those systems that safeguard human life. Check with local authorities for applicable regulations.

Applications

- Navigation Beacons
- Audible Fog Signals
- Highway Warning Signs
- Aircraft Warning Lights
- Railroad Crossing Signals

Users

- Maritime shipping,
- Navy
- Coast Guard
- Oil industry
- Highway departments
- Railroads

- Private owners of communication towers
- Tall buildings on flight paths
- Wharves or structures requiring warning or identification.

Solar Powered Lighting

PV powered lighting systems are installed and operating in many locations. They have proved reliable and are the low cost alternative for many users. Recent improvements in lamp efficiency have allowed system costs to decrease. Security lighting, such as required for military applications, can be powered by PV systems at a fraction of the cost of extending utility lines to remote areas. Lamp control can be implemented with photocells, timers, switches, or sensors such as motion or infrared.

Applications

- Billboards
- Security Lighting
- Emergency Warning
- Area Lighting
- Domestic Use

Solar Powered Commercial Refrigerators

The use of PV powered refrigerator/freezers (R/F) is increasing because of the high reliability they provide. Also, the high efficiency dc refrigerators are being used more in residential applications because their cost is decreasing as larger numbers are manufactured. In most instances, the efficiency of the dc refrigerator is higher than an equivalent size ac unit. This reduces the power requirements accordingly. For PV powered refrigerators, the mode of operation directly affects the total system cost. Factors such as number of users, door opening habits, seasonal use variations, time of loading, temperature of incoming material, and physical location of the unit will significantly affect the amount of power required. User training in proper operation and maintenance should be a part of any project to install R/F systems in remote areas.

Vaccine Refrigeration

The World Health Organization has specified PV power be used for medical vaccine refrigerators in numerous countries around the world. Many dollars worth of vaccine can be ruined if not maintained at the recommended temperature. This requires a reliable power source for the refrigerator.

Agricultural goods and milk cooling refrigeration

Solar PV is a promising alternative solution for cooling and preserving a variety of perishable goods, especially agricultural and dairy products as well, in areas with difficult access to the electricity supply, as is the case in developing countries or isolated rural areas. The simple technology applied to the refrigeration facility and the fact that it lacks complex electronics makes it possible to use and repair the system without external help.

Traditionally solar-powered refrigerators and vaccine coolers use a combination of solar panels and lead batteries to store energy for cloudy days and at night in the absence of sunlight to keep their contents cool. These fridges are expensive and require heavy lead-acid batteries which tend to deteriorate, especially in hot climates, or are misused for other purposes. In addition, the batteries require maintenance, must be replaced approximately every three years, and must be disposed of as hazardous wastes possibly resulting in lead pollution. These problems and the resulting higher costs have been an obstacle for the use of solar powered refrigerators in developing areas. Of late, some companies have come up with more efficient and low cost solar power refrigerators. One such company is Promethean Power Systems, Cambridge, MA.

Promethean Power Systems has developed a solar-powered refrigeration system for commercial cold-storage applications in off-grid and partially electrified areas of developing countries. The technology enables food suppliers to store and preserve perishable food items—such as milk, fruits and vegetables—without the need for expensive diesel-powered generators.

The hybrid solar & grid-powered refrigeration system is designed for mission critical refrigeration applications that must operate 24 hours a day, 365 days a year. The combination of solar and grid power provides a necessary backup mechanism and eliminates the need for a dedicated diesel generator. The company's first product, *Antarctica 250*, is a milk chiller with cooling capacity 250 liters per day and storage capacity of 500 liters.

According to the company, since the system use solar energy for part of energy input, operating cost is 50% lower than the operating cost of an equivalent grid-powered unit and nearly 80% lower than that of a diesel-powered unit.

Technology: The refrigeration system uses a thermal battery system to store cold energy during daytime using solar power and nightime using grid power. A "black-box" electronic control unit runs the entire system, minimizes energy consumption and optimizes the use of available solar and grid power. The hybrid-power optimizer uses proprietary algorithms to efficiently transfer solar and grid power to the thermal battery and electrical loads.

Applications

- Medical

- Commercial
- Residential

Technology Options Involved In Captive Solar

Selecting the best system design for a particular application is important. Often, a combination of techniques can dramatically reduce costs and improve the reliability of a system, or provide the design flexibility to cover a wide range of applications. There are three distinct configurations one can choose from when setting up solar based captive power plant:

- Stand alone PV system
- Grid-tied Captive Power Plant
- Grid-Interactive Only (No Battery Backup)
- Grid-Interactive With Battery Backup
- Hybrid System

Each of these categories has a different connotation, and would need to be treated accordingly, for effectively bringing the surplus capacity into the utilities' network.

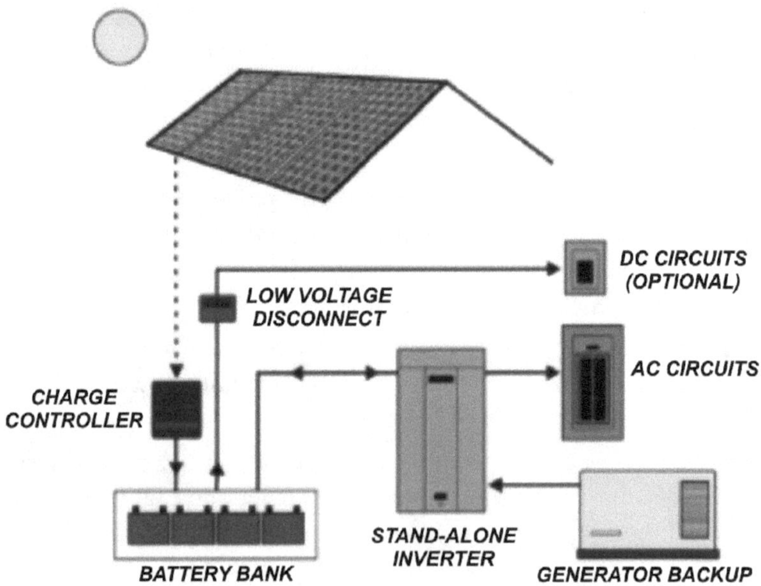

TYPICAL STAND ALONE PV SYSTEM

Stand Alone PV Systems

Poor quality of grid supply (low voltage, fluctuating frequency and frequent interruptions), high tariffs (much higher than actual cost of supply), unfair impositions (peak hour restrictions and unplanned load shedding) and unresponsive attitude of State Electricity Boards have forced many industries to isolate themselves totally from the state grid and be on their own. For a reliable operation of the industry, they necessarily have to employ captive generation with a redundancy.

Stand-alone PV systems are designed to operate independent of the electric utility grid, and are generally designed and sized to supply certain DC and/or AC electrical loads. Worldwide, stand alone solar installations are very popular while in India almost all captive power plants are of the grid-tie. It is often a good idea to start with small and very simple stand alone solar PV system first and then progress from there.

Working

The simplest type of stand-alone PV system is a **"Direct-coupled system"**, where the DC output of a PV module or array is directly connected to a DC load. Since there is no electrical energy storage (batteries) in direct-coupled systems, the load only operates during sunlight hours, making these designs suitable for common applications such as ventilation fans, water pumps, and small circulation pumps.

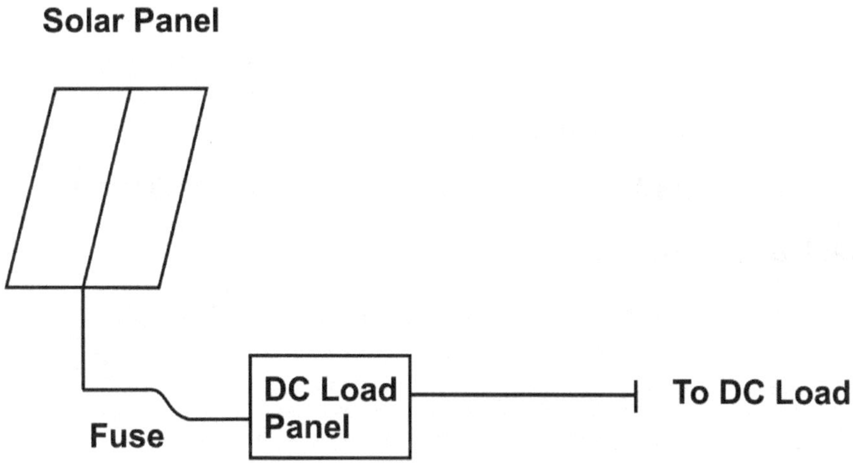

Matching the impedance of the electrical load to the maximum power output of the PV array is a critical part of designing well-performing direct-coupled system. For certain loads such as positive-displacement water pumps; a type of electronic DC-DC converter, called a maximum power point tracker (MPPT) is used between the array and load to help better utilize the available array maximum power output. DC loads can also be connected directly to the battery bank. A more common type of the standalone system is where the PV system with a battery bank powers the AC loads.

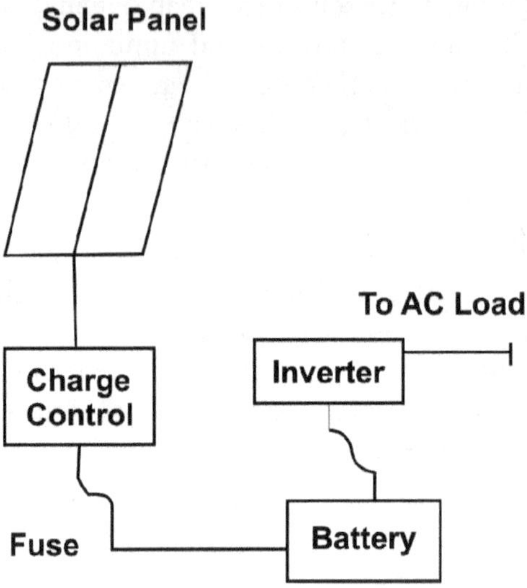

The **"Small stand-alone"** system is an excellent system for providing electricity economically. These systems are used primarily for RV power, lighting, cabins, backup and portable power systems. The size of the photovoltaic array (number of solar panels) and battery will depend upon individual power requirements. The solar panels charge the battery during daylight hours and the battery supplies power to the inverter as needed. The inverter changes the 12 volt batteries DC power into 230V volt AC power, which is the most useful type of current for most applications. The charge controller terminates the charging when the battery reaches full charge, to keep the batteries from "gassing-out", which prolongs battery longevity.

Grid Connected Captive Solar Plants –Without Battery

Typical System Components

Grid-tied system without battery backup consists of just two main components, a PV array and a grid-tied inverter.

In addition, the array frames can be installed as:

1. Fixed, where the frame is fixed at the optimum angle.
2. Adjustable, where the frame can be adjusted manually during the year (often not carried out as years progress)
3. Tracking, where the frames automatically move to receive optimal sunlight during the day and throughout the year.

Grid-interactive PV System without Battery Backup

While trackers are most efficient, they are more expensive and require maintenance.

The most common PV module that is 5-to-25 square feet in size and weighs about 3-4 lbs./sq ft. Often sets of four or more smaller modules are framed or attached together by struts in what is called a panel. This panel is typically around 20-35 square feet in area for ease of handling on a roof.

This allows some assembly and wiring functions to be done on the ground if called for by the installation instructions.

Balance of system equipment (BOS): BOS includes mounting systems and wiring systems used to integrate the solar modules into the structural and electrical systems of the home. The wiring systems include disconnects for the DC and AC sides of the inverter, ground-fault protection, and over-current protection for the solar modules.

Most systems include a combiner board of some kind since most modules require fusing for each module source circuit. Some inverters include this fusing and combining function within the inverter enclosure.

***DC-AC inverter*:** This is the device that takes the dc power from the PV array and converts it into standard ac power used by the house appliances.

Metering: This includes meters to provide indication of system performance. Some meters can indicate home energy usage.

***Other components*:** utility switch (depending on local utility)

The advantages and disadvantages of a grid-tied system without battery include the following:

- Cost-effective for net metering
- Does not provide back-up in case of grid failure
- Simple to install
- No power management opportunities
- Highest efficiency

Grid Connected Captive Solar Plants – With Battery

Grid-tie with power backup combines a grid tie installations with a bank of batteries. Unlike a standard grid-tie system, however, a battery bank provides contingency for power cuts – so that one can continue to use power from solar.

Need for Battery

Batteries are a key component in a grid-tie with back-up or a stand-alone renewable energy system that all of the other components rely on for operation. Without proper maintenance, batteries can fail prematurely and shut the whole system down. The "Best" battery for a particular system is not always the most expensive, but it is seldom the cheapest either. You need to know what your battery storage requirements are.

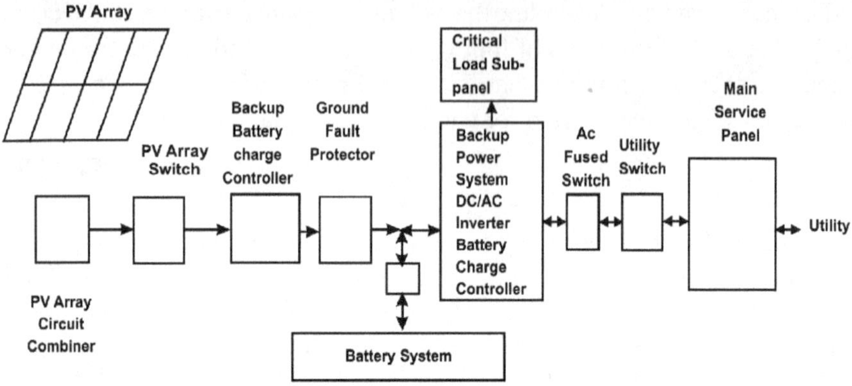

This type of system incorporates energy storage in the form of a battery to keep "*critical load*" circuits in the house operating during a utility outage.

When an outage occurs the unit disconnects from the utility and powers specific circuits in the home. These critical load circuits are wired from a subpanel that is separate from the rest of the electrical circuits. If the outage occurs during daylight hours, the PV array is able to assist the battery in supplying the house loads. If the outage occurs at night, the battery supplies the load. The amount of time critical loads can operate depends on the amount of power they consume and the energy stored in the battery system.

A typical backup battery system may provide about 8kWh of energy storage at an 8-hour discharge rate, which means that the battery will operate a 1-kW load for 8 hours. A 1-kW load is the average usage for a home when not running an air conditioner.

Typical System Components:

In addition to components, a battery backup system may include some or all of the following:

1. Batteries and battery enclosures
2. Battery charge controller
3. Separate sub-panel(s) for critical load circuits

The advantages and disadvantages of a battery based grid-tied system include the following:

- Provides interruptible back-up power
- Batteries are an additional cost.
- Reduces energy cost for utility time of use (TOU) metering.
- Efficiency loss in charging batteries
- Offers power management opportunities
- More component to install

Hybrid Technology Involved In Solar Plants

Systems with more than one source of power are called hybrid systems. It is often desirable to design a system with additional source of power. The most common type of hybrid system contains a gas or diesel powered engine generator. Another hybrid approach is a PV/Wind system. Adding a wind turbine to a PV system provides complementary power generation.

Solar Hybrid Concept

- A hybrid remote power system integrates two or more power sources, using intelligent controls to manage the system operation.
- Inherently reliable due to multiple power sources.
- PV Hybrid systems generally use diesel generating set-capable of providing full rated power on demand as the second energy source.
- The proportion of PV/Battery and Genset can be designed economically i.e reducing of 40% to 60% and to 2-3 days of the autonomous power from solar array and battery respectively depending on the site isolation profile.

Technology Options Prevalent In India and Future Trends

Among the three options that are available, the grid tied captive systems are the most prevalent in India. These are available up to a capacity of 100 kW, and typically do not use batteries.

At the same time, stand alone/captive based power plants in India are evolving fast. Globally, most people do not run their entire load solely off their PV system. The majority of systems use a hybrid approach by integrating another power source. The most common form of hybrid system incorporates a gas or diesel powered engine generator, which can greatly reduce the initial cost. Meeting the full load with a PV system means the array and batteries need to support the load under worst-case weather conditions. This also means the battery bank must be large enough to power large loads. These requirements will make the system unviable owing to the high costs of battery storage. Hence, a diesel-solar PV generator provides the optimal power supply source for India as well, as the generator provides the extra energy needed during cloudy weather and during periods of heavier than normal electricity use, and can also be charging the batteries at the same time. A hybrid system provides increased reliability because there are two independent charging systems at work.

Another hybrid approach is a PV system integrated with a wind turbine. Adding wind turbine makes sense in the locations where the wind blows when the sun does not shine. In this case, consecutive days of cloudy weather are not a problem, so long as the wind turbine is spinning. While in theory this combination appears good, in practice this combination has not delivered the benefits expected out of it, primarily owing to the less-than-optimal efficiencies of micro wind turbines.

For even greater reliability and flexibility while using wind and solar, there are experimentations where a third source – diesel generator – has been included in a PV/Wind system. A generator system will act as a third charging source for the batteries. This three-source hybrid is in its nascent stages in India.

Future Prospects of the Solar Industry

For developing countries like India, Greenpeace has proposed a feed-in-tariff system which would provide the financing to enable massive renewable energy uptake. The scheme proposes a mechanism where the additional costs of renewable energies are financed by a combination of new sectoral emissions trading mechanisms and direct finance from technology funds to be developed in the Copenhagen climate deal.

Especially in developing countries, renewable energy investment and hence total generation costs, remains higher than those of existing coal or gas-fired power stations and this is unlikely to change in the next five to ten years. To bridge this investment and cost gap between conventional fossil fuel based power generation and renewable energy, a support mechanism is required. The Feed in Tariff Support Mechanism (FTSM) is a concept conceived by Greenpeace International. The aim of the mechanism is to expand the use of renewable energy in developing countries with financial support from industrialized nations. It is a mechanism which can allow for rapid deployment of renewable energy technologies via a new sectoral no-lose mechanism or through a technology transfer fund under the United Nations Framework Convention on Climate Change.

In this backdrop, Greenpeace estimated the future installed capacity growth for renewable energy in India, including Solar PV. This estimate is based on two probable scenarios, the reference and the revolution scenario. The reference scenario is comparatively conservative and the revolution scenario assumes aggressive government policies and investments towards the growth of renewable energy.

Reference scenario

In this scenario, the installed capacity of solar PV is estimated to increase to 3GW by 2020 from current installed capacity.

India: Projected Installed Capacity (GW)

Year	Solar PV Installed Capacity (GW)
2020	3
2030	7
2040	11
2050	16

Source: http://www.indiaenvironmentportal.org.in

Revolution scenario

Under the revolution scenario, it is estimated that the installed capacity of solar PV will increase to 10 GW by 2020. The solar PV capacity is projected to outpace the future installed capacity of wind power in 2040.

India: Projected Installed Capacity (GW)

Year	Solar PV Installed Capacity (GW)
2020	10
2030	118
2040	486
2050	1093

Source: http://www.indiaenvironmentportal.org.in

National Solar Mission

Transcending the estimates of the revolution scenario of Greenpeace, the recently launched Jawaharlal Nehru National Solar Mission (NSM) has three successive stages leading up to an installed capacity of 20,000 MW of solar energy including solar thermal by the end of the 13th Five Year Plan in 2022. The solar mission states to achieve off grid solar applications of 200 MW by 2013; 1,000 MW by 2017; and 2,000 MW by 2022. In utility grid power for both solar PV and solar thermal, including rooftop, it targets 1,000-2,000 MW by 2013; 4,000-10,000 MW by 2017; and 20,000 MW by 2022.

National Solar Mission Targets

Year	Target installed capacity (GW)
2013	1-2
2017	4-10
2022	20

Source: Ministry of New and Renewable Energy

Key Challenges in the Growth of Solar PV Technology in India

Key challenges facing the growth and development of PV in India include:

- *Cost and T&D Losses*: Solar PV is some years away from true cost competitiveness and from being able to compete on the same scale as other energy generation technologies. Adding to the cost are T&D losses that at approximately 40 percent make generation through solar energy sources highly unfeasible. However, the government is supporting R&D activities by establishing research centers and funding such initiatives. The government has tied up with world-renowned universities to bring down the installation cost of solar power sources and is focusing on upgradation of substations and T&D lines to reduce T&D losses.
- *Land Scarcity*: Per capita land availability is very low in India, and land is a scarce resource. Dedication of land area near substations for exclusive installation of solar cells might have to compete with other necessities that require land.
- Funding of initiatives like National Solar Mission is a constraint given India's inadequate financing capabilities. The finance ministry has explicitly raised concerns about funding an ambitious scheme like NSM.
- Manufacturers are mostly focused on export markets that buy Solar PV cells and modules at higher prices thereby increasing their profits. Many new suppliers have tie-ups with foreign players in Europe and United States thereby prioritizing export demand. This could result in reduced supplies for the fast-growing local market.
- The lack of closer industry-government cooperation for the technology to achieve scale.
- The need for focused, collaborative and goals driven R&D to help India attain technology leadership in PV.
- The need for a better financing infrastructure, models and arrangements to spur the PV industry and consumption of PV products.
- Training and development of human resources to drive industry growth and PV adoption
- The need for intra-industry cooperation in expanding the PV supply chain, in technical information sharing through conferences and workshops, in collaborating with BOS (balance of systems) manufacturers and in gathering and publishing accurate market data, trends and projections
- The need to build consumer awareness about the technology, its economics and right usage
- Complexity of subsidy structure & involvement of too many agencies like MNRE, IREDA, SNA, electricity board and electricity regulatory commission makes the development of solar PV projects difficult.

- Land allotment & PPA signing is a long procedure under the Generation Based Incentive scheme.

1.2. HYDROGEN ENERGY

Hydrogen is a clean fuel and an energy carrier that can be used for a broad range of applications as a possible substitute to liquid and gaseous fossil fuels. Hydrogen is the most abundant element in the universe, making up 75% of normal matter by mass and over 90% by number of atoms. This element is found in great abundance in stars and gas giant planets. Molecular clouds of H_2 are associated with star formation. Hydrogen plays a vital role in powering stars through proton-proton reaction nuclear fusion. The Hydrogen element in its atomic state consists of a single proton enveloped by a single electron. The above digression is only to emphasize the unique structure and nature of hydrogen and the pivotal role it plays in the energy equation of the universe.

Technically, molecular hydrogen is not a energy source. It can be considered as only a energy carrier since the energy is not created by destruction of mass as in proton fusion reaction. Hydrogen is a very highly combustible gas. It is a fuel that results in high energy output and no greenhouse gas emissions and no toxic wastes. Hydrogen burns violently in air. Pure hydrogen-oxygen flames burn in the ultraviolet color range and as such the flame is nearly invisible to the naked eye,

$$2\ H_2(g) + O_2(g) \rightarrow 2\ H_2O(l) + 572\ \text{kJ/mol}$$

Since the by-product of the above combustion of hydrogen in air is water vapor, it is a highly favored green reaction. Although hydrogen can be produced as a major by-product by many chemical and electrochemical methods, the main problem posed is that of storage. Liquefaction of Hydrogen is not energy efficient since significant energy is consumed. The other major problem posed is that of atmospheric damage such as Ozone depletion if there is significant leakage of Hydrogen into atmosphere. One way to circumvent the storage problems is by storing hydrogen in metal clusters as molecular hydrogen.

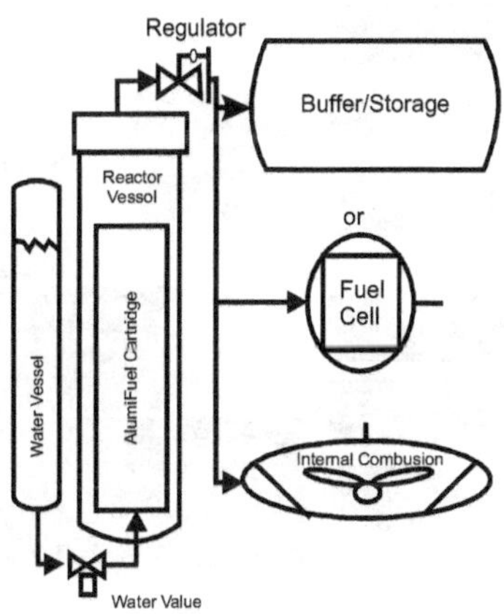

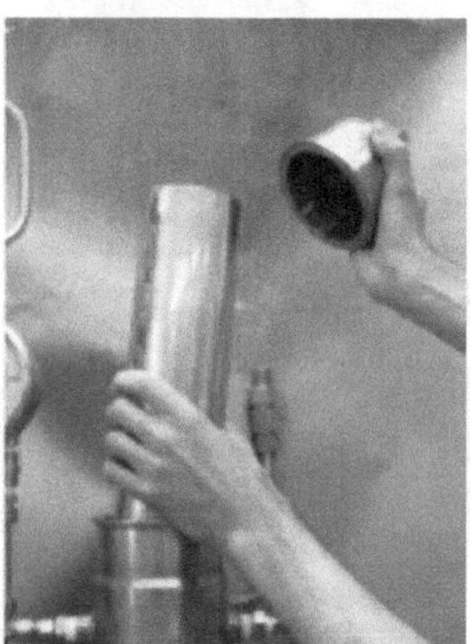

In situ production of hydrogen by chemical and electrochemical methods has been adapted for automobile engine fuel supplement. Hydrogen Power Inc. (HPI) is a Seattle-based alternative energy company that has developed a proprietary method of producing hydrogen called Hydrogen Now™. This patented process safely generates pure hydrogen using aluminum, one of the most abundant and cost-effective natural resources on earth.Hydrogen Now™ combines aluminum, water, and an environmentally friendly catalyst to create a water-split reaction, generating hydrogen on-site and on-demand.

$$2\,Al + 6\,H_2O \rightarrow 2\,Al(OH)_3 + 3\,H_2$$

Electrochemical Synthesis

Currently similar such adaptations for greater fuel economy and greater mileage for petrol is available for a small affordable price wherein the splitting of water by electrochemical means yields on demand hydrogen. $2\,H_2O(aq) \rightarrow 2\,H_2\,(g) + O_2\,(g)$. Both the anode and cathode are made of inert metals such as Platinum so that the nascent oxygen does not oxidize the metal, instead is evolved as molecular oxygen which can then be channeled into the combustion chamber to react with the evolved hydrogen. Such commercially available adaptations have not been tested for long term use yet. However it is a promising technology and has potential for real development.

Hydrogen Energy System

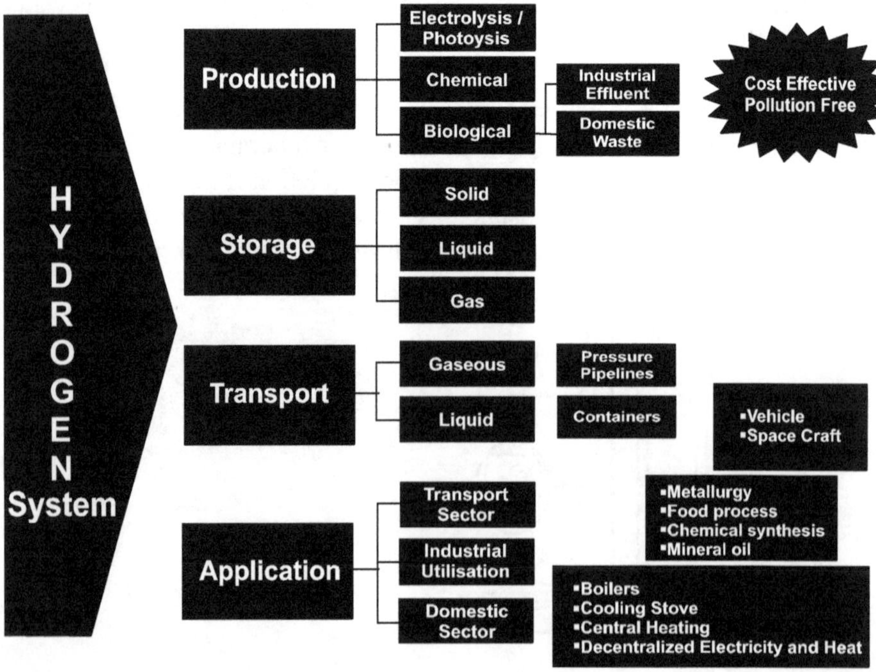

Biological synthesis

H_2 is a product of some types of anaerobic metabolism and is produced by several microorganisms, usually via reactions catalyzed by iron- or nickel-containing enzymes called hydrogenases. These enzymes catalyze the reversible redox reaction between H2 and its component two protons and two electrons. Creation of hydrogen gas occurs in the transfer of reducing equivalents produced during pyruvate fermentation to water.

Water splitting, in which water is decomposed into its component protons, electrons, and oxygen, occurs in the light reactions in all photosynthetic organisms. Some such organisms — including the alga *Chlamydomonas reinhardtii* and cyanobacteria — have evolved a second step in the dark reactions in which protons and electrons are reduced to form H_2 gas by specialized hydrogenases in the chloroplast. Efforts have been undertaken to genetically modify cyanobacterial hydrogenases to efficiently synthesize H_2 gas even in the presence of oxygen.Other rarer but mechanistically interesting routes to H_2 production also exist in nature. Nitrogenase produces approximately one equivalent of H_2 for each equivalent of N2 reduced to ammonia. Some phosphatases reduce phosphite to $H_{2.}$

Fuel Cells

The reverse of electrolysis of water to H_2 and O2 is the classical fuel cell. Here H_2 and O2 are combined in a electrochemical reaction to produce electricity and water. This useful method of electricity production is especially useful for producing electricity in small home units therefore replacing dependence on grid electricity. However there have been many hurdles. Most recently other types of fuel cells have been engineered to use other fuels such as natural gas, biogas etc to produce green electricity.

Fuel Cells have emerged as one of the most promising technologies for the power source of the future. Fuel cell is an electrochemical device that converts energy into electricity and heat without combustion.

Fuel cells are modular in construction, their efficiency is independent of size and have flexibility of using a wide range of fuels to produce hydrogen/ reformate suitable for fuel cell applications. Fuel cells require relatively pure hydrogen free of contaminants such as sulphur and carbon compounds etc. When hydrogen rich reformate gas mixture is used, it results in some emissions similar to lean hydrogen – air mixture burning in IC engines. The fuel cell systems are more efficient than IC engines and turbines. Fuel cells are considered suitable for a broad spectrum of applications ranging from a few milli watts to several kilowatts.

Fuel cells are the long term option for hydrogen applications both for transportation and power generation. Fuel cells especially for vehicular applications are in the development stage and the country needs to identify the path for fuel cell development taking into account technology development efforts going on worldwide and the country's specific priorities and the achievements in this area so far.

Fuel Cell Technologies

There are six major fuel cell technologies of interest viz., Proton Exchange Membrane Fuel Cells (PEMFC), Phosphoric Acid Fuel Cells (PAFC), Alkaline Fuel Cells (AFC), Direct Methanol Fuel Cells (DMFC), Molten Carbonate Fuel Cells (MCFC); and Solid Oxide Fuel Cells (SOFC). These fuel cells operate with different fuels in a wide range of temperatures (600C–10000C) depending on the technology. These technologies are at different stages of development and demonstration.

Phosphoric Acid Fuel Cell (PAFC)

The Phosphoric Acid Fuel cell (PAFC) technology is the most commercially developed fuel cell technology. PAFC stacks use phosphoric acid as an electrolyte. PAFC is being used in applications such as hospitals, hotels, offices, schools, etc. It can also be used in larger vehicles such as buses, etc. The efficiency of PAFC is about 40%. Phosphoric acid fuel cells (PAFC) were the first to be developed in the country more than a decade ago. PAFC power packs of various capacities have been developed, demonstrated and evaluated in actual field conditions.

Proton Exchange Membrane Fuel Cell (PEMFC)

Polymer electrolyte membrane fuel cells (PEMFC) have been developed for use in stationary and transport applications. The mechanism of PEMFC is same as PAFC. They differ in that PEMFCs operate at relatively low temperatures (about 90°C). In view of low operating temperatures PEM fuel cells are considered appropriate for use in automobiles. They have high power density and can vary their output quickly to meet quick shifts in power demand.

Molten Carbonate Fuel Cell (MCFC)

The Molten Carbonate Fuel Cells (MCFC) uses an alkali metal carbonate (Li, Na, K) as the electrolyte. However an alkali metal carbonate must be in the liquid phase to function as an electrolyte. This cell operates at higher temperature of about 600 °C. The high operating temperature is required to achieve sufficient conductivity of the electrolyte. The higher operating temperature of MCFC´s provides the opportunity for achieving higher overall system efficiencies and greater flexibility in the use of available fuels. The high operating temperature, however, impose limitations and constraints on choosing materials suitable for long life time operations. This technology also require significant improvements.

Solid Oxide Fuel Cell (SOFC)

Solid Oxide Fuel cells (SOFC) use solid, nonporous metal oxide electrolytes. The metal electrolyte normally used in manufacturing SOFCs is stabilized Zirconia. This cell operates at a higher temperature of about 1000 0C. This high operating temperature allows internal reforming, promotes rapid kinetics with non-precious materials and produces high quality heat. The solid state character of SOFC components implies that there is no restriction on the cell configuration. It is possible to shape the cell according to the criteria such as overcoming design or application issues. The combined heat and power efficiencies of SOFC could be as high as 80%.

Direct Methanol Fuel Cell (DMFC)

Direct Methanol Fuel Cells use methanol as the fuel. These fuel cells work at lower temperatures and have found application in mobile power generation applications such as laptops etc.

Alkaline Fuel Cell (AFC)

AFC uses alkaline potassium hydroxide as the electrolyte. These cells can achieve power generating efficiencies of upto 70%. The low operating temperatures of Alkaline fuel cells is one of the main advantages for pursuing further improvements in the technology for terrestrial applications.

Hydrogen Energy for India

The Indian economy is dependent on a complex energy mix. About 133,000 MW grid generating capacity has been set up in the country and it is expected that by 2012 this capacity may exceed 200,000 MW. The Indian economy is poised to achieve higher growth rates, which will result in corresponding higher demand for energy.

The share of the transport sector in the total energy consumption in the country is significant. Liquid fossil fuels are the main source of energy supply for the transport sector. India has a very large variety of vehicles, ranging from manually driven bullock carts and cycles to fossil fuel driven light weight vehicles such as two / three wheelers, cars and heavy vehicles like buses and trucks etc. The largest numbers of vehicles are two and three wheelers with an estimated population of more than 40 million, out of the estimated 60 million vehicles in the country. The two / three wheelers are a major source of urban air pollution. Transport sector consumes most of the liquid fossil fuels.

At present coal and petroleum products occupy the central place in the country's overall energy mix. The known resources of liquid fossil fuels are likely to last another 50 years if the consumption pattern continues to grow at existing rate. Its consumption has been increasing at a very steep rate and with the present indigenous production of about 34 MMT, being less than 30% of annual requirement. India is heavily dependent on imported crude oil. With the uncertain and volatile nature of international crude oil prices, which have reached alarming levels in recent months, it has become vitally important to urgently tap the alternative energy sources for ensuring energy security for the country.

Energy security is a major challenge that needs imaginative and innovative solutions. There can be no unique solutions for ensuring energy security for a country like India. All options for diversification of fuels and energy sources need to be pursued vigorously if the Indian economy is to achieve its economic and social goals.

While a number of options are available for decentralized power generation, few alternatives are available for the transport sector, as it requires on-board storage of the fuel. These options include alcohols, bio-diesel and hydrogen. Recently, the use of biofuels has also been taken up in internal combustion engines. Production of bio-diesel would require considerable amount of land area, as compared to an equivalent centralized hydrogen production plant.

Hydrogen as a Fuel

Hydrogen is a clean fuel and an efficient energy carrier. Hydrogen is found in water, organic compounds and hydrocarbons such as petrol, natural gas, methanol and propane. The properties of hydrogen as compared to other conventional fuels. Hydrogen is high in energy content as it contains 120.7 MJ/kg, which is the highest for any known fuel. However, its energy content compared to volume is rather low. This poses challenges with regard to its storage for civilian applications, when compared to storage of liquid fossil fuels. When burnt, hydrogen produces water as a by-product and is, therefore, environmentally benign. Although no CO_2, etc. are produced if hydrogen is burnt in air, yet NOx will be formed at high temperatures. One of the advantages of hydrogen as a fuel is that it can be used directly in the existing internal combustion engines and turbines. It can also be used as a fuel in fuel cells for electricity generation. Hydrogen applications, besides industrial application, cover power generation, transport applications and heat. However, when compared to other alternatives, use of hydrogen in transport sector appears to be more beneficial as it is possible to store hydrogen on-board.

In view of its unique properties, large-scale use of hydrogen in transport sector can help India in achieving energy security through reduction in import of fossil fuels and also reduction in the urban air pollution. Therefore, it is necessary to develop hydrogen energy technologies for large-scale use especially for the transport sector. In the Indian context, apart from substitution of liquid fossil fuels by hydrogen produced from locally available resources, development of hydrogen based decentralized energy systems is relevant for meeting energy needs, in the remote, far-flung and un-electrified regions.

Hydrogen is seen as a potential alternative to fossil fuels, which can produce clean electricity and heat, efficiently. However, the transition to the hydrogen economy from the present fossil fuel based economy will require solutions to many challenges in the areas of production, storage, delivery and applications and spanning infrastructure, technology, economics and large scale public awareness.

Development of Hydrogen Energy Technologies

Several major countries, including Canada, Germany, Japan, UK, USA. etc. are supporting comprehensive research, technology development and demonstration programme for developing and deploying fuel cell systems for stationary, portable and transport applications. The focus of research in these countries is on producing fuel cells for automobiles and also for electricity generation by 2020.

India is one of the few developing countries alongwith China and Brazil, which have strong hydrogen energy research and development programme. In view of the large number of two and three wheelers in the country, apart from development of hydrogen fuel cell vehicles and generators, India is also focusing on the direct use of hydrogen in IC engines. The Ministry of New and Renewable Energy has been supporting research and demonstration activities to develop Hydrogen and Fuel Cell Technologies and their applications for more than a decade. As a result of these efforts, hydrogen operated motorcycles; three-wheelers and small generators have been developed in the country. In addition, Fuel Cells to directly produce electricity from hydrogen and Fuel Cells – Battery Hybrid Van have been developed. Hydrogen production from distillery waste, bagasse and other renewable methods is under development. Hydrogen storage in metal hydrides has also been developed and demonstrated. At present, research is in progress to further improve the technologies for prototype vehicles and generators developed so far. There is need to accelerate the development of hydrogen energy technologies in India as a substitute to petroleum products in partnership with industry and research organizations.

Hydrogen Production / Supply Plans

Hydrogen (H2) is one the most abundant elements available on earth. However, it is not found in elemental form. The richest source of hydrogen is water. The other major sources include fossil fuels like petroleum, natural gas, coal and biomass. Hydrogen energy like electricity is a secondary energy source. A primary energy source is required to produce hydrogen. Hydrogen production technologies in commercial use today are catalytic steam reforming of natural gas, naphtha and other hydrocarbons, partial oxidation of hydrocarbons, gasification of coal and electrolysis of water. Hydrogen is currently being produced in India on large scale in fertilizer and petroleum refining industries, mainly based on steam reforming of naphtha and natural gas. Hydrogen is also produced as a by-product in the chemical industry. The present cost of commercially available hydrogen is high for applications in automobiles and for power generation etc. Several other methods of hydrogen production such as biomass gasification or pyrolysis, dissociation of methanol or ammonia, thermo-chemical and electrochemical splitting of water, biological photosynthesis or fermentation etc. are still at different stages of development. These emerging hydrogen production technologies may provide low cost clean hydrogen in the future. Emphasis of research is on the development of H2 production techniques which do not emit CO2.

It is envisaged that in the coming decades hydrogen will be produced from large centralized plants as well as decentralized plants, close to the point of use. Renewable energy technologies are expected to play a significant role in the production of low cost and carbon free hydrogen on a decentralized basis.

Hydrogen Supply Plans and Production Technologies

Hydrogen supplies for short term and immediate needs

Substantial quantities of hydrogen are available as by-product or excess hydrogen, which is currently being flared in many chemical industries, can be tapped to meet immediate hydrogen requirement of the transport sector. There is a need for estimating the availability of by-product hydrogen from different sources by carrying out a nationwide survey for meeting immediate requirements of hydrogen for transport and power generation applications.

Steam reforming

Steam methane reforming is at present the most common and least expensive method of producing hydrogen. Steam reforming process refers to the endothermic catalytic conversion of light hydrocarbons with water vapour. The reforming reaction is endothermic and requires external heat input. Most of the modern plants use multi-bed pressure swing adsorption (PSA) to remove water, methane, CO2, N2, and CO from the shift reactor to produce a high purity product (>99.99%). This is a commercially proven, cost effective technology, contributing to about 40-50% of total hydrogen production capacity worldwide. This process is extensively used in India in the fertilizer and petroleum refineries. Large numbers of reformers utilizing various feedstock need to be deployed to produce hydrogen in larger quantities. A phased growth of reformers based on different feedstock needs to be planned. Small and medium scale SMR units (capacity ranging from 50 to 24,000 kg/day) are commercially available for distributed production of hydrogen. Efforts for development of skid-mounted reformer for producing hydrogen from methanol have also been initiated.

Electrolysis

Electrolysis is the decomposition of water into hydrogen and oxygen. The major factor in the electrolysis route of hydrogen production is the cost of electricity, which is about three to five times more as compared to the cost of fossil fuel feed stock. In view of the high cost of electrolysis, new techniques such as high temperature steam electrolysis are being developed, where about 40% of the energy required could be supplied as heat. Many agencies in the country are involved in the development of electrolysis -based hydrogen production processes.

Partial oxidation of heavy hydrocarbons

Partial oxidation of hydrocarbons is another method of hydrogen production. In this process a hydrocarbon fuel reacts with limited supply of oxygen to produce a hydrogen mixture, which is then purified. Partial oxidation can be applied to a wide range of hydrocarbons including natural gas, heavy oils, solid biomass, and coal. Its primary by-product is carbon dioxide.

Gasification or partial oxidation of coal

Hydrogen production from gasification of coal is a well-established technology. Gasification can be used to produce syngas from residual oil and coal. More recently, it has been used to process petroleum coke. Coal is ground to a fine powder and then mixed with water to create a 50 - 70% solid content suspension, suitable for pumping. When gasifying liquids, it is necessary to remove and recover soot, ash, and any metals that are present in the feed. Feed preparation and handling steps beyond the basic gasification process are needed for coal, petroleum coke, and other solids such as biomass. CO2 sequestration is necessary to produce large quantities of hydrogen from this method. There are significant coal reserves in India, but Indian coal has around 40% ash content. With appropriate technologies like IGCC, coal can replace natural gas and oil as the primary feedstock for production of hydrogen or synthetic liquid fuel apart from producing electricity. For mid-term supplies, coal gasification is the preferred route for hydrogen production to ensure supplies of large quantities of hydrogen. IGCC for Indian coals is under development. In addition, work related to under ground gasification of coal (UGGC) for producing hydrogen/ synthetic fluid fuel has been initiated by ONGC and NTPC.

Production from biomass

The different methods for hydrogen production from biomass are: gasification / pyrolysis of solid biomass, fermentation of liquid manure and biological hydrogen production. Biomass gasification is similar to coal gasification in many ways. The feedstock is relatively inexpensive. In the pyrolysis method biomass is thermally decomposed at a high temperatures (450-550°C) in an inert atmosphere to form a bio16 oil composed of about 85% oxygenated organics and 15% water. The bio-oil is then steam reformed using conventional technology to produce hydrogen.

The biological processes by which hydrogen is released or appears as an intermediate product can be mainly identified as of two types: Photosynthesis (using algae and photosynthetic bacteria) and fermentation (anaerobic decomposition of organic matter). These processes are at different stages of research and demonstration. Fermentative process is presently considered better due to higher hydrogen yield. In India, production of hydrogen from biomass holds considerable promise. Being agricultural country and having variety of climatic conditions, India has wide range of biomass available.

Hydrogen production from industrial effluents can be a possible production route for mid-term supplies. Distributed hydrogen production can be achieved by using organic industrial waste from distilleries etc. by employing photochemical, electrochemical or biological processes.

Hydrogen Production from Bio-organic Wastes

Many laboratories in the country are involved in the development of technologies for hydrogen production from biomass.

High temperature thermo chemical splitting of water

Thermo-chemical splitting of water by getting heat from an external source such as high temperature nuclear reactor or solar concentrators seems to be the most promising route for providing long-term hydrogen supplies and for large centralized hydrogen production. Large-scale hydrogen production by this process offers quite attractive concept for future CO2 free and efficient energy systems. This process for splitting of water is carried out through multi step chemical reaction at high temperatures in the range of 550-1000°C depending on the chemical processes adopted. Processes like Iodine-Sulfur (I-S), Calcium - Bromine (Ca-Br) and Copper- Chlorine (Cu-Cl) have been considered promising for further development. High temperature nuclear reactors are suitable for supplying heat to endothermic process steps involved in these processes. Department of Atomic Energy through its Bhabha Atomic Research Centre (BARC) is involved in developing technologies related to high temperature reactors.

Low temperature water splitting

Photo-catalytic processes involve semiconducting powders spread on water containing solutions, which produce hydrogen on exposure to sunlight. These techniques are still in the early stages of development. Photo-electrochemical processes involving wet photovoltaic systems to produce hydrogen through splitting of water in one step.

Hydrogen can also be produced from water using alkali metal sodium. During the reaction, sodium is transformed to sodium hydroxide. However, the reaction is not reversible and sodium can be recovered from sodium hydroxide using solar furnace. Such processes hold promise for future as viable processes for hydrogen production.

Postproduction cleaning processes

In the post production cleaning stage, all remaining unwanted elements are separated from the hydrogen gas. This especially applies to the products of incomplete reforming like CO, H2O, O2, NH3 and CO2. The catalytic processes serve exclusively for the removal of CO, while the other processes like adsorption process / membrane process / metal hydrides can also be applied for removal of other elements, depending on the materials used.

Carbon dioxide sequestration

CO2 is a by-product in many methods to produce hydrogen from fossil fuels. This CO2 has to be sequestered / stored so that the total process is nearly clean from the environmental emissions. The main options include (i) use of deep saline reservoirs, (ii) injection of CO2 into hydrocarbon deposits to enhance oil recovery (EOR) or production of coal-bed methane (CBM), and (iii) injection into the deep ocean. Without capture and storage of CO2, the reforming or gasification processes would normally release this gas into atmosphere. Capture of CO2 would add about 25 – 30% to the cost of producing hydrogen.

Synthetic fluid fuel

Production of synthetic fluid fuel along with hydrogen production from coal, biomass, etc., which can be used as fuel in IC engines, also needs to be looked into. A synthetic fluid fuel i.e. methanol would be easy to produce, transport and utilize efficiently in IC engines.

Green Initiative for Future Transport (GIFT)

The Green Initiative for Future Transport (GIFT) is aimed at developing and demonstrating hydrogen powered IC engine and fuel cell based vehicles ranging from small two/three wheelers to heavy vehicles through different phases of development. Hydrogen based IC engines have the potential to provide a useful bridge to future pure hydrogen and fuel cell vehicles, particularly through the cost effective introduction of a hydrogen infrastructure. Market drivers will determine, if and when fuel cell technology is commercially viable for transport applications. Moreover, pure electric vehicle technology is also improving rapidly and would help with introduction of fuel cell based power trains. It is recognized that the performance of the hydrogen fuelled vehicles have to be at par with the commercially available options to the consumer in performance, safety, convenience and also in the cost. This would require a well planned and coordinated industry driven action plan. The Indian automobile industry is committed and geared to take up the challenges in this task. It is envisaged that by 2020 about one million vehicles would be on Indian roads that would use hydrogen as a fuel. The ultimate aim by 2020 should be to introduce such vehicles which are capable of providing technical performance matching with conventional petroleum driven vehicle.

Green Initiative for Power Generation (GIP)

The Green Initiative for Power Generation (GIP) envisages developing and demonstrating hydrogen powered IC engine/turbine and fuel cell based decentralized power generating systems ranging from small milli watt capacity to MW size systems through different phases of technology development and demonstration. High temperature fuel cells offer a promising option for decentralized generation of efficient and clean power. This initiative would help in providing clean energy in a decentralized manner to rural and remote areas, apart from power generation in urban centres. The ultimate goal by 2020 would be to introduce such power generating systems in large numbers, which are capable of providing technical performance matching with a conventional fossil fuel driven generator.

It is envisaged that by 2020 a large number of decentralized power generating systems with a cumulative capacity of 1000 MW would be set up in the country that would use hydrogen as a fuel.

Hydrogen Safety, Codes and Standards

Hydrogen is already being produced, stored, transported and consumed in various chemical and industrial processes. The use of hydrogen as an energy carrier is yet to be exploited. During its usage in industrial processes, several relevant safety codes and standards have been developed. In addition, most of the large gas manufacturers have developed their own supplementary standards. These standards are predominantly concerned with the industrial applications of hydrogen. The present regulations involve transportation of hydrogen to and from sites. However, for hydrogen applications in power generation, mobile and transport sector, existing codes and standards would need major additions and up-gradations.

Development of suitable standards for hydrogen and fuel cells will not only help ensure safety but also facilitates business in hydrogen as an energy carrier / commodity and in the products, services and systems that are being developed to make hydrogen easily available and acceptable especially for consumer applications.

Status of Standards

International standards for hydrogen technologies

Several international organizations like International Standards Organization (ISO) and International Electrotechnical Commission (IEC) have been working on the development of standards and codes relevant to use of hydrogen energy and fuel cells. The main objective of developing these standards is to facilitate use of hydrogen energy technologies in a user-friendly manner.

Indian Codes and standards for hydrogen

Hydrogen has been in use in Indian industry for a long period. During this period several regulations and codes for safe handling of hydrogen have been developed. The Bureau of Indian Standards (BIS) has also issued specification for compressed gaseous hydrogen storage (IS – 1090). The Department of Explosives is entrusted with the administration of Explosives Act, 1884, Petroleum Act, 1934, Inflammable Act, 1952 and other rules framed under these acts which also includes static and mobile pressure vessel (unfired) rules, 1981 and the gas cylinder rules, 1981. These rules are published & administered by the Chief Controller of Explosives, Department of Explosives, Nagpur. Recently this organization has been renamed as Petroleum and Explosives Safety Organization (PESO). The Oil Industry Safety Directorate (OISD) has formulated and coordinated implementation of a series of self-regulatory measures aimed at enhancing the safety in oil and gas industry in India.

1.3. FISSION ENERGY

Nuclear Fission - Age Old Dream Of Infinite Power; Power To Destroy!

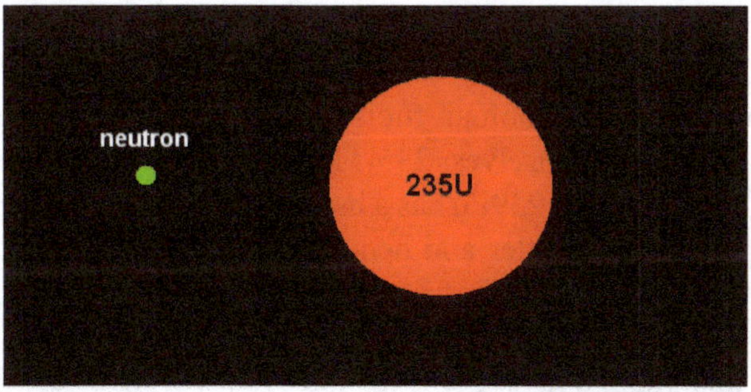

Nuclear power is produced by controlled nuclear fission reaction. Nuclear fission is a nuclear reaction in which the nucleus of an atom splits into smaller parts (lighter nuclei), often producing free neutrons and photons. The amount of free energy contained in nuclear fuel is millions of times the amount of free energy contained in a similar mass of chemical fuel such as gasoline, making nuclear fission a very tempting source of energy.

Mostly Uranium 235 is used as fuel for the fission reactions in nuclear power reactors. The average energy associated with a single reaction of a Uranium 235 is 215Mev. Commercial and utility plants currently use nuclear fission reactions to heat water to produce steam, which is then used to generate electricity. Now nuclear energy is also being used to power ships and other similar large transport vessels. A typical working Diagram of a nuclear power reactor is as shown:

Schematic of a Nuclear Power Plant

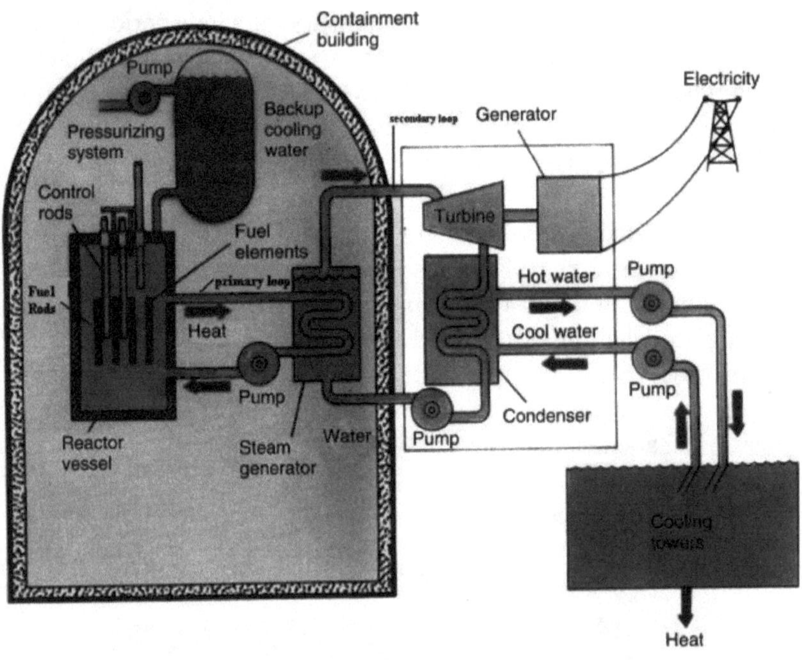

The most common nuclear fuels, 235U and 239Pu, are not major radioactive hazards by themselves: 235U has a half-life of approximately 700 million years, and although 239Pu has a half-life of only about 24,000 years, it is a pure alpha particle emitter and hence not particularly dangerous unless ingested. Once a fuel element has been used, the remaining fuel material is intimately mixed with highly radioactive fission products that emit energetic beta particles and gamma rays. Some fission products have half-lives as short as seconds; others have half-lives of tens of thousands of years, requiring long-term storage in facilities until the fission products decay into non-radioactive stable isotopes.

Most recently beryllium oxide is being seen as a viable nuclear fuel. Uranium pellets have the disadvantage of poor heat conduction which makes it unstable during fission reaction as the core of the pellet heats too quickly.

There have been a few costly nuclear power station disasters that have happened in the past. Also irresponsible governments can easily misuse the enriched Uranium for nuclear arms production.

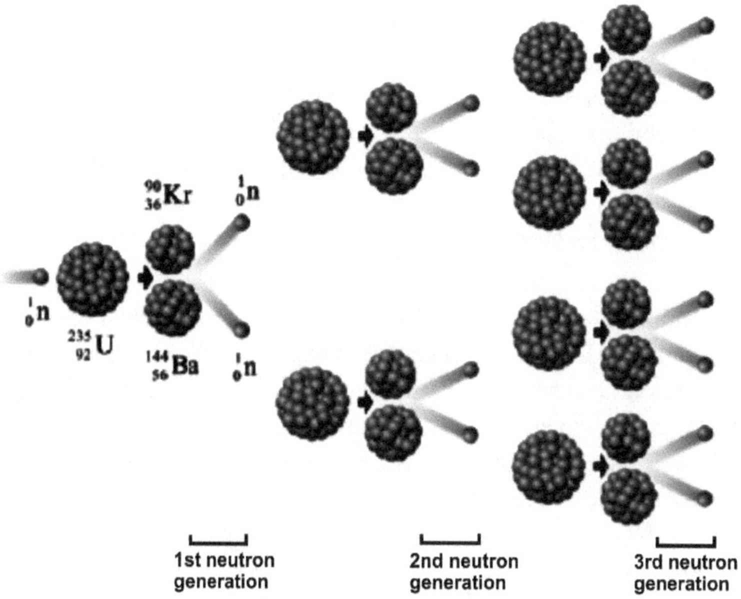

Movements such as greenpeace have denounced the use of nuclear fuels as alternate energy in the past. The recent APEC report also shows that greenpeace had rejected nuclear fuels on the basis that current day nuclear technology does not warrant its use even for peaceful purposes.

All radioactive disposals are indeed expensive and short-sighted. Till this problem is solved in a satisfactory and energy efficient manner, nuclear fuels cannot be used for peaceful purposes in a effective way. However with the immediate and urgent need for finding alternate energy resources in most countries, nuclear power is still a very attractive option. The research and development in disposal and recycling of radioactive wastes is still a very high priority effort.

India's Nuclear Development

"As long as the world is constituted as it is, every country will have to devise and use the latest devices for its protection. I have no doubt India will develop her scientific researches and I hope Indian scientists will use the atomic force for constructive purposes. But if India is threatened, she will inevitably try to defend herself by all means at her disposal."

These words were said by our great Prime Minister Jawahar Lal Nehru on 26th June 1946. Since then we have been developing our nuclear Systems to provide both energy sufficiency and security to the nation. When India became a free country in 1947, the world was already into the nuclear age. In 1948 India set up its own atomic energy commission under the chairmanship of Homi.J.Bhaba. Later on the Department of Atomic Energy (DAE) was created under the Office of the Prime Minister Jawahar Lal Nehru. The atomic energy commission then set up the Uranium Corporation of India Limited (UCIL) later that year as the PSU. The UCIL, under the administrative control of India's atomic energy commission, began its uranium operations in 1968 at Jaduguda with ore mining and processing facilities, each with 1,000 metric tons per day capacity. India completed negotiations to build a nuclear reactor with the aid of the US and Canada in 1956. The US agreed to supply the "heavy water" for the 40 megawatt research reactor. The 1st commercial reactor began operation in 1969 at Tarapur.

In 1954 India called for a standstill agreement on all nuclear testing and signed the Partial Test Ban Treaty in 1963. It was also one of the members of the Eighteen Nation Disarmament Commission which started negotiating the NPT in July 1965. However, as the negotiations unfolded, Indian excitement diminished. The treaty allowed possession of nuclear weapons to states that had imploded nuclear devices before 1 January 1967. However, it did not address the question of reductions of the arsenals of the Nuclear Weapons State (NWS) adequately. India also felt threatened when China, was included in the treaty as a NWS since China had conducted nuclear tests in 1964 because it had a border dispute with it. So India finally refused to sign the global Treaty on the Non-Proliferation of Nuclear Weapons (NPT). As a result, the 45-member Nuclear Suppliers Group (NSG) banned India from global nuclear trade. The NPT's failure in meeting India's expectations provided it with a motivation to go nuclear. Being out of the NSG also had some benefits for the country:

- The support of the Indian government to help the development of nuclear fuel and technology.
- Creation of a pool of nuclear scientists, engineers and technicians who have developed unique systems in the fast breeder reactor systems, the Thorium fuel cycle, nuclear fuel reprocessing and Tritium extraction & production.

Nuclear power technology in India has reached a state of maturity. The Department of Atomic Energy continues to take steps to further its development. Today, the Nuclear Power Corporation of India Ltd (NPCIL) is responsible for design, construction, commissioning and operation of thermal nuclear power plants. The Nuclear Power Corporation is a triple A-rated company and has been highly commended for its excellent commercial performance, both in building power plants as well as in their operation. The Indian nuclear development programme is divided into 3 stages of development as described below:

STAGE 1: Pressurized Heavy Water Reactor using:

- Natural Uranium di-oxide is used as the fuel matrix
- Heavy water is used as moderator and coolant
- Natural U isotopic composition is 0.7 % fissile U-235 and the rest is U-238.

STAGE 2: Fast Breeder Reactor

- In this Pu-239 serves as the main fissile element
- A blanket of U-238 surrounding the fuel core undergoes nuclear transmutation to produce fresh Pu-239 as more and more Pu-239 is consumed during the operation.
- Besides a blanket of Th-232 around the FBR core also undergoes neutron capture reactions leading to the formation of U-233
- It is technically feasible to produce sustained energy output of 420 GWe from FBR.

STAGE 3: Breeder Reactor

- U-233 is obtained from the nuclear transmutation of Th-232 which is used as a blanket in the second phase Pu-239 fuelled FBR.
- U-233 fuelled breeder reactors will have a Th-232 blanket around the U-233 reactor core which will generate more U-233 as the reactor goes operational thus resulting in the production of more and more U-233 fuel
- These U-233/Th-232 based breeder reactors are under development and would serve as the mainstay of the final thorium utilization stage of the Indian nuclear programme

India's Current Nuclear Potential and Standing

India's Current Nuclear installed capacity is 4183Mwe. This serves 2.5% of the country's energy needs. The ban on India from the NSG group was lifted on September 2008 when Washington pushed through a "waiver" that freed India from 34 years of sanctions. The Civil nuclear cooperation agreements have been signed with the USA, Russia, France, UK and Canada, as well as Argentina, Kazakhstan, Mongolia and Namibia. There are plans for eight 1000 MWe units at the Kudankulam site, and in January 2007 a memorandum of understanding was signed for Russia to build four more there, as well as others elsewhere in India. The new units are expected to be the larger 1200 MWe AES-2006 versions. Russia is reported to have offered a 30% discount on the

$2-billion price tag for each of the phase 2 Kudankulam reactors. This is based on the plans to start a serial production of reactors for the Indian nuclear industry, with much of these equipments and components proposed to be manufactured in India, thereby bringing down costs. In 2005 four sites were approved for eight new reactors. Two of the sites, Kakrapar and Rajasthan, would have 700 MWe indigenous PHWR units, Kudankulam would have imported 1000 or 1200 MWe light water reactors alongside the two being built there by Russia, and the fourth site was greenfield for two 1000 MWe LWR units - Jaitapur in the Ratnagiri district of Maharashtra state, on the west coast. The plan has since expanded to six 1600 MWe EPR units.

Reactor	**State**	**Type**	**MWe net, each**	**Commercial operation**
Tarapur 1 & 2	Maharashtra	BWR	150	1969
Kaiga 1 & 2	Karnataka	PHWR	202	1999-2000
Kaiga 3	Karnataka	PHWR	202	2007
Kakrapar 1 &2	Gujarat	PHWR	202	1993-95
Kalpakkam 1 & 2 (MAPS)	Tamil Nadu	PHWR	202	1984-86
Narora 1 & 2	Uttar Pradesh	PHWR	202	1991-92
Rajasthan 1	Rajasthan	PHWR	90	1973
Rajasthan 2	Rajasthan	PHWR	187	1981
Rajasthan 3 & 4	Rajasthan	PHWR	202	1999-2000
Rajasthan 5 & 6	Rajasthan	PHWR	202	Feb & April 2010
Tarapur 3 & 4	Maharashtra	PHWR	490	2006, 05
Total (19)			**4183 MWe**	

Challenges hindering Nuclear Growth in the Country

There a lot of challenges or problems that nuclear power faces, that have hindered its development over the period of time. Some of the major challenges faced by the industry are:

Accidents at Nuclear Power Plants

There have been numerous accidents and mistakes at Nuclear Power plants and reprocessing facilities that have made the issue of the safety in the plants one of the major challenges to be tackled in the setting up of any nuclear plants in the country. In India, there have not been any severe accidents leading to core meltdown or large radiation exposures to the public until now. On measures of occupational exposure to workers, India's nuclear facilities perform poorly. For example in the 1980s, radiation exposures to power plant workers were ten times the world average for each unit of electricity and twice the world average for each monitored worker. Some of the major examples of nuclear power plant accidents are:

- Three Mile Island, U.S in 1979
- Chernobyl, Ukraine in 1986
- Narora, India in 1993

Biological Effects of Radiation

The current scientific data suggests that there is no safe minimum, or threshold, for adverse radiation effects on the DNA of biological systems and those, even small doses can produce consequences for the organism.

The biological effects fall into the following categories:

- Cell Death
- Cancer Induction
- Genetic Damage to Future Generations
- Dose-Response Tissue Reactions

These Issues with the effect of radiations on individuals living close to the plant and working in them is another very big cause of concern. As recently as 2003, there have been accidents involving high radiation exposures to workers in India.

Storage and Disposal of High Level Nuclear Reactor Waste

Since the spent nuclear reactor (SNF) fuel is highly radioactive initially it is too dangerous to handle and thus it is very important to shield the radioactivity from humans and the environment. The radioactive material in the SNF generally falls into three categories:

- Un-reacted fuel, usually uranium
- Fission products
- Activation products, most notably plutonium

Usually the storage and disposal of the SNF is done by putting the nuclear waste into large pools of water. The water cools the radioactive isotopes and shields the environment from the radiation. Nuclear waste is typically stored in these supervised pools between 20-40 years. As the SNF ages the radioactivity decreases, reaching the point where it does not need to be water cooled and can be placed in dry storage facilities. Throughout this time there is a great reduction in heat and radioactivity and this makes handling of nuclear waste safer and easier. Then these can be processed or disposed off as required.

Safety of Nuclear Power Plants

Safety of nuclear power plant installations has also been a point of concern to the nuclear power industry. The Government has come up with regulations and laws to ensure the safety of these nuclear installations.

The Nuclear Liability Bill

The 123 agreement (Indo-US) in August 2008, ended India's isolation from global atomic commerce and opened up its foreign market for foreign players, but the system cannot be implemented until India put in place a compensation regime that limited the liability of private companies in case of an accident. This gave birth to the Civil Liability for Nuclear Damage Bill 2010, which stipulates the compensation burden on the state-run reactor operator, the liability of the federal government and the responsibility of private suppliers and contractors. The bill is very important for foreign players to enter the Indian market, because if such a bill is not in place, then the compensation claims from a nuclear accident can be enough to bankrupt a private company. Finally the nuclear liability bill was passed in the Lok sabha after a lot of debate on the cap provided. The cap has been finally set to $320 million for the operator and $450 million by the government.

1.4. NUCLEAR FUSION

Nuclear Fusion - Cold or Hot, Still A Hot Topic of Discussion

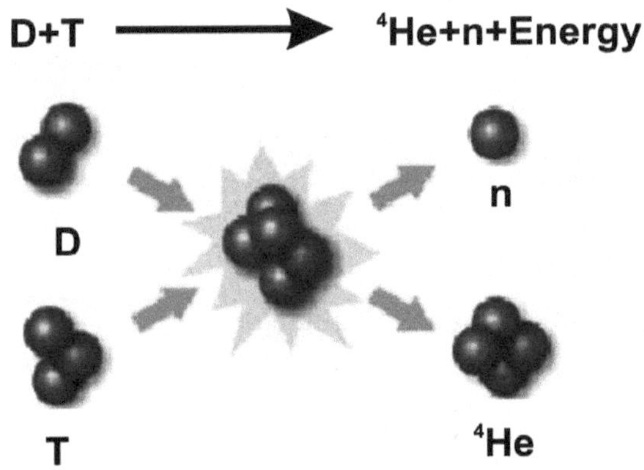

Fusion Reactions

Fusion reaction is a nuclear process by which nuclei of two light elements fuse to produce a fast, heavier nucleus and an even faster nucleon, i.e. a neutron or a proton. There is a small mass difference, say m, between the initial and the final reaction products which gets converted into energy through Einstein's equation E=mc2, c being the speed of light. This energy comes out in the form of kinetic energy of the product particles and can be converted into electricity by conventional technologies.

For such a reaction to occur, the reacting nuclei need to have enough kinetic energy to overcome the repulsive electrostatic barrier between any two of them. For this to happen in laboratory experiments, the reacting particles need to be heated to very high temperatures, more than the temperature at the core of the sun. At such high temperatures, matter remains in plasma state, a collection of charged particles.

A Deuterium and a Tritium nucleus fuse to produce a Helium nucleus and a neutron. The reaction produces 17.6 MeV of energy, out of which the Helium carries 3.5 MeV and the neutron 14.1 MeV. In a plasma undergoing fusion, the reactions can be self sustained, as part of the kinetic energy of the resulting charged Helium can be used to maintain the very high temperatures required to sustain the fusion reactions.

Fusion of Hydrogen atoms to Helium as it occurs naturally in the Stars, is well known due to centuries of spectroscopic study. The light and warmth we get from the Sun is due to this reaction being maintained by a chain process over millions of years. The figure on the left shows the kind of fusion reaction that happens between isotopes of hydrogen to yield He. The exact amount of energy released is calculated by the famous E=mC2 equation of Einstein. The exact energy in MeV is given the table below.

To achieve a controlled fusion reactor for energy purposes is no easy task. The advantage of fusion over fission is that there are no toxic radioactive wastes to worry about. The main difficulty is that to trigger the process the threshold energy needed is quite enormous.

Reactants		**Products**	**Q**	**n/MeV**
First Generation Fusion Fuels				
21H + 21H (D-D)	→	32He + 10n	3.268 MeV	.306
21H + 21H (D-D)	→	31H + 11p	4.032 MeV	0
21H + 31H (D-T)	→	42He + 10n	17.571 MeV	.057
Second Generation Fusion Fuels				
21H + 32He (D-3He)	→	42He + 11p	18.354 MeV	0
Third Generation Fusion Fuels				
32He + 32He	→	42He+ 211p	12.86 MeV	0
115B + 11p	→	3 42He	8.68 MeV	0
Complete Deuterium Fusion - Sum of first 4 rows				
6D	→	2(4He + n + p)	43.225 MeV	.046
Current popular nuclear reaction				
235U + n	→	2 FP+ 2.5n	~200 MeV	.001

In the above table, n/MeV is the ratio of neutrons released to energy release. Low ratio of this is preferred. This is because the high energy neutrons released during a nuclear reaction would react with other products to result in radioactive by-products. The ideal is to have zero radioactive by-products. In this regard the third generation fusion fuels such as 3He with zero neutrons and a high 12.86 MeV is a very much preferred nuclear reaction. There are no radioactive by-products to bother with. The high energy proton released is normally used in generating electricity using electromagnetic fields which also act to contain it.

Recently there has been increased interest in 3He which is abundantly present on the Moon in high concentration as compared to Earth. One of the main reasons why the bombing of Moon surface to get information on the water content within the Moon crust. Although far fetched in terms of cost and effort involved, it has been seen as a future project to have a full time manned station on the Moon to excavate and transport 3He for fusion reactors on Earth.

There have been a few attempts at a laboratory fusion attempt. The method used is electrochemical wherein the hydrogen produced in situ by splitting of water is fused by the high temperature and pressure built-up within collapsing micro-bubbles. These experiments are generally referred to as 'Cold Fusion'. It does not mean the threshold energy is reduced. It simply means the high energy needed is achieved in a small way within collapsing micro-bubbles.

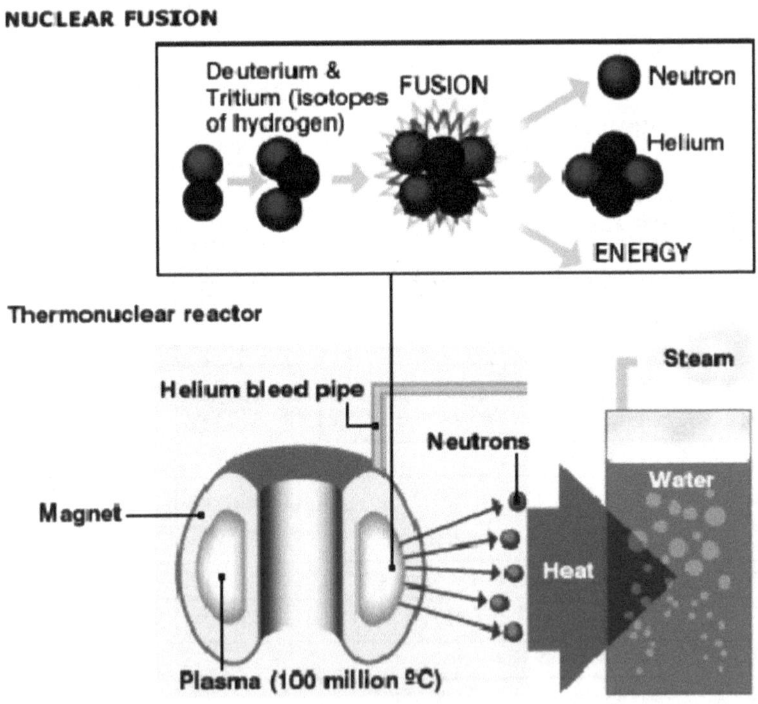

There have been attempts at achieving fusion explosives such as was attempted with 'Hydrogen Bomb' experiments. There have been other fusion explosives that have been experimented with such as neutron bomb and cobalt bomb. Whereas neutron bomb has no radioactive fallouts, 60Co is less attractive because of radioactive fallouts. The splitting of water by electrochemical method is the most promising of current day technologies for achieving cold fusion.

Creating Starfire on Earth

The brightest example of fusion reactions in nature is the Sun and the stars in which hydrogen nuclei, bound together by strong gravitational force, fuse in a chain of reactions shown in the below table to produce finally Helium.

Fusion reactions in the Sun

p+p > D + e^+	First two protons (hydrogen nuclei) fuse to produce a deuterium and a positron
p+D > He^3 + gamma Radiation	A proton and a deuterium fuse to produce a light isotope of Helium, He^3 (He with one neutron)
He^3+He^3 > He^4 + D+D	Two He^3 fuses to produce He^4 (He with 2 neutrons), for each of this reaction to happen, the first two reactions have to occur twice

In laboratory experiments, the fusion reaction that is least difficult to achieve is that between a deuterium and a tritium nucleus, because it is the one that occurs at relatively lower temperatures, as is evident from the various reaction probabilities as shown in Figure 1. However, several fusion reactions are possible between the lightest of nuclei, namely hydrogen (H) and its isotopes (Deuterium (D) and Tritium (T) with one and two extra neutrons respectively) isotope of helium, He3 or even boron (B), Lithium (Li) and so on.. Some of these reactions and their products are shown in the belowFigure .

Unlike in the Sun, where particles are tightly bound together by the enormous gravitational pull of the huge mass of the Sun, on earth, it takes enormous effort to keep the charged particles together (note that like charges repel). This is the major area of fusion research - that of confinement, i.e., how to maintain a plasma of large enough density of Deuterium and Tritium at a high enough temperature for a sufficiently long time so that the particles fuse and produce net energy, larger than that required to produce and hold the plasma in the first place.

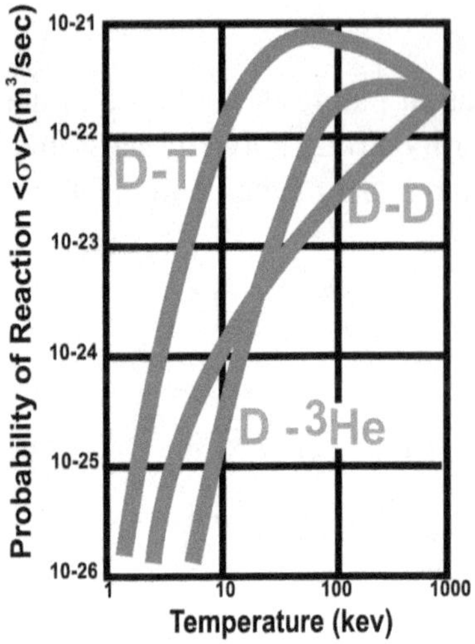

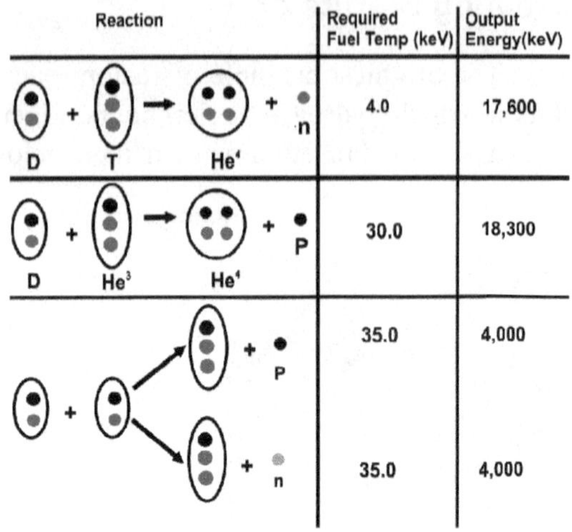

Examples of Fusion Reactions

Fusion Fuels

Fusion energy, when it becomes available, will practically be a source of unlimited amount of energy. For example, just a kilogram of D-T fuel would release 108 kWh of energy (3.39´1011 J per gram) and would provide the requirements of a 1GW (electrical) power station for a day. Deuterium is contained naturally in water, one D atom out of 6700 H atoms and can be separated out. Tritium is unstable by nature, with a half-life of 12.3 years, and has to be manufactured from lithium. In a reactor, once the initial start-up inventory of tritium (manufactured elsewhere) has been used up, tritium can be obtained by neutron bombardment lithium contained in the blanket. Lithium is widely distributed throughout the earth's crust. Fusion will consume very small quantities of these fuels, 0.5-5 tonnes per GW(e).a, depending on the efficiency of using the natural lithium. The total reserves of lithium are estimated to be 1016 Gigajoules in land, and 1019 Gigajoules in the sea, sufficient for thirty thousand, and thirty million years respectively, at today's energy consumption rate.

Advanced Future Fusion Fuels

The D-T reactions have the disadvantages that 80% of the energy is carried out by high energy neutrons and that tritium must be generated inside the reactor. The high velocity neutrons impose massive shielding requirements, produce radiation damage and are a source of undesired activation of the reactor structure. To generate tritium, a highly complex breeding blanket must surround the reactor core. Other reactions, having a highly reduced or completely absent neutron output and utilizing fuels that do not require breeding have therefore been considered. For example, in a D-D reactor, tritium would only be produced in small amounts by a secondary reaction and most of the neutrons resulting from this process would have much less energy and thus would be easier to shield. Similarly a reactor operating on H-B fuel would virtually suppress neutron production and could even lead to efficient direct conversion to electricity.

A D-He3 mixture would not have tritium breeding requirements but would give neutron yields several orders of magnitude below those from the D-T reaction (furthermore He3 is virtually non-existent on earth and may have to be transported from the moon). However, the use of these so-called advanced fuels faces many difficulties. Because of their lower fusion reactivity, the power density in the plasma for a given plasma pressure would be 50-100 times smaller for any other fusion fuel than for D-T and the required confinement time would be 25-50 times larger. This would require either operation at much higher values of density and temperature. There are several other complexities involved. For the first generation of fusion reactors, the fuel will certainly be D-T, and the neutron problems will be tackled by using low activation structural materials, presently under development. Advanced fuels will therefore be investigated only as a next generation option.

Conditions for Fusion

The closeness of plasma to power plant conditions is measured in terms of the triple product nTtE, the product of density, i.e. the number of fuel particles per unit volume (n), the temperature (T) and the energy confinement time (tE). For a 50-50 D-T plasma at about 20 keV, to achieve ignition condition in a power plant, (i.e., when the fusion reaction is self-sustained through alpha particle heating), one would need this triple product to have the value.

$$n_{DT} T_i \tau_E > 6x10^{21}\ m^{-3}\ keV\ s$$

Another important parameter for fusion based power plant is Q, the ratio of fusion power to input auxiliary heating power. While fusion power plant generating electricity would need Qe"10, an ignited power plant would correspond to Q=" , since there is no externally injected heating power in such a device. Present day fusion experiments have brought the triple product to within a factor of 3-5 of its final required value and have already exceeded conditions equivalent to a Q=1 operating power plant.

Importance of Fusion Energy

At the beginning of the 21st century, human society is faced with a precarious situation of increasing energy demands, especially from growing third world economies like India and China, coupled with a fast depleting conventional energy resources which has been dominated by fossil fuel in the past century. Figure 1 highlights the difference between the demand and the available supply which has already started widening. This has led to and can potentially lead to in future conflicts of human societies which can become a serious problem unless a viable extractable alternative energy resource(s) is not obtained quickly.

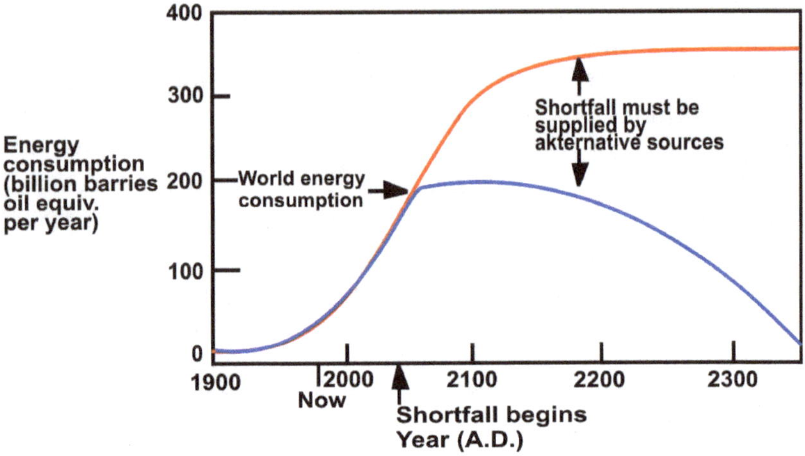

Energy Demand (red curve) and available Fossil Fuels (blue curve)

1.5. HYDRO ENERGY

Hydro Energy - Flow with the Tide

Introduction

Water (Hydro) has two very interesting properties. It being a fluid can carry energy as both heat and as kinetic energy. It also has capacity to do work if its potential energy can be effectively used. Hydropower is a renewable energy resource because it uses the Earth's water cycle to generate electricity. Water evaporates from the Earth's surface, forms clouds, precipitates back to earth, and flows toward the ocean. The movement of water as it flows downstream creates kinetic energy that can be converted into electricity. 2700 TWH is generated every year. Hydropower supplies at least 50% of electricity production in 66 countries and at least 90% in 24 countries. [ii]Hydropower is by far the single largest renewable energy source in India, accounting for over 10% of total electricity generation. . While most of this energy is from large hydro-electric plants, small hydro plants (up to 25 MW capacities) have also started making a dent in India.

The kinetic energy of water flow has been used for electrical power generation for over several decades. There are quite a few hydro-electric power stations in operation. Man made structures such as dams built across rivers serve dual purpose of storage and power generation. Initial installation and construction costs and maintenance costs are offset by its utilization for irrigation, water supply and power generation. Only where there is perennial water supply such as rivers and reservoirs fed by the seasonal rain and snow can be effectively used for this purpose. In the last few years due to drastic climatic changes in several countries, there are draught conditions that have made many of these power-stations non-functional or dependent on fossil fuel for their operation.

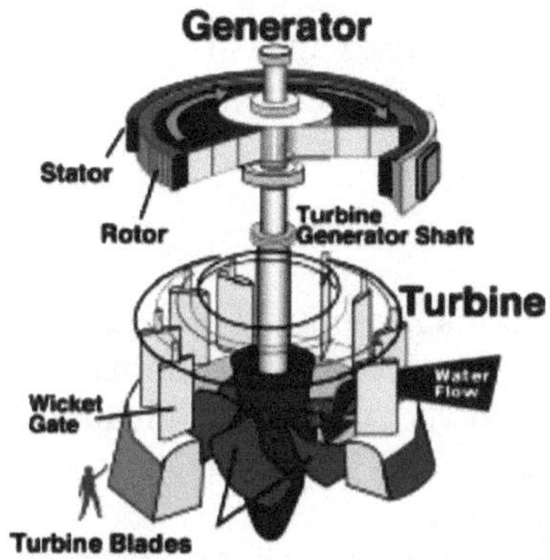

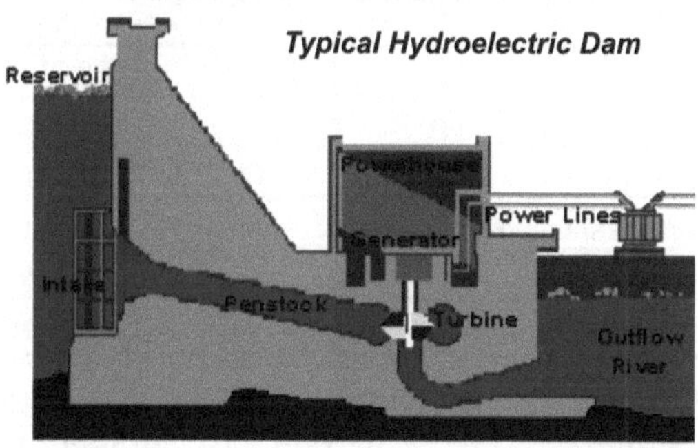

The other form of kinetic energy from water is the tidal power. Turbines built on the ocean bed can be used to generate electricity. There are a few such generators around the world which uses existing strong ebb and flow of the tides. A tradition of research into propeller turbines in both air and water has given rise to expertise in this area. Successful civil engineering and marine biology departments also contribute to the relevant skills.

The other form of kinetic energy is the surf or waves. But this is not so regulated and adaptation for turning the turbine is difficult. A few stations have been built which utilizes this energy in a clever way. One is to adapt a blow-hole which pushes the air periodically as the water fills a enclosed chamber with in-coming wave. The other adaptation is the driving of a piston on the ocean bed when the wave passes the surface.

Technology

A hydroelectric power plant consists of a high dam that is built across a large river to create a reservoir, and a station where the process of energy conversion to electricity takes place. The first step in the generation of energy in a hydropower plant is the collection of run-off of seasonal rain and snow in lakes, streams and rivers, during the hydrological cycle. The run-off flows to dams downstream. The water falls through a dam, into the hydropower plant and turns a large wheel called a turbine. The turbine converts the energy of falling water into mechanical energy to drive the generator After this process has taken place electricity is transferred to the communities through transmission lines and the water is released back into the lakes, streams or rivers. This is entirely not harmful, because no pollutants are added to the water while it flows through the hydropower plant.

Potential in India

India is blessed with immense amount of hydro-electric potential and ranks 5th in terms of exploitable hydro-potential on global scenario. As per assessment made by CEA, India is endowed with economically exploitable hydro-power potential to the tune of 1 48 700 MW of installed capacity. The basin wise assessed potential is as under :-

Basin/Rivers	Probable Installed Capacity (MW)
Indus Basin	33,832
Ganga Basin	20,711
Central Indian River system	4,152
Western Flowing Rivers of southern India	9,430
Eastern Flowing Rivers of southern India	14,511
Brahmaputra Basin	66,065
Total	**1,48,701**

In addition, 56 number of pumped storage projects have also been identified with probable installed capacity of 94 000 MW. In addition to this, hydro-potential from small, mini & micro schemes has been estimated as 6 782 MW from 1 512 sites. Thus, in totality India is endowed with hydro-potential of about 2 50 000 MW.

Projects

Major Hydropower generating units

NAME	STATE	CAPACITY (MW)
BHAKRA	PUNJAB	1100
NAGARJUNA	ANDHRA PRADESH	960
KOYNA	MAHARASHTRA	920
DEHAR	HIMACHAL PRADESH	990
SHARAVATHY	KARNATAKA	891
KALINADI	KARNATAKA	810
SRISAILAM	ANDHRA PRADESH	770

Top ten countries (in terms of capacity)

COUNTRY	POWER CAPACITY (MWh)	INSTALLED CAPACITY (MW)
TAJIKISTAN	527000	4000
CANADA	341312	66954
USA	319484	79511
BRAZIL	285603	57517
CHINA	204300	65000
RUSSIA	160500	44000
NORWAY	121824	27528
JAPAN	84500	27229
INDIA	82237	22083
FRANCE	77500	77500

Barriers

The energy of running water has been exploited for very many years. However, traditional approaches have suffered disadvantages due to environmental factors. For example:

- Building a dam across a river floods the land that would otherwise be available for use, alters the landscape, affects the local community that would have lived and worked on the flooded land, alters the character of the river, and prevents the free movement of fish;
- Diverting a river affects the nature of the countryside and does not lend itself to use on a large scale.
- Permanent complete or partial blockage of a river for energy conversion is adversely affected by variations in flow.
- Building large-scale hydro power plants can be polluting and damaging to surrounding ecosystems. Changing the course of waterways can also have a detrimental effect on human communities, agriculture and ecosystems further downstream.
- Hydro projects can also be unreliable during prolonged droughts and dry seasons when rivers dry up or reduce in volume.

Hydro research centres

Alps Power Technologies (P) Limited

The company is manufacturing small turbines and genset up to 1000 KW, complete with microprocessor based static excitor system,microprocessor based digital governor, remote operation and telemetry and telecontrol system, chartless recorder for data etc. The company has its own manufacturing and testing facilities at its works, in ghunna industrial area, Saharanpur, India

Flovel Mecamidi

Flovel Mecamidi Energy Private Limited (FMEPL) is a joint venture between Flovel MG Holdings Private Limited, India and Mecamidi S.A., France. Promoters of Flovel MG Holdings Private Limited along with its core team have decades of experience in marketing, design, manufacture, supply, erection, commissioning & servicing of hydro power projects of all types both for local as well as export markets.

Karshni Intertech Pvt.Ltd

Karshni Intertech Pvt.Ltd is a manufacturer, wholesale supplier, exporter of hydro energy products. Their range of products include hydro energy system components (small), hydroelectric turbines (small), solar charge controllers, water pumping windmills, wind energy system components (large), backup power systems, 100% renewable energy farming , fully integrated systems.

Multitek Consortium

Multitek Consortium is a hydro energy based company located in Delhi, India. Their range of products hydro energy system components (small), water pumps, turbine machines, gates and hoists, penstock etc.

Nagalaxmi Industries

Nagalaxmi Industries are manufacturers of industrial structures for thermal, hydel, nuclear power station, food industries, pharmaceutical, chemical, cement etc.

SBA Hydro Systems Pvt. Ltd

SBA Hydro Systems Pvt. Ltd is a manufacturer, wholesale supplier, exporter of hydro energy products. Their range of products include hydro energy system components (small), hydro energy system components (large), hydro energy systems (large), hydro energy systems (small), hydroelectric turbines (small), hydroelectric turbines (large).

1.6. WIND ENERGY

Wind Energy - Not Gone with the Wind

The wind has been a powerful source of alternative energy for a long time; being used by the Babylonians and Chinese 4,000 years ago to power irrigation pumps. The use of wind for simple machines such as wind mills is well known. Its use for electricity generation is still not so well adapted. Although there has been increase in percentage power generation using wind turbines, more development in this technology needs to be promoted. One of the main draw backs is that it can be noisy and as such not easy to have suburban installations. In large farms where there is abundance of high speed winds throughout the year, substantial percentage power supply can be achieved using wind turbines. Old style wind turbines were housed in sturdy not so high installations. However the current trend is for a series of very high installations. The wind speed being more at greater heights. Wind is a attractive form of renewable energy that can be used, especially in windy countries. The machine and engineering required is quite simple and not very costly. There is also increasing investor participation and interest in wind technology.

Wind turbines are increasingly used in large farms for their energy requirements. Especially with increase in investor interest in this technology. Countries like Australia and New Zealand have been very successful in developing this technology. Their climatic condition is especially useful because of the high winds they have all the year round. With the improvement and innovations in novel composite materials it has been possible to improve on material fatigue and the development of light weight robust materials, has made it possible to develop wind mills with wing span as large as a football field. Siemens is a world leader in renewable energy innovations. The maximum power generation that was possible in the first Siemens wind turbines that were built in the early 80's was only 22 kilowatts. Now there are Siemens wind turbines that produce as much as 3.6 megawatts.

Introduction

Wind is a form of solar energy. Winds are caused by the uneven heating of the atmosphere by the sun, the irregularities of the earth's surface, and rotation of the earth. Wind flow patterns are modified by the earth's terrain, bodies of water, and vegetation. Humans use this wind flow, or motion energy, for many purposes: sailing, flying a kite, and even generating electricity.

The terms wind energy or wind power describes the process by which the wind is used to generate mechanical power or electricity. Wind turbines convert the kinetic energy in the wind into mechanical power. This mechanical power can be used for specific tasks (such as grinding grain or pumping water) or a generator can convert this mechanical power into electricity.

Wind Energy Technology

Simply stated, a wind turbine works the opposite of a fan. Instead of using electricity to make wind, like a fan, wind turbines use wind to make electricity. The wind turns the blades, which spin a shaft, which connects to a generator and makes electricity. Wind turbines generally have three rotor blades, which rotate with wind flow and are coupled to a generator either directly or through a gear box. The rotor blades rotate around a horizontal hub connected to a generator, which is located inside the nacelle. The nacelle also houses other electrical components and the yaw mechanism, which turns the turbine so that it faces the wind. Sensors are used to monitor wind direction and the tower head is turned to line up with the wind. The power produced by the generator is controlled automatically as wind speeds vary. The rotor diameters vary from 30 metres (m) to about 90 m, whereas the towers on which the wind electric generators (WEGs) are mounted, range in height from 25 to 80 m.

Wind has considerable amount of kinetic energy when blowing at high speeds. This kinetic energy when passing through the blades of the wind turbines is converted into mechanical energy and rotates the wind blades and the connected generator, thereby producing electricity. A wind turbine primarily consists of a main tower, blades, nacelle, hub, main shaft, gearbox, bearing and housing, brake, and generator. The main tower is 50–100 m high. Generally, three blades made up of fiber reinforced polyester are mounted on the hub, while in the nacelle the major parts are housed. Under normal operating conditions, the nacelle would be facing the upstream wind direction. The hub connects the gearbox and the blades. Solid high carbon steel bars or cylinders are used as main shaft. The gearbox is used to increase the speed ratio so that the rotor speed is increas-ed to the rated generator speed it is the most critical component and needs regular maintenance. Oil cooling is employed to control the heating of the gearbox. Gearboxes are mounted over dampers to minimize vibration. Failure of gearbox may put the plant out of operation for an entire season as spares are often not available. Thus, new gearless configurations have become attractive for wind plant operators. The above

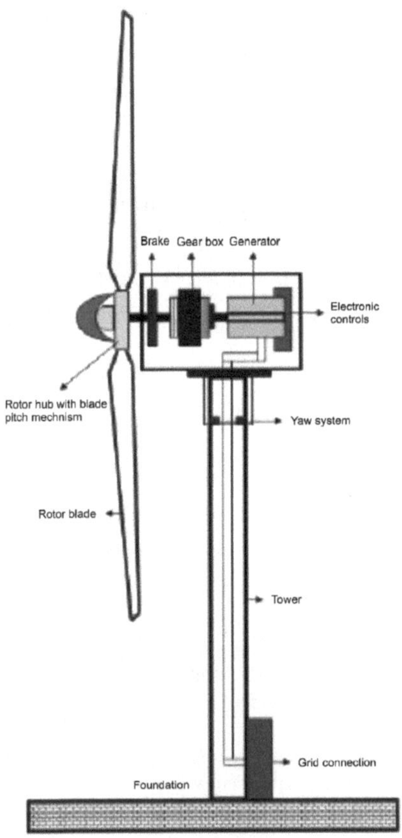

Schematic of Wind Turbine

Figure presents a schematic of a wind turbine. The most dramatic improvement has been in the increasing size and performance of wind turbines. From machines of just 25 kW 20 years ago, the commercial size range sold today is typically from 600 up to 2.5 MW, with 80 m diameter rotors placed on 70–100 m high towers. In 2003, the German company Enercon erected the first prototype of a 4.5 MW turbine with a rotor diameter of 112 m.Wind turbines have a design lifetime of 20–25 yr, with their operation and maintenance costs typically about 3%–5% of the cost of the turbine. At present, wind electric generators are being manufactured in the country by several manufacturers, through i) joint ventures under licensed production, ii) subsidiaries of foreign companies, under licensed production, and iii) Indian companies with their own technology. An indigenization level of up to 70% has been achieved in machines of unit sizes up to 500 kW. The import content is somewhat higher in higher capacity machines. The current annual production capacity of domestic wind turbines is about 2500 MW, which is expected to grow by 10 000 MW until 2010. For grid-interactive power, two types of wind turbines, viz., stall regulated and pitch regulated, are deployed in the country. The stall regulated wind turbines have fixed rotor blades, whereas pitch regulated wind turbines have adjustable rotor blades that change the angle of attach depending on the wind speed. Both technologies have their own advantages and disadvantages.

Wind turbines are also available with lattice, steel tubular, and concrete tubular towers. At present, the wind industry is market driven and competitive. Most of the wind turbine manufacturers in India provide operation and maintenance support and also monitor the field performances of the wind turbines installed by them. With better wind data and the use of analytical tools and experience in siting wind farms, it is expected that the capacity factor for the new wind plants would exceed 20%. The initial phase of growth of the wind industry was based on imported designs and relatively low research and development inputs. India has a solid domestic manufacturing base, including global leader Suzlon, accounting for over half of the market, Vestas Wind Tech and RRB. In addition, international companies have set up production facilities in India, including Enercon, Repower, Siemens, and LM Glasfiber and the new entrants such as ReGen Power Tech, WinWinD, Kenersys, and Global Wind Power. Over the past few years, both the government and the wind power industry have succeeded in injecting greater stability into the Indian market. This has encouraged larger private and public sector enterprises to invest in wind. It has also stimulated a stronger domestic manufacturing sector; some companies now source more than 80% of the components for their turbines in India. Indian company Suzlon, the world's fifth largest turbine manufacturer, is now also well established in the international wind market beyond India, operating in 20 countries around the world and supplying turbines to projects in Asia, North and South America, and Europe. Wind turbines of up to 2.5 MW are presently manufactured in India.

Government Wind Projects

National wind power programme

The Wind Power Programme in India was initiated towards the end of the Sixth Plan, in 1983–84. The programme aims at survey and assessment of wind resources, setting up demonstration projects, and provision of incentives to make wind electricity competitive. As a result, wind electricity has emerged as an option for grid-quality power generation. The costs in respect of wind monitoring stations are shared between the Ministry of Non-Conventional Energy Sources (MNES) and the state nodal agencies in the ratio of 80:20 (90:10 for north-eastern states).

Wind Resource Assessment Programme

The Wind Resource Assessment Programme is being implemented by C-WET (Centre for Wind Energy Technology) in coordination with state nodal agencies. An annual mean wind power density greater than 200 W/m2 (watts per square meter) at 50-metre height has been recorded at 211 wind monitoring stations, covering 13 states and union territories, namely Andaman and Nicobar Islands, Andhra Pradesh, Gujarat, Karnataka, Kerala, Lakshadweep, Madhya Pradesh, Maharashtra, Orissa, Rajasthan, Tamil Nadu, Uttaranchal, and West Bengal.

Master plans

Master plans are available for 97 potential sites for wind power in Andhra Pradesh, Gujarat, Karnataka, Kerala, Madhya Pradesh, Maharashtra, Orissa, Rajasthan, Tamil Nadu, and West Bengal. The master plans provide information on the availability of wind, land, grid availability, and accessibility to the site, which enables project promoters and state nodal agencies to undertake proper planning and implementation of the projects. The master plans have been provided to the state nodal agencies and are made available to project promoters, developers, and consultants through C-WET at a nominal cost.

Wind Energy for Water Pumping and Off-grid Power Generation Projects

Water-pumping windmill A water-pumping windmill pumps water from wells, ponds, and bore wells for drinking, minor irrigation, salt farming, fish farming, etc.

Aerogenerator

An aerogenerator is a small wind electric generator having a capacity of up to 30 kW.

Wind–solar hybrid systems

When an aerogenerator and an SPV system are interfaced, the power generation from these is mutually supplemented, and the resultant hybrid system offers a reliable and cost-effective electric supply in a decentralized mode.

Type	Description
Water-pumping windmills	Three water-pumping windmills of AV-55 type installed in and around Auroville have become the exclusive source of drinking water.
Aerogenerator	• The West Bengal Renewable Energy Development Agency (WBREDA) has installed six aerogenerators of 3-kW capacity each in the existing SPV power plants at Sagar and Mousani islands. • A number of aerogenerators have been installed by the Maharashtra Energy Development Agency (MEDA), and are working satisfactorily. An aerogenerator of 3.2-kW capacity, installed at the Manashakti Research Centre, Lonawala, is supplying electricity to illuminate 22 streetlights.
Wind–solar hybrid systems	• A 5-kW capacity wind–solar hybrid system installed on Vagator beach in Goa, which has become a destination point for tourists. The system illuminates 60 CFLs (compact fluorescent lamps) of 18 watts rating each. • A 15-kW wind–solar hybrid system has recently been installed at the famous pilgrimage site of Bhimashanker Deosthan, in Pune district, Maharashtra. This system provides electricity to meet the needs of the entire temple complex.

Barriers

- Initial cost for wind turbines is greater than that of conventional fossil fuel generators.
- Noise produced by the rotor blades.
- There is interference on television signals.It causes significant bird and other avian deaths.
- Wind resources might not be available near cities and, even so, the space might be used for other purposes that can generate larger profits.
- Wind cannot be stored (unless batteries are used)

- Not all winds can be harnessed to meet the timing of electricity demands.

1.7. BIOENERGY

Bio-Energy - Nature's Organic Generators

Fuels got from either live plant products such as wood, mulch, algae and animal products such as microbes, animal excreta have been in use in some form or other over the centuries. While some of these fuels are not entirely green, they are cost saving and can even be classified as 'renewable'. A liquid known as bio-oil can be created from biomass found in forestry and agricultural residues. The biomass is thermo-chemically converted to bio-oil by using processes called direct liquefaction or fast pyrrolysis. Although bio-oil has a high heating value, it is best suited for direct combustion in large boilers because of its high viscosity. The high water and oxygen content of bio-oils reduces their heating value to less than half the value of petroleum. However, bio-oils are low in viscosity and have been successfully burned in boilers, kilns, turbines and diesel engines. In the future, bio-oil might be burned with a small diesel pilot fuel in large engines for electrical generation or in locomotives or ships.

Certain strains of bacteria produce a combustible gas when they digest biomass in the absence of oxygen. This process is called anaerobic digestion. When the bacteria digest biomass such as animal manure or landfill waste, they produce biogas. Cured cow dung is a fuel which emits methane which is combustible gas. This is therefore used in small and large fuel and electricity generators. In large cattle farms with large output of dung, generators using this fuel can supply all the power supply for the farm. This has been effectively used in farms in developing countries too since it is cost effective.

Ethanol which is the main component in alcohol that is consumed as drink is now additive in Car engine fuel. The maximum 10% can be used safely without damaging the engine. The main recommendations being reductions in greenhouse gas emissions. It can be manufactured by fermentation of molasses, wheat or corn.

Biomass characterization

From the perspective of development of commercial power plants, biomass can be classified under the following different categories:

- Sources of biomass
- Physical characteristics
- Combustion properties
- Ash characteristics

Source of biomass – Different sources include agroresidue, agro-industrial residue, forest residue and municipal solid waste. The market for agro-industrial residues like bagasse, rice husk, etc., is now established and it is possible to make a reasonable forecast on price and availability. For the other biomasses, uncertainty would remain. Financial and risk analysis must always be carried out to take care of these uncertainties.

Physical characteristics – Biomass can be either in woody/granular form like chips, shells, husks or leafy form like straw, stalks, trash, etc. These characteristics play a very important role in the design of:

- Biomass harvesting and collection strategy
- Transportation and storage system
- Fuel feeding system for the boiler and
- Combustion system

Stalk-leafy

Shells-woody

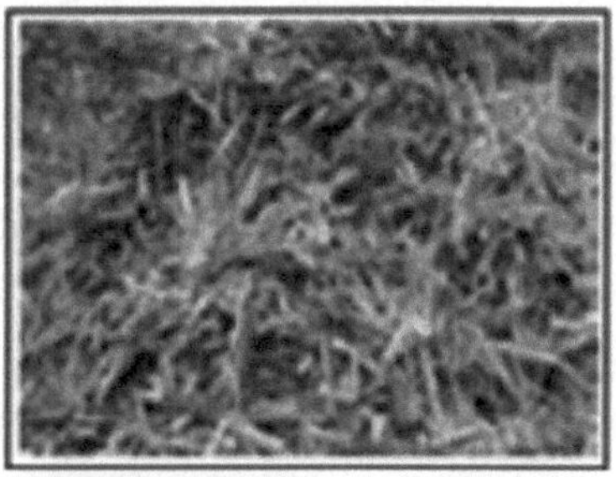

Bagasse-mixed

Chips-woody

Riverside green-leafy

Straw/stalks-leafy

Different types of biomass

The bulk density of woody biomass on 'as received' basis usually ranges from 200 to 400 Kg/M3, whereas that of leafy biomass is around 20 to 30 Kg/M3. Thus, without densification, a truck of about 30 M3 carrying capacity would be able to transport 12 MT of woody biomass as against only about 1 MT of leafy biomass. Similarly, for storage too, enormous space would be required. Some densification can be carried out simply by sizing and binding, as is the age old practice by farmers. Densification technology like pressure baling is widely practiced in the sugar industry. Pelletization is also quite a common practice in the west. However, the energy cost of pelletization is too high to make it economical for the power plant. Presently, integrated reaper cum field baling system is the most commonly used method for harvesting and simultaneous densification of agro-residues like straw and stalks.

In addition to densification, use of these machines helps in improving collection efficiency too. In Europe, most of the straw based power plants feed bales directly into the boiler thereby reducing the need for additional fuel preparatory system in the power plant. In the first demonstration, a straw fired plant was set up at Jalkheri in Punjab, India, with support from the Danish Government and MNRE, where a similar system was used. However, the system was found too complex and costly to maintain. Eight conveyors were used, four from either side of the boiler; from the main bale conveyors, diverters were used to load the individual conveyors. These diverters tend to malfunction with the slightest irregularity in the bale geometry/solidity, causing jamming of the conveyors. The binding threads used for the bales are supposed to melt immediately as the bale enters the furnace, so that the bale gets dislodged and loosened fibers catch fire. Developing a nylon thread with such fine characteristics became quite a challenging task. This plant had to be modified with traditional fuel feeding arrangement for better reliability. The fluidized bed system used also created problems due to the ash characteristics creating difficulty in draining ash through the holes provided in the bed deck.

In the 12 MW project being constructed in Punjab, the system has been designed keeping in mind learning from the European projects, the Jalkheri project and a few mustard residue based projects in Rajasthan. A large number of reaper baler machines have been procured for harvesting and baling of the available straw in the shortest possible time, so as to free the farmers' land for the next crop. Bale shredding and belt conveying systems are being installed so that loose straw is fed and fired in the boiler. Travelling grate stoker system has been used instead of the fluidized bed system.

Combustion properties

Moisture, ash and net calorific values are the important parameters; the moisture content usually varies from 15-50 percent, depending on the type of biomass and impact of natural drying. Most of the biomass, on a bone dry basis, has heat content of about 4,000 kCal/Kg and about 3,200 kCal/Kg on air dry basis. The moisture content in bagasse is about 50 percent.

For the purpose of project design, the calorific value may be taken at 2,000 kCal/Kg for bagasse and 3,000 kCal/ Kg for other biomasses. MSW is different from naturally available biomass depending upon the characteristics of the city garbage. It is therefore, very important to carry out a detailed investigation, over an extended period, during all the seasons and covering all the zones for characterization. Technology choice (Incineration of as received biomass vs preparation of residue derived fuel, RDF, for conventional combustion) would be dependent upon the characteristics.

Ash characteristics

Ash content in most of the biomasses is quite low ranging from 2-6 percent except in husks and some woods, wherein it could be upto 18 percent. More importantly, it is the chemistry of ash, which plays a key role in deciding the steam parameters and design of the boiler furnace. Ash content in MSW is more a function of external impurities like inerts. For certain biofuels, the ash melting temperature is a relevant driving force for combustion process, since a high process temperature initiates ash melting and slag expansion, resulting in plant breakdown and high maintenance. Low ash melting temperatures are characteristic for most of the leafy biomasses and energy grain, while woody biomass has less ash melting problems. Ash fusion temperature and the ratio of basic and acidic salts are the two important factors influencing clinker formation. On the other hand presence of alkali salts, particularly oxides of sodium and potassium causes fouling in the convection zones. MSW ash may contain heavy metals and other toxins. This may require incorporation of special treatment facilities for conformance with environmental regulations. Most of the leafy biomass as well as MSW contains significant amounts of chlorides and sulphates. The presence of chlorides promotes corrosion in the high temperature zones like superheaters, whereas sulphates have an adverse impact in the low temperature zones like economizers, air preheaters, etc. The design and engineering has to be done for maintaining the desirable temperatures at various zones. Adequate on-line cleaning arrangement should also be provided in the various zones, which are prone to fouling.

Why Biomass Power?

Electricity has today become a basic necessity for not just the developed world, but also for the developing and underdeveloped countries. At the same time, the feedstocks used for power generation have been primarily fossil fuel based and non-renewable in nature. Not only will these fuels be exhausted, but they also give rise to harmful pollution, especially in the form of greenhouse gases that lead to climate change and global warming.

This makes it imperative for all countries concerned to consider greener and more renewable sources for power production. Biomass based power production is one such. While there are multiple pathways to produce power using biomass, all these utilize a variety of biomass in order to either derive power directly or indirectly.

With serious concern globally and in India on the use of fossil fuels, it is important for India to start using renewable energy sources. It is equally important for India to explore sources that can bring power in a distributed manner and on small scales so that over 60,000 villages that have no access to power can benefit from electricity. This is where biomass power, and especially biomass gasification based power, will come useful.

Biomass gasification, with its capability to work in kW scales (as low as 20 kW) and its ability to utilize a wide and diverse range of biomass feedstock, is ideally suited for the power needs of many segments. This would serve rural areas where access to power is minimal but an easy access to significant amount of cheap (and many times no cost) biomass is prevalent.

Indian Power Production Scenario

The average electricity consumption in India is still among the lowest in the world at just 630 kWh per person per year, but this is expected to grow to 1000 kWh in the near future. According to Central Electricity Authority (CEA), the peak electricity demand in 2008 was 120 GW of power, while only 98 GW could be supplied. According to an analysis by the Indian PV project developer Astonfield, this deficit is likely to grow to 25 GW by 2012. The Ministry of Power has set an agenda of providing "Power to All" by 2012.

India plans to bridge the peak deficit using a number of avenues. Many of them rely on increasing the fossil fuel footprint and hence indeed increase our reliance and dependence on these fossil fuels. At the same time, the government also making serious efforts to accumulate the growth of renewable's contribution to power.

Some of the highlights of the current power production status in India:

- India's current installed capacity (end of 2010): 1,70,229 MW, from all sources
- Power generation capacity is mainly based on thermal and hydro, with about 11% from renewable energy.
- In 2010, peak power shortage was 12 %.
- Electricity demand is expected to rise by 7.4% a year during the next quarter of a century. This will see generation capacity increase five-fold in India is to supply this growing demand.

Status of Indian Renewable Power Generation

Total installed capacity of renewable power sources

As of Feb 2011, India has over 18.3 GW of installed renewable energy capacity. Wind represents about 13 GW, small hydro represents 2.8 GW, and the majority of the remainder is from biomass installations.

Total Electricity Installed Capacity: 171.9 GW (Feb 2011)

Energy source	% Share in installed capacity
Thermal	64.75%
Nuclear	2.78%
Hydro (large hydro)	21.73%
Other renewable energy sources	10.73%

Source: CEA

Need for Biomass Power in India

More than 70% of India's population depends on biomass and about 32% of the total primary energy use in the country mainly in rural areas is still derived from biomass. Biomass gasification based power production, is relevant today especially in the Indian context mainly because of its potential to provide distributed power at rural level, especially for small remote villages that have good access to biomass but no access to grid power, and which require only small scale power production. Biomass based power is also relevant in the context of climate change and global warming as biomass based power production is net carbon neutral.

- In 1999 to 2000, more than 85 percent of India's rural population was dependent on traditional fuels (biomass and cow dung-cake) for their basic energy needs. The use of these fuels in inefficient cooking stoves led to high levels of indoor air pollution, causing wide-spread respiratory and eye diseases, particularly among women. India's goal is to provide cleaner fuels or other means of cooking to the entire population by 2012.
- Because of the high costs of connecting these remote villages to the national grid, it is economical to promote projects based on solar energy, biomass gasifiers and small hydro power plants. The government provides up to 90 percent financial assistance for non-conventional energy schemes in these areas.

Benefits of Biomass Power

Biomass-based power shows many potential benefits, some of which are listed below:

- Distributed generation
- Base load power
- Suited for rural areas
- Ability to have small, kW scale power production
- Rural economic upliftment
- Carbon neutral
- Efficient utilization of renewable biological sources
- Efficient utilization of renewable biological sources
- Reduces methane, a major GHG gas
- Low Cost Resource

Distributed generation – Because biomass is available in almost all places, and especially in rural areas, and more important, as gasification based power production can be done on small scales (as low as 20 kW), this process can be used for distributed generation of power as against the centralized power production method followed today.

Base load power – Many renewable energy sources such as solar and wind cannot be used for base load power generation due to their intermittency and variability. Biomass based power generation, on the other hand, can be used for base load power generation.

Suited for rural areas – Biomass based power is well suited to remote villages with no access to grid but access to significant amounts of biomass.

Ability to have small, kW scale power production – Biomass gasification based power production can be done at small scales – as small as 20 kW – unlike other sources of power (say, nuclear) that require much larger scales. This will ideally suit small villages that have only a few households.

Rural economic upliftment - Also the possibility of increasing the prosperity of rural areas especially if dedicated energy crops become common for biomass based power production – Currently, most biomass based power production uses waste biomass such as agro waste and waste from agro processing units. However a trend is emerging in which companies are exploring the use of dedicated energy crops for biomass power production. This has the twin benefits of a more reliable biomass supply chain and at the same time providing the much needed employment for the rural masses. Given that a 1 MW biomass based power generation could require biomass growth in over 150 hectares, the opportunities for rural employment are indeed significant.

Carbon neutral - Biomass power results in no new net GHG emissions as it is part of the carbon cycle. Unlike coal and other forms of fossil fuel which have been buried millions of years ago and burning them adds to carbon in the atmosphere, whereas biomass energy generation results in no new carbon emission or pollution.

Efficient utilization of renewable biological sources - Biomass power is an efficient process which results in the use of mostly animal and crop wastes which would be converted into carbon dioxide anyway.

Large variety of feedstock – Biomass power can use a large variety of feedstock such as wood pellets, rice husk, bagasse etc.

Reduces methane, a major GHG gas – Decomposition of organic matter releases methane. Capturing this methane yields energy while protecting the atmosphere. The animal industry and landfills produce significant amounts of methane.

Low Cost Resource – Biomass power can be produced economically, at costs competitive to grid power, if there is a good availability of feedstock.

Potential For Biomass Power In India

As India has a large amount of biomass, there is a high biomass potential in India. The table below provides an estimate of the current biomass potential in India.

Estimate of Current Biomass Potential in India (2010)

Biomass Type	Potential (MWe)	Percentage
Agro potential	18728	54
Livestock	9332	27
Fruits	660	2
Vegetables	1220	3
Industrial Wastes	1470	4
Subtotal	31410	90
	Urban Wastes	
MSW	3190	9
MLW	361	1
Subtotal	3551	10
Grand Total	34961	100

Total Amount of Energy Crops or Waste Biomass Available in Various States

State	Area (KHa)	Crop Productivity (million T/ yr)	Biomass Generation (million T/ yr)	Biomass Surplus (million T/yr)	Power (Mw)
Andhra Pradesh	2,540.20	3.23	8.30	1.17	150.20
Assam	2,633.10	6.08	6.90	1.40	165.50
Bihar	5,833.10	13.82	20.44	4.29	530.30
Chhattisgarh	3,815.50	6.14	10.12	1.91	220.90
Goa	156.30	0.55	0.83	0.13	15.60
Gujarat	6,512.90	20.63	24.16	7.51	1,014.10
Haryana	4,890.20	13.52	26.16	9.80	1,261.00
Himachal Pradesh	710.30	1.33	2.67	0.99	128.00
Jammu	368.70	0.65	1.20	0.24	31.80
Jharkhand	1,299.80	1.51	2.19	0.57	66.80
Karnataka	7,277.30	38.64	23.77	6.40	843.40
Kerala	2,041.70	9.75	9.42	5.70	762.30
Madhya Pradesh	9,937.00	14.17	26.50	8.03	1,065.40
Maharashtra	15,278.00	51.34	36.80	11.80	1,585.00
Manipur	72.60	0.16	0.32	0.03	4.10
Meghalaya	0.80	0.01	0.04	0.01	1.10
Nagaland	27.10	0.09	0.15	0.03	3.10
Orissa	2,436.60	3.63	5.35	1.16	147.30
Punjab	6,693.50	27.81	46.34	21.27	2,674.60
Rajasthan	12,537.50	93.65	204.89	35.53	4,595.00
Tamil Nadu	2,454.00	24.54	15.98	6.66	863.70
U.P	12,628.20	46.80	50.42	11.73	1,477.90
Uttaranchal	66.40	0.14	0.16	0.05	6.60
West Bengal	5,575.60	21.06	23.32	2.96	368.30
	105,786.4	399.25	546.41	139.35	17,982.0

Rajasthan, Punjab, Maharashtra and Haryana are states with high biomass potential. Together, they comprise close to 50% of the total estimated potential for biomass in India.

Future Potential of Power Generation from Biomass in India

Biomass Type	Realistic			Optimistic			Pessimistic		
	10-13	14-20	Beyond 2020	10-13	14-20	Beyond 2020	10-13	14-20	Beyond 2020
Agro potential	19295	20687	21743	21680	30506	38934	18172	16937	16107
Live stock	9332	9767	10470	18183	19126	20639	6994	7356	7938
Fruits	738	963	1165	764	1084	1392	498	570	627
Vegetables	1292	1481	1633	1416	2008	2578	896	960	1008
Industrial Wastes	1679	2289	2857	1878	2918	3998	1472	1722	1926
Subtotal	32337	35188	7868	43921	55642	67541	28032	27545	27606
Urban Wastes									
MSW	3992	6773	9781	4277	7818	12029	3204	4181	5057
MLW	397	492	574	442	622	794	362	404	436
Subtotal	4389	7225	10355	4719	8440	12823	3566	4585	5493
Grand Total	36725	42413	48223	48640	64082	80364	31598	32129	33099

Note: All Numbers in Mega Watts

Biomass Power In India – Key Highlights

The table gives an overall view of the potential of biomass power, installed capacities, government incentives, and major barriers for biomass based power production in India.

Total available potential	**19500 MW**
Exploited potential (production /installed capacity)	• Direct Biomass 901 MW • Cogeneration (bagasse and non-bagasse) – 1649 MW installed • Gasification: 125 MW
Specific government incentives	• Customs Duty Exemption/Reduction on parts of Biomass Operated Electricity Generator • Excise Duty Exemption on parts of Biomass Operated Electricity Generator • Exemption in Central Sales Tax • 100 % accelerated depreciation • Income Tax Holiday for ten years (can be availed within 15 years). • Power sector reforms have encouraged investment in grid-connected biomass projects.

Contd.

Amount of investments happening in this now, expected in future	In the current Five Year Plan period (2007 to 2012), the government's target for biomass power capacity is 1200 MW and 500 MW for cogeneration plants
Key bottlenecks and barriers	• Feedstock supply and price security • A less concentrated form of energy, making it less efficient • Emergent competing usage: Recently developed plastics from biomass are cheaper and meet or even exceed most performance standards, but lack the water resistance or longevity as conventional plastics.
Cost of power generation - and trends in the same over years	Cost of electricity production – Rs 2.25-3.25 / kWh. This includes all costs, including capital depreciation, O&M, insurance and interest costs. This cost could increase over the years as the cost of biomass increases.

Methods of Power Production from Biomass

Biomass based power production methods

There are multiple ways to produce power from biomass. While the most obvious way is to use it to produce steam that runs a turbine, this may not be the most efficient or the most feasible. In fact, most biomass power plants in India (as well as in many other parts of the world) are following the rankine cycle route for biomass based power production. But other well-known technologies – especially gasification – are also being increasingly used. Emerging processes such as pyrolysis could also start contributing in future.

Primary Routes for Power from Biomass

The three primary routes for biomass to power are: Combustion, Gasification and Anaerobic Digestion. Combustion is easy to understand – instead of coal or other fossil fuels, biomass is used to produce steam that runs a turbine. Combustion of biomass for power could either be in the form of co-firing (when it is burned along with coal) or pure play biomass based combustion.

In the case of gasification, the biomass is first gasified and this gas in turn produces power in a gas engine.

Anaerobic digestion is usually applied to biomass that typically has a high amount of water in them (anaerobic digestion is commonly used for treating organic waste such as kitchen waste and sewage waste into energy). Under this route, microorganisms act upon the organic matter present in the biomass under anaerobic (absence of air) conditions and convert it into biogas.

An emerging route for biomass based power is pyrolysis. In this, the biomass is rapidly heated to 450 - 600°C in the absence of air, and results in a bio-oil called the pyrolysis oil, which in turn could be used for firing the boilers.

Typically, 50 - 75 % (by weight) of the feedstock is converted into pyrolysis oil.

- Combustion
- Gasification
- Anaerobic Digestion
- Pyrolysis
- Comparison of Different Biomass-based Power Production Technologies

Combustion

- Typically works well beyond 5 MW
- Well established technology works on the regular rankine cycle
- Comprises over 85% of installed capacity for biomass based power production in
- India (excluding biomass cogeneration)
- Works well for most types of biomass

Co-firing – This is a sub-set of combustion based power production. Some of the modern coalfired power plants use biomass for co-firing along with coal. It is quite efficient, cost-effective and requires moderate additional investment. In general, combustion efficiency of biomass can be 10 percentage points lower than for coal at the same installation, but co-firing efficiency in large-scale coal plants (35%-45%) is higher than the efficiency of biomass-dedicated plants. In the case of co-combustion of up to 5%-10% of biomass (in energy terms) only minor changes in the handling equipment are needed and the boiler is not noticeably de-rated. For biomass exceeding 10% or if biomass and coal are burned separately, then changes in mills, burners and dryers are needed. Many co-firing technology options have been demonstrated in several countries (Northern Europe, United States and Australia) in some 150 installations using different feedstock (wood biomass, residues and crops).

Cogeneration – When bagasse is also used as a feedstock for steam generation in boilers in sugar mills, the main objective is process heating, and thus power production is only an ancillary benefit (which is why the term cogeneration – generation of both heat and power). As a result, the capacity of the power production is set based on the heating requirements. Thus, during the cane season, these mills have enough bagasse to be used for both heating and power production. During the non-cane season, typically coal is used for power production, as there are no heating requirements.

Gasification

In the case of combustion, the biomass is fired to generate steam which turns a turbine for power production. In the case of gasification, the biomass is gasified into a mixture of CO and H2 in a gasifier. This gas is fed to a gas engine that produces electricity. Biomass gasification refers to the incomplete combustion of biomass resulting in production of combustible gases consisting of Carbon monoxide (CO), Hydrogen (H2) and traces of Methane (CH4). This mixture is called producer gas. Producer gas can be used to run internal combustion engines (both compression and spark ignition) for power production, or can be used as substitute for furnace oil in direct heat applications.

Gasifiers can work at low scales – as low as 20 kW, and works well up to 2 MW, with current technology.

Technology uses a combination of gasifier and gas engines. The technology has been in vogue for decades, but is still evolving. Currently, less than 125 MW of cumulative installed capacity in India (less than 15% of total biomass power, excluding biomass cogeneration). Works best for woody biomass, but latest gasifiers also work reasonably well with nonwoody (including fine biomass).

Anaerobic Digestion

In the absence of air, organic matter such as animal manures, organic wastes and green energy crops (e.g. grass) can be converted by bacteria-induced fermentation into biogas (a 40%-75% methane-rich gas with CO2 and a small amount of hydrogen sulphide and ammonia). Anaerobic digestion is also the basic process for landfill gas production from municipal green waste. It has significant potential in India as well as worldwide. Anaerobic digestion is increasingly used in smallsize, rural and off-grid applications at the domestic and farm-scale. The rising cost of waste disposal may improve its economic attractiveness. Anaerobic digesters are used both at small-scale and large-scale levels. Small scale biogas for household use is a simple, low-cost, low-maintenance technology, which has been used for decades. It usually concerns rural areas and communities without connection to the grid.

Industrial applications mainly process huge amounts of feedstock. This would require a welldeveloped logistical system for feedstock collection and effluent disposal. The feasibility of such plants depends on the availability of cheap and free feedstock due to costs.

While a significant number of the existing anaerobic digestion plants are processing residual sludge from wastewater treatment plants, many other industries have potential for this. Most small-scale units such as tanneries, textile bleaching and dying, dairy, slaughterhouses cannot afford effluent treatment plants of their own because of economies of scale in pollution abatement. Recycling/recovery/re-use of products from the wastes of such small-scale units by adopting suitable technology could be a viable proposition. Generation of energy using anaerobic digestion process has proved to be economically attractive in many such cases. Overall, power production from anaerobic digestion is quite well established as a technology, though the economics of this route are still evolving.

Pyrolysis

Pyrolysis as a method for power production is not well established currently in India or elsewhere in the world. The two main methods of pyrolysis are "fast" pyrolysis and "slow" pyrolysis. Fast pyrolysis yields 60% bio-oil, 20% biochar, and 20% syngas, and can be done in seconds, whereas slow pyrolysis can be optimized to produce substantially more char (~50%) along with organic gases, but takes on the order of hours to complete. In either case, the gas or oil can be used as a fuel for firing the boiler for steam production and subsequent power production. Typically pyrolysis plants work well beyond 2 MW scale, while gasification plants work well until 2 MW scale, at the current technological progress. Thus, it can be said that pyrolysis takes off where gasification ends.

Slow Pyrolysis

In the case of slow pyrolysis when you get an organic gas and charcoal. The gas can be cooled and fed to a gas engine for power production. Cooling this gas however results in a significant amount of hydrocarbons being removed. Thus most of the energy is wasted away. A more efficient idea that is being explored is to use this heterogeneous gas straight for combustion of boilers and running a steam cycle. Charcoal is a valuable product, which fetches anywhere between Rs 10-Rs 25 per Kg. It has a much better calorific value than coal and people in many places use charcoal because coal might not be available in those places.

Fast Pyrolysis

Fast pyrolysis is a process in which organic materials are rapidly heated to 450 - 600°C in absence of air. Under these conditions, organic vapours, permanent gases and charcoal are produced. The vapours are condensed to pyrolysis oil. Typically, 50 - 75 wt % of the feedstock is converted into pyrolysis oil. The pyrolysis oil can be used as a replacement for furnace oil.

Comparison of Different Biomass-Based Power Production Methods

Parameter	Combustion	Anaerobic Digestion	Gasification	Pyrolysis
Resource	Mainly solid Biomass	Wet biomass	Mainly solid Biomass	Mainly solid Biomass
Example of Raw Materials	Wood logs, chips, agricultural residues, energy crops	Manure, sewage Sludge	Wood chips and pellets, agricultural residues	Wood chips and pellets, agricultural residues
Technology Status	Commercial	Commercial	Commercial	Demonstration
Temperature (°C)	700–1400	Not applicable	500–1300	380–530
Pressure (MPa)	> 0.1		> 0.1	0.1–0.5
Drying	Not essential, but may help	Not essential	Necessary	Necessary
Advantages		Anaerobic digestion is a very effective method of treating high moisture content organic wastes, and many implementations of anaerobic digestion are driven by waste management needs, with biogas as a valuable by product	Advantages compared to combustion in terms of economies of scale, higher electrical efficiencies of up to 50% are possible. Up to 25% efficiency in small scale applications (between few tens of KW up to 5 MW) This makes gasification especially for small scale application interesting, because there is no efficient technology for solid biomass for power production available	The main advantages compared to combustion or gasification is the fact that the main product is a liquid (especially for fast pyrolysis) with high energy content, easy to store and transport, and can be used for different uses

Biomass Gasification Technology

Gasification plants consist of several process steps. The solid biomass fuel delivered needs to be adjusted (fuel conditioning and handling) to the fuel characteristics (particle size, water content) required for the gasification process. The conditioned fuel enters the gasification process, which produces raw product gas. The raw product gas needs to be cleaned in order to achieve the product gas quality needed for further utilization. The cleaned product gas is used for the production of electric power, heat and fuel based on different technologies.

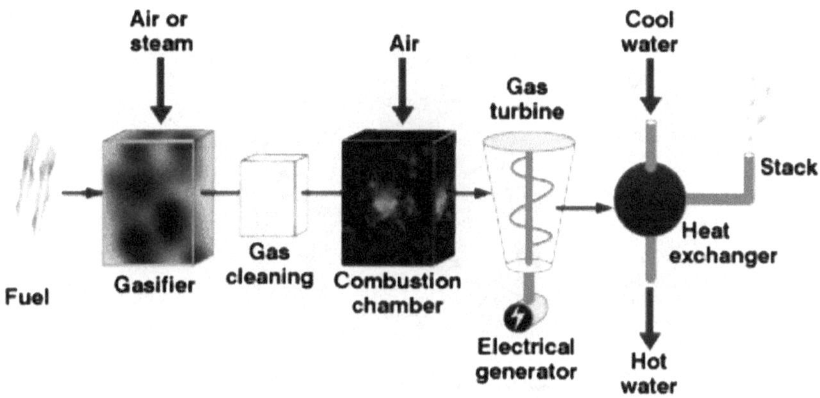

During the thermo-chemical biomass gasification process solid biomass is cracked by thermal energy and a fumigator and converted into a product gas. The product gas is cleaned and used for the production of heat and power e.g. by gas engines (biomass CHP).

Components of a Biomass Gasification System For Power Production

Gasifiers

Biomass gasifiers are reactors that heat biomass in a low-oxygen environment to produce a fuel gas that contains from one fifth to one half (depending on the process conditions) the heat content of natural gas. The gas produced from a gasifier can drive highly efficient devices such as gensets, turbines and fuel cells to generate electricity.

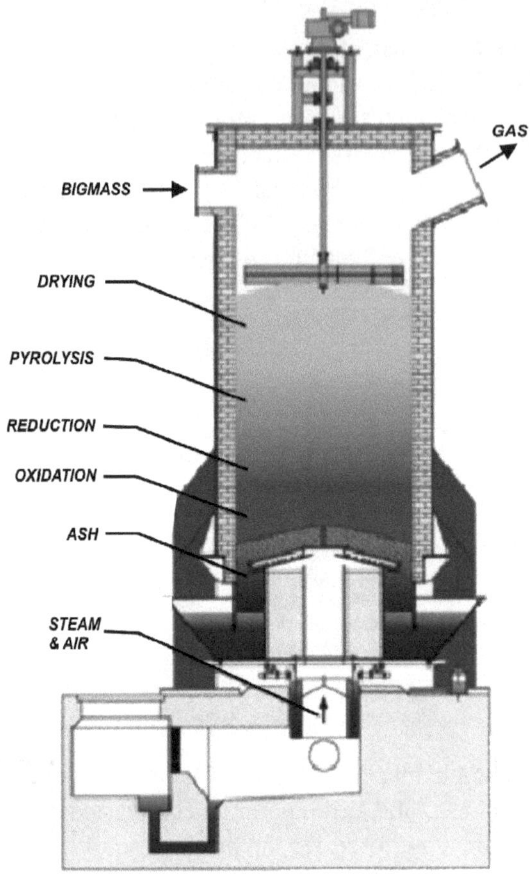

Biomass Gasifier

Gas engines

Gas engines used in the gasification power plants run on producer gas to produce power. These engines have reasonable efficiencies. Producer gas has a very low air to fuel ratio (1.3:1) compared to other gases (Natural gas 17:1). Hence the engine has to be operated with a different carburetor for producer gas and natural gas. Also, the producer gas can be operated in an engine which has a higher compression ratio. Engines used for producer gas have generally lower in efficiency and they are cheaper. The efficiency of these engines is more than 30%.

Power evacuation system

Suitable evacuation systems need to be provided in order to transmit the electricity to the grid (if it is grid connected) or to the location where it is required (if it is captive)

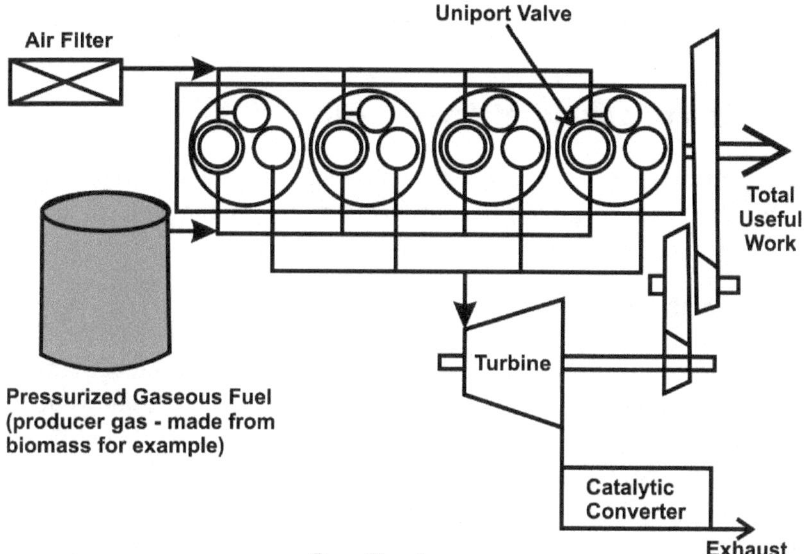

Gas Engine

Types of Gasifiers

There are two principal types of gasifiers, namely:

- Fixed-bed type
- Fluidized-bed type

Fixed Bed Gasifiers

The fixed bed gasification system consists of a reactor/gasifier with a gas cooling and cleaning system. The fixed bed gasifier has a bed of solid fuel particles through which the gasifying media and gas move either up or down. It is the simplest type of gasifier consisting of usually a cylindrical space for fuel feeding unit, an ash removal unit and a gas exit. In the fixed bed gasifier, the fuel bed moves slowly down the reactor as the gasification occurs. The fixed bed gasifiers are of simple construction and generally operate with high carbon conversion, long solid residence time, low gas velocity and low ash carry over. In fixed bed gasifiers, tar removal used to be a major problem, however recent progress in thermal and catalytic conversion of tar has given credible options.

Fixed bed gasifiers are the most commonly ones. These are in turn available under two important categories depending on the direction of the gas flow through the reactor:

- Updraft gasifiers
- Downdraft gasifiers

Updraft – mainly done for coal gasification; Indian gasifiers are mainly downdraft. For updraft, the tar formation will be much higher (10 times or more) than for the downdraft. In India, most gasifiers used are of the downdraft type.

Advantages of downdraft over updraft

Downdraft – gas with less tar, but with some particulates, so producer gas more suitable for use in gas engines Updraft – more suitable with some thermal applications

Updraft Gasifiers

Fuel flexibility is the main feature of updraft multifuel gasifiers. These gasifiers can operate on either coal or biomass and fuel switching does not require any changes in the reactor. Updraft gasifiers tolerate higher ash content, higher moisture content and greater size variation in fuel as compared to downdraft gasifiers.

In updraft gasifiers, gas is drawn out of the gasifier from the top of the fuel bed while the gasification reactions take place near the bottom. As the producer gas passes through the fuel bed, it picks-up volatile matter (tars) and moisture from the fuel. Therefore, the gas from the updraft gasifier contains condensable volatiles. The design and operation of the gasifiers is such that the gas comes out at 200-400 C temperature. At this temperature, most of the volatile hydrocarbons are in vapor form, which add to the energy content of the gas. It is most appropriate to utilize updraft gasifiers in close-coupled-hot gas mode for direct heating applications. However, if the application warrants, the scrubbing of gas to remove the volatiles/tars is also carried out.

Downdraft Gasifiers

Downdraft gasifiers are fuel specific. Downdraft wood gasifiers can operate on wood like biomass materials and biomass briquettes with a minimum bulk density of 250 kg/m3 and ash content of less than 5%. In downdraft gasifiers, gas is drawn from the bottom of the reactor while the hottest reaction zone is in the middle. The volatile matter in the fuel gets cracked within the reactor and therefore the output gas is almost tar-free. However, the gas, as it comes out of the reactor, contains small amounts of ash and soot. The gas comes out of the gasifier at 250-450° C. This gas can also be used either in hot condition (after preliminary cleaning) or in cold-clean condition (after appropriate gas clean-up arrangement). The gas from the downdraft gasifiers can be cleaned to very high purity such that it can be used in IC engines or for direct heating applications where purity of gas is a critical requirement.

Fluidized Bed Gasifiers

In fluidized bed gasifiers, the biomass is brought into an inert bed of fluidized material (e.g. sand, char, etc.). Such systems are less sensitive to fuel variations but produce larger amounts of tar and dust. They are more compact but also more complex, and usually used at larger scales. Fluidized bed gasifiers are operated with significantly higher gas flow velocities than fixed bed gasifiers. The fuel bed and a carrier material (e.g. sand) are fluidized by the gas flow (fumigator and recirculated product gas). Thus, the gasification reaction takes place in a fluidized bed but only 5-10% wt of the bed is fuel.

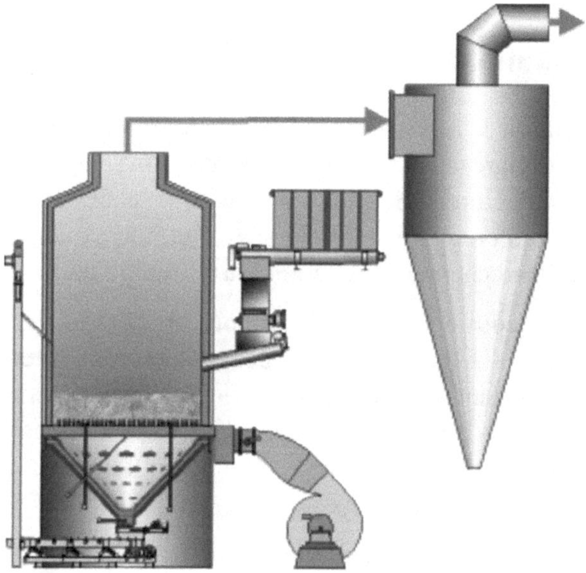

Fluidized bed Gasifier

The fuel is fed into the system either above-bed or directly into the bed, depending upon the size and density of the fuel and how it is affected by the bed velocities. During normal operation, the bed media is maintained at a temperature between 1000EF and 1800EF. When a fuel particle is introduced into this environment, its drying and pyrolyzing reactions proceed rapidly, driving off all gaseous portions of the fuel at relatively low temperatures. The remaining char is oxidized within the bed to provide the heat source for the drying and de-volatilizing reactions to continue. In those systems using inert bed material, the wood particles are subjected to an intense abrasion action from fluidized sand. This etching action tends to remove any surface deposits (ash, char, etc.) from the particle and expose a clean reaction surface to the surrounding gases. As a result, the residence time of a particle in this system is on the order of only a few minutes, as opposed to hours in other types of gasifiers. Thus, higher fuel throughput rates are achievable.

Since the fluidized bed allows an intensive mixing and a good heat transfer, there are no distinguished reaction zones. Hence, drying, pyrolysis, oxidation and reduction reactions take place simultaneously. The temperature distribution in the fluidized bed is relatively constant and typically ranges between 700°C and 900°C. The large thermal capacity of inert bed material plus the intense mixing associated with the fluid bed enable this system to handle a much greater quantity and, normally, a much lower quality of fuel.

Major Constraints Associated With Gasifiers

Biomass Gasification process has some common limitations and technology-specific limitations, some of which are given here.

Common Limitations

- Gasification is a complex and sensitive process. There exists high level of disagreement about gasification among engineers, researchers, and manufacturers. Several manufacturers claim that their unit can be operated on all kinds of biomass. But it is a questionable fact as physical and chemical properties varies fuel to fuel.
- Gasifiers require at least half an hour or more to start the process. Raw material is bulky and frequent refueling is often required for continuous running of the system. Handling residues such as ash, tarry condensates is time consuming and dirty work. Driving with producer gas fueled vehicles requires much more and frequent attention than gasoline or diesel fueled vehicles.
- Getting the producer gas is not difficult, but obtaining in the proper state is the challenging task. The physical and chemical properties of producer gas such as energy content, gas composition and impurities vary time to time. All the gasifiers have fairly strict requirements for fuel size, moisture and ash content. Inadequate fuel preparation is an important cause of technical problems with gasifiers.
- Gasifier is too often thought of as simple device that can generate a combustible gas from any biomass fuel. A hundred years of research has clearly shown that key to successful gasification is gasifier specifically designed for a particular type of fuel. Hence, biomass gasification technology requires hard work and tolerance.

Gasifiers - Technology Specific Limitations

Fixed Bed - Updraft fixed bed gasifiers

Major drawbacks are the high amounts of tar and pyrolysis products that occur because the pyrolysis gas does not pass the hearth zone and therefore is not combusted. This is of minor importance if the gas is used for direct heat applications in which the tar is simply burned. But when the gas is used for engines, extensive gas cleaning is required.

Fixed Bed - Downdraft fixed bed gasifiers

- High amounts of ash and dust particles remain in the gas because the gas has to pass the oxidation zone, where it collects small ash particles
- Fuel requirements are relatively strict; fuel must be uniformly sized from 4 to 10 cm so as not to block the throat and allow pyrolysis gases to flow downward and heat from the hearth zone to flow upward; therefore, pelletization or briquetting of is often necessary.
- The moisture content of the biomass must be less than 25 percent (on a wet basis).
- The relatively high temperature of the exit flue gas results in lower gasification efficiency.

Fluidized bed gasifiers

- High tar and dust content of the producer gas could result in problems while using the gas in the engines.
- High producer-gas temperatures, which leave alkali metals in the vapor state
- Incomplete carbon burnout results in lesser energy output
- Complex operation because of the need to control the supply of both air and solid fuel
- Need for power consumption for the compression of the gas stream.

Current Status of Biomass Gasification in India

Even though biomass gasification provides the benefits of a well proven technology that can produce power at small scales using locally available resources, the total amount of power production from biomass gasification in India is relatively low. EAI estimates that the total installed capacity of biomass gasification based power production in India will be about 140 MW, out of a total of about 2600 MW of biomass based power (cumulative of grid connected and off grid). Of the total, bagasse based power generation has the lion's share (about 1400 MW), followed by combustion-based biomass power production (about 875 MW).

Currently, most power production systems in India using biomass gasification are off-grid and have been for captive consumption for an industry or for a community.

Size (Capacity) distribution for Gasification and Combustion Technologies

	Combustion	Gasification
Size		
Small(10 kW – 25kW)	Not prevalent	Prevalent
Small-medium(25kW – 250kW)	Not prevalent	Prevalent
Medium(250 kW – 2MW)	Not prevalent	Prevalent
Large (2 MW and above)	Prevalent	Not prevalent

Type of system	Gasification	Combustion
Small Systems(10 kW – 25 kW)	• The smaller systems are more prominent in the rural area where availability of feedstock is not an issue; emphasis is on power generation despite lower efficiencies. • The efficiency (energy output/energy input) for a 25 KW system is about 12%. • The number of installed systems in this range is the maximum.	Combustion technology is not used in this range owing to very lower efficiencies.
Medium Systems(25 kW – 250 kW)	• In terms of cumulative capacity installed, this range is the maximum • Installed systems around the 500 MW capacities are much fewer in comparison to the 25-250 kW categories.	Same reason as above.
Large Systems(1MW and above)	• Gasifiers work well up to 2 MW, beyond which multiple engines can be used, or pyrolysis technology can be implemented for higher capacities. • 36-40% efficiencies possible for 2 MW gas engines • There are fewer than 10 installations in India • The ideal minimum capacity requirement for combustion technology to be employed is 3MW-5MW.	

Contd.

	• When considering bulk inputs the capacity can range between 5MW-10 MW. • Maximum capacity installed in this sector is about 20 MW.

State Wise Installation of Biomass Power Plants

Biomass gasification plants in India

The table below provides the total capacity of biomass based power plants operating in the various Indian states. Please note that this list includes all forms of power production –combustion, gasification and cogeneration. Of the total (2600 MW), biomass gasification forms only a small part (less than 125 MW).

State-wise/Year-wise list of commissioned biomass power/co-generation projects as on 30.06.2010

State	Upto 31.3.2003	2003-2004	2004-2005	2005-2006	2006-2007	2007-2008	2008-2009	2009-2010	2010-2011	Total (MW)
Andhra Pradesh	160.05	37.7	69.5	12	22	33	9	20	--	363.25
Bihar	--	--	--	--	--	--	--	--	9.5	9.5
Chattisgarh	11	--	--	16.5	85.8	33.5	9.8	43.8	--	199.9
Gujarat	0.5	--	--	--	--	--	--	--	--	0.5
Haryana	4	--	2	--	--	--	--	1.8	28	35.8
Karnataka	109.38	26	16.6	72.5	29.8	8	31.9	42	--	336.18
Madhya Pradesh	--	1	--	--	--	--		--	--	1
Maharashtra	24.5	--	11.5	--	40	38.5	71.5	33	10	288.5
Punjab	22	--	--	6	--	--	--	34.5	--	62.5
Rajasthan	--	7.8	--	7.5	8	--	8	--	28	59.3
Tamil Nadu	106	44.5	22.5	--	42.5	75	43.2	62	23.5	419.2
Uttar Pradesh	46.5	12.5	14	48.5	--	79	172	194.5	14	581
West Bengal	--	--	--	--	--	--	--	16	--	16
Total	483.93	129.5	136.1	163	228.1	266	345.4	447.6	113	2312.63

Source: http://www.mnre.gov.in/

1.8. GEO ENERGY

Geo Energy - Earth... A Powerhouse If We Can Tap It

Use of hot-water springs for local residential home heating and also to a limited extent for electricity generation has been successfully attempted in some regions of geothermal activity. Since the cost of such adaptations is very low, it is very attractive for extensive commercialization. There may be even greater focus for energy efficient homes in the future due to greater public awareness and concern for use of alternate energy where ever possible.

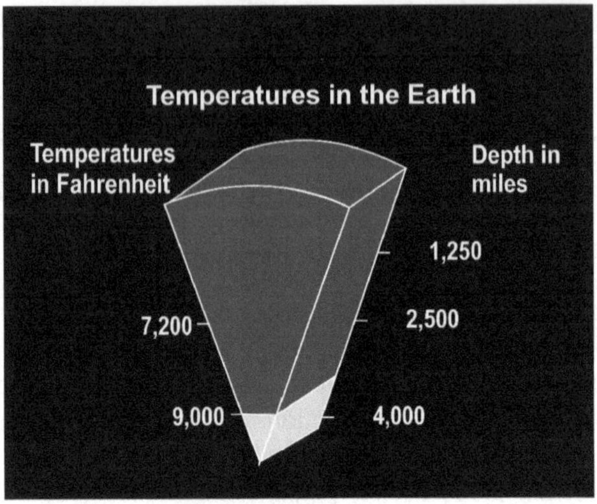

Earth's Temperatures
Source : Geothermal Education Office (GEO)

The improvement in the technology for detection of this resource has received focus in the recent years. Eg. detection of geothermal activity in northern basin and range province of the western U.S.A. The possibilities are many for such developments. With improvements in deep drilling technology and engineering the possibility of using geothermal energy for electricity generation is becoming increasingly attractive option.

Geothermal Energy in India

India Professes direct use of geothermal energy within a cited capacity of 203 MW. Though there is yet to be any geothermal electricity generated. Over 300 hot spring locations have been identified by the Geological Survey of India, and estimates put India at about 10,600 MW of geothermal power potential.47 Potential sites have been identified in Puga Valley (J&K), Tatapani (Chhattisgarh), Godavari Basin Manikaran (Himachal Pradesh), Bakreshwar (WBengal), Tuwa (Gujarat), Unai (Maharashtra), and Jalgaon (Maharashtra).

Geothermal Development Highlights

- Glitnir Bank of Iceland announced exploration in India in February 2008.
- In January 2010, India and Iceland announced a cooperation on geothermal energy development including technologies used in deep drilling, reservoir assessment, and geothermal demonstration power plants.

National Policies

Policy (Year)	Description
Geothermal Energy R&D Program(2010)	Ministry of New and Renewable energy seeking proposals for geothermal energy projects based on results of assessment studies5
India- Brazil –South Africa Declaration on Clean Energy (2007)	Agreement to work together in the promotion of nuclear energy, clean energy technologies, other renewable energies and climate change mitigation.
Integrated Energy Policy (2006)	Address all aspects of energy including energy security, access and availability, affordability and pricing, efficiency and the environment
Traffic Policy (2006)	Included provisions for renewable energy such as percentage for energy purchase made application for tariffs.
National Electricity Policy (2005)	Released in accordance with the Electricity Act of 2003 and promoted non- conventional energy sources.
Electricity Act (2003)	Comprehensive framework for power development with key provisions

Advantages of Geothermal Energy

Geothermal energy is a domestic energy resource with cost, reliability and environmental advantages over conventional energy sources. It contributes both to energy supply, with electrical power generation and direct-heat uses.

For generation of electricity, hot water is brought from the underground reservoir to the surface through production wells, and is flashed to steam in special vessels by release of pressure. The steam is separated from the liquid and fed to a turbine engine, which turns a generator. Spent geothermal fluid is injected back into peripheral parts of the reservoir to help maintain reservoir pressure. In the absence of steam, heat from hot water is extracted through a secondary fluid and the high pressure vapour from the secondary fluid is utilized to run the turbine.

If the reservoir is to be used for direct-heat application, the geothermal water is usually fed to a heat exchanger and the heat thus extracted is used for home heating, greenhouse, vegetable drying and a wide variety of other small scale industries. Hot water at temperatures less than 120 °C can be used for this purpose. Further, the spent hot water, after generating electricity can also be used for direct application.

As a result of today's geothermal production, consumption of exhaustible fossil fuels is offset, along with the release of acid-rain and greenhouse gases that are caused by fossil-fuel use. Systems for use of geothermal energy have proven to be extremely reliable and flexible. Geothermal electric power plants are on line 97% of the time, whereas nuclear plants average only 65% and coal plants only 75% on-line time. Geothermal plants are modular, and can be installed in increments as needed. Because they are modular, then can be transported conveniently to any site. Both baseline and peaking power can be generated. Construction time can be as little as 6 months for plants in the range 0.5 to 10 MW and as little as 2 years for clusters of plants totaling 250 MW or more.

The competing goals of increased energy production for worldwide social development and of mitigating release of atmosphere-polluting gases are not compatible using today's fuel mix, which relies heavily on coal and petroleum. Development of geothermal energy has a large net positive impact on the environment compared with development of conventional energy sources. Geothermal power plants have sulphur-emissions rates that average only a few percent of those from fossil-fuel alternatives. The newest generation of geothermal power plants emits only ~135 gm of carbon (as carbon dioxide) per megawatt-hour (MW-hr) of electricity generated. This figure compares with 128 kg /MW-hr of carbon for a plant operating on natural gas (methane) and 225 kg/MW-hr of carbon for a plant using bituminous coal. Nitrogen oxide emissions are much lower in geothermal power plants than in fossil power plants. Nitrogen-oxides combine with hydrocarbon vapours in the atmosphere to produce ground-level ozone, a gas that causes adverse health effects and crop losses as well as smog. There are other environmental advantages to geothermal energy. Geothermal power plants require very little land, taking up only a fraction of that needed by other energy sources. Thus emission of CO_2 and SO_2 by geothermal power plants is far less compared with conventional fossil fuel based power plants.

World geothermal energy status

Currently there are an estimated 12,000 MW of direct use and over 8,000 MW of generating capacity in geothermal resources world-wide. To put geothermal generation into perspective, this generating capacity is about 0.4% of the World total installed generating capacity. The USA, Philippines, Italy, Mexico, Iceland Indonesia, Japan and New Zealand are the largest users of geothermal energy resources (both direct and indirect). Table 2 shows the location of present electric power generation from geothermal energy in order of size per country. The 1999 capacity of 8246MW electricity was a 40% increase from the capacity installed in 1990.

*Other countries with less than 20 MW generation are: Argentina, Australia Ethiopia, France (Guadeloupe) ,Greece, Portugal(Azores), Russia, Thailand (World Geothermal Congress, 2000).*Currently geothermal resources in over 30 countries provide directly used heat capacity of over 12,000 MW. These countries include: Algeria, Austria, Belgium, Bulgaria, China, Denmark, England, France, Georgia, Germany, Greece, Hungary, Iceland, Indonesia, Ireland, Italy, Japan, Latvia, Nicaragua, Philippines, Poland, Portugal, Romania, Russia, Slovakia, Sweden, Switzerland, Thailand and Turkey.

The majority of the earlier geothermal plants were funded and operated by National Power agencies around the world with the exception of California where the development of the Geysers geothermal field was carried out by privately funded utility companies. With the recent international trend towards de-regulation in the power industry, private developers have become more directly involved in both resource assessment and development. This has been particularly so in Indonesia and the Philippines.

Indian Geothermal Provinces

In India nearly 400 thermal springs occur, distributed in seven geothermal provinces. These provinces include The Himalayas: Sohana: West coast; Cambay: Son-Narmada-Tapi (SONATA): Godavari and Mahanadi. These springs are perennial and their surface temperature range from 37 to 90° C with a cumulative surface discharge of over 1000 l/m. Figure 7 shows the location of these geothermal provinces. These provinces are associated with major rifts or subduction tectonics and registered high heat flow and high geothermal gradient (Figure 7) For example the heat flow values and thermal gradients of these provinces are 468 mW/m^2; 234° C/km (Himalayas); 93 mW/m^2; 70° C/km (Cambay); 120 - 260 mW/m^2; 60-90°C/km (SONATA); 129 mW/m^2; 59° C/km (west coast); 104 mW/m^2; 60° C/km (Godavari) and 200 mW/m^2; 90° C/km (Bakreswar, Bihar). The reservoir temperature estimated using the above described geothermometers are 120° C (west coast), 150° C (Tattapani) and 200° C (Cambay). The depth of the reservoir in these provinces is at a depth of about 1 to 2 km. These geothermal systems are liquid dominated and steam dominated systems prevail only in Himalayan and Ta ttapani geothermal provinces. The issuing temperature of water at Tattapani is 90° C; at Puga (Himalaya) is 98° C and at Tuwa (Gujarat) is 98° C. The power generating capacity of these thermal springs is about 10,000 MW. These are, as mentioned above, medium enthalpy resources. From the point of power generation technology described above in Part I, these resources can be utilized effectively to generate power using binary cycle method. Since majority of these springs are located in rural India, these springs can support small scale industries in such areas. Dehydrated vegetables and fruits have a potential export market and India being an agricultural country, this industry is best suited for India conditions. An example of the cost involved in dehydration of fruits using conventional heat and geothermal heat, from Central America, is given in the following table 4. This gives an idea about the economic potential of geothermal resource.

Showing the cost of dehydrated fruits using conventional and geothermal heat

PRODUCT	CAPACITY (Kg)	TIME (hours)	HEAT COST. GEOTHERMAL SYSTEM	HEAT COST CONVENTIONAL SYSTEM
PINEAPPLE	800	18	900	5000
APPLE (SLICES)	700	16	800	4500
APPLE (CUBES)	900	16	800	4500
BANANA	800	24	1300	6000
PLANTAIN	700	30	1500	6500

Courtesy: M/s Eco-Fruit Agro Industry,Gautimala, Central America (Cost in rupees).

Technology and Resource Type

Geothermal resources vary in temperature from 30-350 ° C, and can either be dry, mainly steam, a mixture of steam and water or just liquid water. In order to extract geothermal heat from the earth, water is the transfer medium. Naturally occurring groundwater is available for this task in most places but more recently technologies are being developed to even extract the energy from hot dry rock resources. The temperature of the resource is a major determinant of the type of technologies required to extract the heat and the uses to which it can be put. The below Table lists the basic technologies normally utilized according to resource temperature.

Basic technology commonly used

Reservoir Temperature	Reservoir Fluid	Common Use	Technology commonly chosen
High Temperature >220°C	Water or Steam	Power Generation Direct Use	Flash Steam; Combined (Flash and Binary) CycleDirect Fluid Use Heat Exchangers Heat Pumps
Intermediate Temperature 100-220°C.	Water	Power Generation Direct Use	Binary CycleDirect Fluid Use; Heat Exchangers ; Heat Pumps
Low Temperature 50-150°C	Water	Direct Use	Direct Fluid Use; Heat Exchangers; Heat Pumps

Power Generation Technology

High temperature resources

High temperature geothermal reservoirs containing water and/or steam can provide steam to directly drive steam turbines and electrical generation plant. More recently developed binary power plant technologies enables more of the heat from the resource to be utilised for power generation. A combination of conventional flash and binary cycle technology is becoming increasingly popular.

High temperature resources commonly produce either steam, or a mixture of steam and water from the production wells. The steam and water is separated in a pressure vessel (Separator), with the steam piped to the power station where it drives one or more steam turbines to produce electric power. The separated geothermal water (brine) is either utilised in a binary cycle type plant to produce more power, or is disposed of back into the reservoir down deep (injection) wells. The following is a brief description of each of the technologies most commonly used to utilise high temperature resources for power generation.

Flash Steam Power Plant

This is the most common type of geothermal power plant. The illustration (Fig. 3) below shows the principal elements of this type of plant. The steam, once it has been separated from the water, is piped to the powerhouse where it is used to drive the steam turbine. The steam is condensed after leaving the turbine, creating a partial vacuum and thereby maximizing the power generated by the turbine-generator. The steam is usually condensed either in a direct contact condenser, or a heat exchanger type condenser. In a direct contact condenser the cooling water from the cooling tower is sprayed onto and mixes with the steam. The condensed steam then forms part of the cooling water circuit, and a substantial portion is subsequently evaporated and is dispersed into the atmosphere through the cooling tower. Excess cooling water called blow down is often disposed of in shallow injection wells. As an alternative to direct contact condensers shell and tube type condensers are sometimes used, as is shown in the schematic below. In this type of plant, the condensed steam does not come into contact with the cooling water, and is disposed of in injection wells.

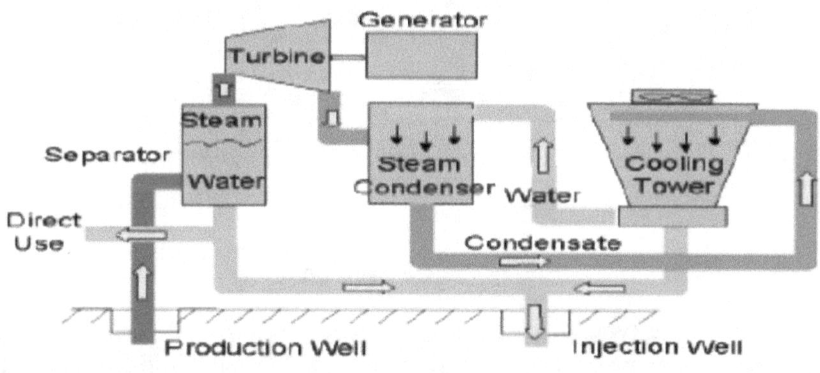

Single Flash Power Plant

Typically, flash condensing geothermal power plants vary in size from 5 MW to over 100 MW. Depending on the steam characteristics, gas content, pressures, and power plant design, between 6000 kg and 9000 kg of steam each hour is required to produce each MW of electrical power. Small power plants (less than 10 MW) are often called well head units as they only require the steam of one well and are located adjacent to the well on the drilling pad in order to reduce pipeline costs. Often such well head units do not have a condenser, and are called backpressure units. They are very cheap and simple to install, but are inefficient (typically 10-20 tonne per hour of steam for every MW of electricity) and can have higher environmental impacts.

Binary Cycle Power Plants

In reservoirs where temperatures are typically less than 220° C. but greater than 100° C binary cycle plants are often utilised. The illustration (Fig. 4) shows the principal elements of this type of plant. The reservoir fluid (either steam or water or both) is passed through a heat exchanger which heats a secondary working fluid (organic) which has a boiling point lower than 100° C. This is typically an organic fluid such as Isopentane, which is vaporised and is used to drive the turbine. The organic fluid is then condensed in a similar manner to the steam in the flash power plant described above, except that a shell and tube type condenser rather than direct contact is used. The fluid in a binary plant is recycled back to the heat exchanger and forms a closed loop. The cooled reservoir fluid is again re-injected back into the reservoir.

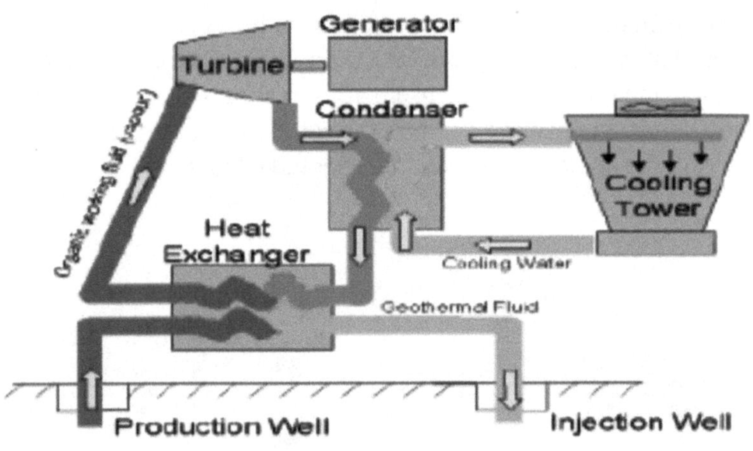

Binary Cycle Power Plant

Binary cycle type plants are usually between 7 and 12 % efficient, depending on the temperature of the primary (geothermal) fluid. Binary Cycle plant typically varies in size from 500 kW to 10 MW. The curves (Fig. 5) give an indication of the electrical power output from a binary plant over a range of flows and geothermal reservoir temperatures.

Combined Cycle (Flash and Binary)

Combined Cycle power plants are a combination of conventional steam turbine technology and binary cycle technology. By combining both technologies, higher overall utilization efficiencies can be gained, as the conventional steam turbine is more efficient at generation of power from high temperature steam, and the binary cycle from the lower temperature separated water. In addition, by replacing the condenser-cooling tower cooling system in a conventional plant by a binary plant, the heat available from condensing the spent steam after it has left the steam turbine can be utilized to produce more power.

Medium Temperature Resources

Medium temperature resources are normally hot water with temperatures ranging from 100° C to 220° C. The most common technology for utilising such resources for power generation is the binary cycle technology. This technology is described above under high temperature resources.

Direct Use Technology

Direct use technologies are where geothermal heat is used directly rather than for power generation and are built around the extraction of heat from relatively low temperature geothermal resources, generally of less than 150° C. Because geothermal heat is non-transportable, (except short distances by fluid pipeline) any applications must generally be sited within10 km or less of the resource. For many resources, the relatively low temperatures and/or pressures in the reservoirs means that they have insufficient energy and/or pressure differences to naturally carry the fluids to the surface and pumps are frequently used (either down-hole or at the surface).

The type of technology selected for utilising geothermal heat for direct use applications is dependent on the nature of the geothermal fluid and the type of direct use planned. In many direct use applications, the geothermal fluid cannot be used directly, such as in drying processes or where clean steam or hot water is necessary, as geothermal fluid often contains chemical contaminants. In such cases heat exchangers are utilised to extract the heat from the hot geothermal fluid and transfer it to either clean water, or in the case of drying processes, to air.

There are two main types of heat exchangers commonly used. They are plate heat exchangers and shell and tube. The heat exchanger technology employed in the geothermal industry is the same as is commonly used over a wide range of industries where heat exchangers are utilised.

Commonly used heat pump technology can also be employed in order to utilise geothermal heat for air conditioning and refrigeration applications.

Technological Issues with Geothermal Developments

Whether geothermal energy is utilized for power production or for direct use applications, there are issues in geothermal utilization that often have technical implications. Geothermal fluids often contain significant quantities of gases such as hydrogen sulphide as well as dissolved chemicals and can sometimes be acidic. Because of this, corrosion, erosion and chemical deposition may be issues, which require attention at the design stage and during operation of the geothermal project. Well casings and pipelines can suffer corrosion and /or scale deposition, and turbines, especially blades can suffer damage leading to higher maintenance costs and reduced power output.

However, provided careful consideration of such potential problems is made at the design stage, there are a number of technological solutions available. Such potential problems can be normally overcome by a combination of utilising corrosion resistant materials, careful control of brine temperatures, the use of steam scrubbers and occasionally using corrosion inhibitors.

Provided such readily available solutions are employed, geothermal projects generally have a very good history of operational reliability. Geothermal power plants for example, can boast of high capacity factors (typically 85-95%).

Application of Chemical techniques in geothermal exploration

The application of chemical techniques has become an integral part of any geothermal exploration programme. During the pre-drilling stages of exploration, geochemistry of thermal waters and gases may provide information on deep conditions and processes not obtainable by geological or geophysical techniques. The dissolved constituents in the thermal waters can be grouped into two major groups i.e. a) chemically, non-reactive and b) chemically reactive groups. The first group may be called tracers and the second, the geo-indicators.

The tracers, once enter the fluid phase, ideally remain unchanged, providing a tag allowing their origin to be traced back to their. These include noble gases like He and Ar and other conservative elements like Cl, Li, B, Rb, Cs and N_2 .

Geo-indicators are reactive species, responding to changes in their environment (especially temperature and type of rock with which the fluids interact) in a controlled and well understood manner. These include Na, K, Mg, Ca and SiO_2, which take part in temperature dependent reactions with Al-silicate rocks which house geothermal systems, and H_2, H_2S, CH_4 and CO_2 which are involved in temperature -pressure dependent redox reactions within them or redox systems of the rock phase such as FeII/FeIII reaction.

Out of the constituents mentioned above, Na, K, Mg, Ca, SiO_2, Cl, Li, B, Rb and Cs enter the liquid phase while He, Ar H_2, H_2S, CH_4 and CO_2 enter the vapour phase in geothermal systems. These constituents are very useful in estimating the thermal reservoir conditions and the reservoir temperature. We shall see how these constituents are used in estimating the reservoir temperature. Those chemical constituents that are used in estimating the reservoir temperature are known as geochemical thermometers. Two such important geothermometers, the silica and cation geothermometers, are discussed below. They are known as water geothermometers because they enter the liquid phase in geothermal systems.

Silica and Cations as geothermometers

Water geothermometers are classified into two groups i.e. 1) based on temperature dependent variations in solubility of individual minerals and 2) based on temperature dependent exchange reactions which fix the ratios of certain dissolved constituents (Fournier, 1991). The silica minerals are ideal members under group 1 while other cations such as Ca, Mg, Na and K are ideal under group 2. Temperature estimation based on group 2 members require evaluation of activity coefficients for two or more dissolved species in order to calculate the temperature at which solution-mineral equilibrium was last attained. The calculation of activity coefficients must take into account the total composition of the fluid and the result vary as a function of temperature. Simple techniques for estimating the reservoir temperatures based on silica and cations are described here.

Silica geothermometer

The solubility of silica mineral decreases drastically and linearly as temperature decreases below 340° C. If temperature vs silica concentration in thermal waters are plotted, they define a straight line within this temperature limits. Similarly the dissolved silica in liquid after steam separation (90 - 250° C) also defines a similar line. The equations for such straight lines results in the following equations:

Quartz -no steam loss $t^{\circ}C = (1309/5.19 - \log S) - 273.15$ (1)

Quartz -max. steam loss $t^{\circ}C = (1522/5.75 - \log S) - 273.15$ (2)

Silica- enthalpy diagram

It is useful to use enthalpy instead of temperature in the silica- temperature diagrams to estimate the reservoir temperatures. This is because, the combined heat contents (enthalpies) of two types of waters at different temperatures are conserved when they mix, thus the dilution effect is eliminated here. Enthalpy-silica diagrams can be used to correct silica concentrations for adiabatic cooling with single stage steam loss at any temperature.

Cation geothermometers

Cation geothermometers are widely used to calculate the reservoir temperatures from surface thermal waters. This technique is based on ion exchange reactions with temperature dependent equilibrium constants. An example is the exchange of Na and K between co-existing alkali feldspars:

$$\text{Na Al Si}_3\text{ O}_8 + \text{K} = \text{K Al Si}_3\text{ O}_8$$

The equilibrium constant K_{eq} for the above reaction is

$$K\ eq = \frac{\text{KAISi308 Na}}{\text{NaAISi308 K}} \tag{3}$$

The above equation can be written as

$$K\ eq = Na / K \tag{4}$$

Similar equation can be written for monovalent and divalent ions such as K and Mg , thus

$$K\ eq = K / \text{Ö}\ Mg$$

The variation of K eq with temperature can be obtained by an integrated form of van't Hoff equation

$$\text{Log}\ K_{eq} = 1\ H^o / 2.303\ RT + C$$

Where 1 H° is the enthalpy of the reaction, T is temperature in Kelvin, R is the gas constant and C is a constant of integration.

Since 1 H° changes little with temperature in the range of 0 to 300° C, a plot of log Na/K versus temperature will approximately be a straight line. Equations for straight line, like that develpped for silica geothermometery have been proposed by several workers and two most widely used equations are given below:

$$\text{Na - K} \quad t^o\ C = 1217 / 1.483 + \log (Na/K) - 273.15 \tag{5}$$

$$\text{Na - K} \quad t^o\ C = 1390 / 1.750 + \log (Na/K) - 273.15 \tag{6}$$

Equation 5 is proposed by Fournier (1983) and 6 is proposed by Giggenbach et al., (1983). Besides these two, several other equations such as Na-K-Ca and K-Ca, Na -Ca and K- Mg have also been proposed and are in use. Giggenbach (1988) evolved a new geothermometer where both K/Na (t_{kn}) and K/Mg (t_{km}) geothermometers are combined. This geothermometer, represented in the form a figure by Giggenbach (1988) is wide used for the above purpose. Selecting suitable thermal water samples is very essential in estimating reservoir temperatures using geochemical thermometers.

1.9. VACUUM ENERGY

VACUUM ENERGY - In the beginning there was nothing and from nothing came everything

Vacuum energy is an underlying background energy that exists in space even when the space is devoid of matter (free space). The concept of vacuum energy has been deduced from the concept of virtual particles, which is itself derived from the energy-time uncertainty principle. The effects of vacuum energy can be experimentally observed in various phenomena such as spontaneous emission, the Casimir effect, thevan der Waals bonds and the Lamb shift, and are thought to influence the behavior of the Universe on cosmological scales. Using the upper limit of the cosmological constant, the vacuum energy in a cubic centimeter of free space has been estimated to be $10^{''15}$Joules. However, in both Quantum Electrodynamics (QED) and Stochastic Electrodynamics (SED), consistency with the principle of Lorentz covariance and with the magnitude of the Planck Constant requires it to have a much larger value of 10^{113} Joules per cubic meter.

The art of transmitting electrical energy through natural mediums - Patent by Nikola Tesla. This is a patent that was issued to Nikola Tesla by the US Patent office in the year 1905. This scan of the original document of the famous electrical energy transmission through air is worth reading by anyone interested in the history of science. Apparatus for transmitting electrical energy - Patent by Nikola Tesla. This was issued by the US Patent office to Nikola Tesla in the year 1914 although originally filed in the year 1902. This contains the original diagrams of the apparatus.

Vacuum is not just empty space. It is that matrix that always existed before the Universe as we know it came into being. Interestingly the visible matter is only about 5%. The so called 'Dark Matter' which although not visible is experienced as gravitational effect in galaxy clusters. This is a significant 25%. 'Dark Energy' which is considered to be the intrinsic property of vacuum itself is a huge 70%. Unlike normal matter and energy, 'Dark Energy' being an intrinsic part and property of vacuum does not dilute in an expanding universe. In an ever expanding universe the sum total of 'Dark Energy' increases.

Tesla through his own experimentation and because of his research in Hindu Philosophy (Vedas), he knew how to harness this subtle energy. He died in poverty totally unknown to the masses for his great contributions which were confiscated by the government on his death. Part of his misfortunes was due to his feud with Edison. His discoveries or re-discoveries have been a well kept secret in all these years. Just few adventurers and free energy enthusiasts tinker with these experiments in secret. One thing is certain. Whether it is the unorthodox scientist doing his own backyard science or it is the spiritual holy man demonstrating extra-ordinary abilities, there is a world of energy unknown and unacknowledged by the general academia.

The ultimate nature of 'space' is difficult to determine and understand. The ability to harvest the intrinsic vacuum reservoir is not beyond human capability. Why can we not solve the energy problem of the world? Unlimited cost free energy and perpetual machine have been the dream of many. But to tinker with God's best kept secrets is to invite trouble. That is in case we as humans are not ready for it. To be able to harness this unlimited energy there has to be a change in human consciousness. That is the main teaching of the Vedas. The 'Brahman' or consciousness is the single entity which encompasses the entire universe. It is eternal, infinite and more subtle than even the vacuum which it encompasses. The Vedas known to have originated from the Bramhan itself, is the science of Bramhan, the ultimate reality of existence. It is not hard to imagine this as the only source of all energy.

❑❑❑

Chapter–2

Sustainable Landscape

Sustainability has recently become an important factor in the engineering world. Landscape architecture is a discipline that attempts to improve the way humans interact with the environment. That interaction can be improved in various ways such as water conservation, energy conservation, or urban planning. landscape architecture encompasses urban design, community and regional planning, interior and exterior garden design, parks and recreation, historic site and natural area preservation, energy and water conservation, landscape restoration and management, among others. The varied list is an example of the dynamic essence of landscaping and provides insight into the many areas which can be improved by implementing sustainable practices.

Sustainable development practices aim to protect the quality of life of future generations. This can only be done by understanding how the natural environment operates as well as how human interactions affect it. Sustainable Landscape Architecture focuses on enhancing the holistic knowledge of the surrounding landscapes, including the complex processes which naturally occur to maintain it. Employing this knowledge within the planning phases of development should result in the reduction of negative environmental impacts due to the same. The traditional consequences of land development can be eliminated or mitigated when developers are able to foresee the consequences of their work. Many times, replicating undeveloped conditions and/or native landscapes within the overall site design will prove very useful in achieving the goals of sustainability. All of the sustainable topics covered in this chapter involve the application of a technology that resulted from better understanding the natural environment.

Green Roofs

Green Roofs are flat or slightly pitched roofs of buildings which have been converted to or originally designed to be a habitat for plant life. The goal of a green roof is usually to have as much of the roof covered with foliage as possible. Green roofs all consist of the same general structure to give them the ability to support plant life without damaging the structure beneath: Roof decking (metal or concrete), Insulation, Waterproof Membrane, Drainage Layer, Growing Medium / Soil, Plant Life. Depending on the performance expectations of the green roof the properties of these layers will be designed.

There are three main varieties of green roofs; extensive, intensive, and semi-intensive. Extensive refers to smaller scale green roofs which usually have thinner layers of soil and support smaller plants. Intensive roofs are the opposite, supporting large plants (even trees) with thick layers of soil. Semi-intensive green roofs are those roofs which fall in the middle of the two extremes, sharing some qualities of both.

One of the main benefits of green roofs is their thermal properties. A green roof cools the air above them, reduces the temperature of the roof, and reduces the amount of heat transferred into the building interior. These effects can significantly reduce cooling load for the building. Reducing thermal strain on the roofing material also lengthens the life of the roof as such as by 30 years.

Green roofs also provide a significant benefit with respect to storm water mitigation. In an urban area rainstorms often produce large quantities of runoff from the many impermeable surfaces in a city. Green roofs help to reduce the flow of storm water by absorbing significant amounts of rain before they begin to produce runoff. Green roofs may also positively affect the air quality of the surrounding area. The presence of greenery in an area can reduce concentrations of ozone, carbon dioxide, and other pollutants, while providing indirect benefits such as smog reduction through heat island mitigation.

Green Walls

Green walls are interior and exterior walls that have vegetative covering and come in a variety of designs and sizes with a wide range of practical decorative vegetation. They utilize almost any type of plant, depending on the region. Orientation, climate, sunlight, wind exposure, and maintenance regimes all influence the palette of plants suitable for any given project. There are two major types of green walls. A green façade, which uses climbing, plants to form a wall covering, and a living wall, which uses modular plants in a panel system.

Green walls are also known as bio-walls, vegetated walls, eco-walls, and vertical gardens.

Green façades refer to a guidance structure that provides support for vines or climbing plants to grow up the side of a wall. Most systems use wire fencing, modular trellis systems, or stainless steel cables as support systems. Different types of supports are used for different kinds of plants, and there are four main types of climbing plants; self-clinging climbers, vines-climbing plants, leaf-twining climbers & tendril climbers, and ramblers & scrambling plants.

Living walls are walls, indoors and outdoors, composed of individual planting cells attached to a supporting panel system. Mounting systems for interior and exterior living walls are generally the same. The panels are usually hung on a bracket system that can attach to most surfaces and a waterproof membrane should be attached directly behind the brackets. Typically, panels are not stacked or interlocked. Instead, each panel is hung individually and can be hung next to each other to cover a wall. When crops are in the planting cells, it is uncommon for the panel to be above six feet high. This allows for easier care by working in an upright standing position.

Green walls benefit the people and surrounding environment by removing over 80% of Volatile Organic Compounds (VOCs) and other harmful toxins. The walls can also assist with sound absorption and building insulation. Greenery on walls provides an ascetically pleasant environment that can have positive mental health impacts and be a useful advertising technique. Maintenance, aside from typical maintenance associated with most type of plants, is not a necessity in order to maintain a green wall.

Storm water Runoff Infiltration

Storm water run-off infiltration systems such as bioretention areas and vegetated swales are stormwater management tools promoted by Low-Impact Development. These environmentally-conscience practices aim to mitigate some of the detrimental consequences of land development, specifically those linked to impervious surface area. Increases in impervious surface area typically lead to increased run-off volume, increased run-off contamination, and decreased ground water recharge. These can then create additional consequences such as erosion, and downstream flooding. The chain of negative impacts can continue as these affect the quality and stability of eco-systems, harming a variety of native vegetation and species. Stormwater run-off infiltration systems are incorporated onto sites in an attempt to reduce and ideally prevent this chain from occurring. Therefore, the main goal of stormwater infiltration systems is to reduce imperviousness and restore undeveloped conditions. By creating vegetated areas which replicate pre-development conditions the natural hydrologic cycle can be better maintained thus inhibiting a long list of potential, harmful consequences at the source.

Infiltration systems are typically shallow depressions which include a ponding area, vegetation, and a mix of mulches, sand, and soil. However, they can be designed and altered to achieve very specific project goals. Their particular designs depend greatly on several site criteria such as soil permeability and ground slope and factors such as drainage area and climate can further limit their use.

Proper maintenance is crucial to the infiltration systems' performance over time. Inadequate maintenance has been the cause of numerous unsuccessful projects which usually result in aesthetically unpleasant sites. However, properly designed and maintained infiltration systems have shown to consistently reduce run-off volume and improve run-off quality.

Constructed Wetlands

Constructed wetlands are wetlands that have been constructed for the purpose to treat wastewater. This is done by subjecting the water to wetland vegetation, soils, and the associated microbial assemblages to treat wastewater. The vegetation, soils, and microbial assemblages in the wetland will treat the wastewater through natural processes such as aerobic and anaerobic digestion

There are three main types of constructed wetlands. They are surface flow (SF) wetlands (also known as free water surface wetlands), subsurface flow (SSF) wetlands, and vertical flow (VF) wetlands. The difference between these types of wetlands relates to how the wastewater flows through the system. Figure 1 illustrates the difference between SF, SSF, and VF wetlands.

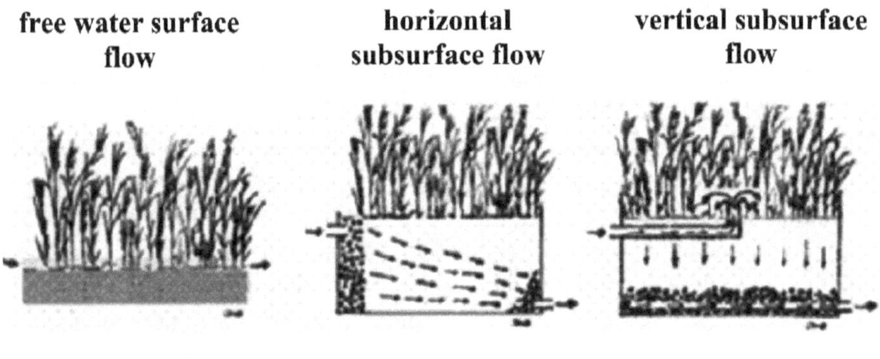

Figure 1: The Difference between ST, SSF, and VF Wetlands

By using constructed wetlands to treat wastewater harmful pollutants such as pathogens, minerals, dissolved solids, heavy metals, and organic contaminants are removed from the water. Constructed wetlands also help reduce the need for potable water, as water from a constructed wetland can be used to irrigate plants, flush toilets, or cleaning purposes. Wetlands are also said to provide social benefits by providing a place for education (for nature study) and recreational activities such as walking, jogging, hunting, and picnicking. The biggest drawback to using constructed wetlands for wastewater treatment is securing enough land for the wetland. Therefore constructed wetlands are often used as a low cost low energy alternative to mechanical treatment plants in rural areas where the cost of land is less. Other potential drawbacks that need to be considered are the potential for wetland overflow, the potential for mosquitoes to breed in the wetland, odor control, and the negative effect of lower temperatures on the wetlands effectiveness.

Rainwater Harvesting

Rainwater harvesting is the process of capturing rainwater and using it instead of potable water for either potable or non-potable uses. By doing this a building is able to reduce its potable water usage. The amount of potable water that is conserved using this method varies greatly depending on various characteristics such as volume and consistency of rainfall, rainwater catchment area, rainwater storage tank size, and the buildings potable water usage. These factors also dictate the cost of installing a rainwater harvesting system as well as its operating costs.

Typically rainwater harvesting systems consist of a catchment area, a treatment process, a storage tank, and piping to the intended use. For most domestic rainwater harvesting systems the catchment areas consists of the buildings roof. The treatment, size of the storage tank, and the extensiveness of the rainwater's piping system all depend on the final use of the rainwater.

After the rainwater is caught by the catchment system the water is typically filtered to prevent debris from entering the water storage tank. This help ensuring the quality of the water. The storage tank size greatly affects the economic feasibility of the system, as the cost of tank instillation tends to be the largest component of rainwater harvesting system's cost. Therefore when designing a rainwater harvesting system it is very import to size the storage tank correctly.

The quality of rainwater collected also needs to be monitored if it is to be used for drinking. This is because rainwater can be contaminated with microbes, metals, or chemicals. Also, the physical qualities (such as appearance and odor) of the water must also be taken into account. Depending on the quality of rainwater at a site and the intended use, a variety of filtration and/or disinfection methods can be used to improve the quality of rainwater.

Xeriscaping

Xeriscaping became popular in the 1980s as a new theory for landscaping and farming during droughts. The purpose of xeriscaping is to produce fruitful vegetation and beautiful landscaping with minimal water consumption.

Xeriscaping has seven chief principles that contribute to the overall goal: planning and design, soil improvement, minimizing turf, appropriate plant selection, efficient irrigation, use of mulch, and maintenance. Important aspects of xeriscaping are grouping plants with similar needs together and minimizing the amount of lawn grass. People might want a large manicured lawn, however they use a great amount of water, and xeriscaping encourages reduction of lawn areas and switching to low maintenance alternative covering. Proper planning and plant selection are also vital to reduce the amount of maintenance and water required to sustain the landscaping. In order to ensure maximum growth, suitable nutrients in the soil must be provided for the plants via mulching and irrigation. Applying these techniques encourages water conservation and improved water quality while maintaining a beautiful garden.

The most beneficial results are found when all aspects of xeriscaping are applied and work together. Water consumption can be reduced up to 50% and healthier plants can result from not over or under watering. Xeriscaped areas are typically lower maintenance than land with traditional landscaping. Xeriscaping is not only good for the environment, but they are also good for the owners by increasing the land value and heightening the curb appeal.

2.1. GREEN ROOFS

The idea of green roofs has been around for centuries, with many houses in Scandinavia and Germany having home made green roofs throughout history. The idea of "greening" the rooftops in urban areas however is a relatively new idea which has gained much support in the last decade or so. Green roofs are continuing to gain popularity. Green roof technology has been shown to have significant benefits in certain circumstances for the environment and for the building occupants and owners and the use of green roofs is being constantly increased. Green roofs are seen as a possible solution to short and long term energy reduction and water conservation goals.

Technical Description

Green Roofs are flat or slightly pitched roofs of buildings which have been converted to or originally designed to be a habitat for plant life. The goal of a green roof is usually to have as much of the roof covered with foliage as possible. Green roofs all consist of the same general structure to give them the ability to support plant life without damaging the structure beneath. A typical green roof consists of at least the following layers from bottom to top: roof decking (metal or concrete), insulation, waterproof membrane, drainage layer, growing medium / soil, plant life.

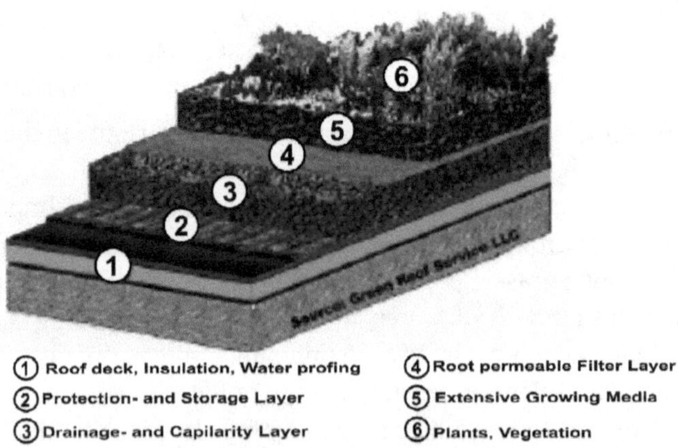

Figure 2: Extensive Green Roof Diagram

There are many varieties of this basic design, but several features are essential. The waterproof membrane is necessary to protect the structure from any undrained water, and the drainage layer is needed to eliminate excess water that is unable to be absorbed by the soil or growing medium. Soil is used in cases where more load can be carried by the roof, but sometimes lightweight growing medium, or substrate, replaces it Substrate usually consists of a nutrient rich mixture of organic material and minerals designed to be as lightweight as possible.

There are three main varieties of green roofs; extensive, intensive, and semi-intensive. Extensive refers to smaller scale green roofs which usually have thinner layers of soil and support smaller plants. Intensive roofs are the opposite, supporting large plants (even trees) with thick layers of soil. Semi-intensive green roofs are those roofs which fall in the middle of the two extremes, sharing some qualities of both. Due to the variation in definition of semi-intensive roofs only extensive and intensive green roofs will be addressed here. The reader should keep in mind that in some instances it may be the best option to create a semi-intensive roof by choosing properties that do not fall into either of the other two categories.

Extensive Green Roofs

Extensive green roofs are "smaller scale" green roofs. They generally utilize a growing medium or substrate instead of soil in order to remain lightweight. Extensive roofs usually have a substrate thickness of between 2cm to 20cm, depending on the types of plants being used. Typically herbaceous plants, grasses, moss, and sedum are used to cover an extensive roof. This type of roof is designed to be low maintenance and typically requires little or no watering. Usually access to the roof is limited to occasional maintenance to protect the plants and to limit the live loading on the roof. This type of roof is more common due to its lower cost and reduced structural demands. An extensive green roof ranging from 4cm to 10cm will have a loading ranging from 50kg/m2 to 100kg/m2. Another study on extensive green roofs estimated structural requirements to be an additional 70kg/m2 to 170kg/m2 in addition to the weight of the roof below the waterproof membrane.

Extensive roofs are appropriate for retrofitting to an existing structure due to their relatively light weight. Extensive green roofs have less aesthetic appeal than intensive roofs but still may be more visually pleasing than a traditional flat roof covered with gravel ballast or rubber mat.

Figure 3: Extensive Green Roof

Intensive Green Roofs

Intensive Green roofs are systems which tend to house larger plants with deeper layers of growing medium. Intensive green roofs can have a strong aesthetic appeal and often times are accessible to the public with paths, benches, or other features of a normal outdoor park. Medium sized trees, large shrubs, and other large plants are common features of intensive green roofs along with small ponds or pools. The growing medium on intensive roofs ranges from 15 cm deep up to several meters deep in order to support the larger trees. Intensive roofs often require regular maintenance and irrigation, so they may incur some operation and maintenance costs on the building owner. The weight of such a system can vary greatly and intensive roofs typically require their own structural support system to prevent overloading the roof. This makes intensive roofs unsuitable for retrofitting to an existing structure, as the beams that support the roof of a building are not easily removed or replaced.

Intensive green roofs are worth the cost to building owners because they offer significant energy savings due to their increased thermal performance as compared to extensive green roofs. They absorb greater volumes of storm water and better regulate the air temperature and quality allowing them to provide increased environmental benefits.

Potential Benefits

One great benefit of green roofs is their thermal properties. Green roofs have the effect of cooling the air above them, as opposed to traditional roofs which tend to greatly increase ambient temperature above them. The reason for this is that plant life tends to absorb sunlight and turn the radiation into energy and reflect excess sunlight. The plants also cool themselves through the process of transpiration in which they release water that is evaporated, similar to animals sweating. Moisture also evaporates directly from the soil. Evapotranspiration is a term used to describe the combined affect of direct evaporation and plant transpiration. Regular roofs absorb the sun's rays, heat up, and radiate that heat back out to the air. This produces an effect where the air heats up directly above rooftops and contributes to the heat island effect. The heat island effect is where the air temperature in an urban environment is higher due to the aggregate effect of many manmade surfaces absorbing solar radiation. Green roofs can locally reduce this effect, and widespread use of green roofs in a city has the possibility to mitigate the heat island effect substantially. Another thermal effect of green roofs is to significantly reduce the temperature of the roof itself. As a traditional roof absorbs solar radiation throughout the day it can gain significant amounts of heat.

Reducing thermal strain on the roofing material lengthens the life of the roof. Research estimates that the average membrane roof lasts about 15 years, but an average extensive green roof lasts 45 to 50 years, due to the greenery and soil protecting the roofing materials from sunlight, rain, wind, and other detrimental weather. In addition to lengthening the life of the roofing material regulating the temperature of the roof will also regulate the temperature inside the building. In cold climates green roofs provide added insulation to the roof. Some studies find that in very dry and cold environments the transpiration process can cancel much of the added insulating benefits. Still, most research finds at least some prevention of heat flow through the roof in the cold months, which helps keep the internal building temperature warmer. One study in Ottawa found a reduced heat flow through the roof of 26% in the winter. Heat gain in the summer through the roof was reduced by 95%. In Toronto a study found reduced heat flow through the roof averaging from 10% to 30% in winter, and from 70% to 90% in summer.

Green roofs provide a significant benefit with respect to stormwater mitigation. In an Urban area rainstorms often produce large quantities of runoff from the many impermeable surfaces in a city, as impermeable surfaces can make up as much as 45% of total ground area in a built up city. This runoff must be collected and treated as wastewater because it often carries many harmful chemicals and other hazards with it. Green roofs help to reduce the flow of stormwater by absorbing significant amounts of rain before they begin to produce runoff.

Since the stormwater benefits of a green roof are based largely on the thickness of the soil extensive roofs tend to be less effective at absorbing rainwater than intensive roofs. One study found that roofs with 15 to 20 cm of growing medium absorbed 60% or water annually, where roofs with 2 to 4 cm absorbed only 40%. Similarly, extensive roofs tend to have less plant cover than intensive roofs so their thermal benefits will be reduced compared to intensive roofs.

Economic Benefits - cost savings opportunities for the building owner include:

- Protection of roof membrane resulting in a longer material lifespan (it is estimated that green roofs will last up to twice as long as conventional roofs), resulting in decreased maintenance and savings in replacement costs;
- Savings on energy heating and cooling costs, depending on the size of the building, climate and type of green roof.

Sound Insulation

- Soil, plants and the trapped layer of air can be used to insulate for sound. Sound waves that are produced by machinery, traffic or airplanes can be absorbed, reflected or deflected. The substrate tends to block lower sound frequencies and the plants block higher frequencies.
- A green roof with a 12 cm (4.7 inches) substrate layer can reduce sound by 40 decibels; a 20 cm (7.9 inches) substrate layer can reduce sound by 46-50 decibels.

Economic Benefits

- Potential to reduce the size of HVAC equipment on new or retrofitted buildings (capital and operational savings).
- Potential to reduce the amount of standard insulation used.
- Potential to incorporate cooling and/or water treatment functions.
- Potential for local, regional, and national market exposure, depending on the uniqueness of the project.
- Potential to reduce or eliminate roof drains.
- Potential to meet regulatory requirements for stormwater management.
- Potential to reduce community resistance to new developments.

Amenity Space and Aesthetics

- Provision of amenity space for day care, meetings, and recreation;
- Aesthetic appeal, increasing the value of the property and the marketability of the
- Building as a whole, particularly for accessible green roofs. For example, American and British studies show that "good tree cover"

adds between 6 to 15 per cent to the value of a home. Green roofs offer the same visual and environmental benefits.

- Satisfying the aesthetic needs of people looking down upon the roof from adjacent buildings.
- Potential to improve employee productivity.

The following benefits may be achieved, depending on the type of public policy support for green roof installations in the area.

- Potential for reduced stormwater/wastewater charges from your municipality or utility.
- Potential to reduce the size of stormwater management ponds or cisterns, resulting in cost savings.
- Potential for grants related to energy efficiency and/or green roofs.
- Potential for density bouncing / larger floor area ratio.
- Potential to satisfy regulatory requirements for green roofs.
- Potential to score more than 7 credits under the Green Building Council LEED certification system.
- Potential for satisfying minimum parkland / green space set aside, requirements.
- Potential for greenhouse gas emissions trading credits, stemming from energy savings.

Public Benefits

Public policies that support green roof installations will create jobs for the following:

- Suppliers and manufacturers of roofing membranes and root repellent layers;
- Suppliers and manufacturers of drainage layers, landscaping cloth, curbs, irrigation systems and other specialty products;
- Suppliers and manufacturers of substrate, light-weight soils and amendments;
- Garden nurseries specializing in plants specifically for green roofs;
- Design and engineering professionals;
- Contractors and landscapers; and,
- Companies supplying maintenance contracts.

Community cost savings opportunities include:

- Cost savings from increased stormwater retention and decreased need to expand or rebuild related infrastructure.
- Decreased cost of meeting greenhouse gas reductions and adapting to climate change by reducing the "Urban Heat Island Effect" and the need for interior building insulation.
- Decreased need for health care services from reductions in ground level ozone resulting from a reduction in the urban heat island.
- Increased worker productivity and creativity.
- Decreased need for health care services and medication due to the benefits of passive experiences with nature and vegetation.
- Extending the lifespan of landfill sites by reducing re-roofing material waste.
- Opportunities to recycle aggregate and compost.

Improved Air Quality

Filtration of Airborne Particulates:

- A green roof will not only absorb heat, decreasing the tendency towards thermal air movement, but will also filter the air moving across it.
- 1 m^2 (10.76 ft^2) of grass roof can remove up to 2 kg (4.4 lbs) of airborne particulates from the air every year, depending on foliage type.

Carbon Dioxide/Oxygen Exchange:

- Through the process of photosynthesis, plants convert carbon dioxide, water and sunlight/energy into oxygen and glucose. This cyclical process supplies animals and humans with oxygen and food.
- 1.5 m^2 (16.15 ft^2) of uncut grass, produces enough oxygen per year to supply 1 human with their yearly oxygen intake requirement.

Temperature Regulation

Moderation of the Urban Heat Island Effect:

- Through the daily dew and evaporation cycle, plants on vertical and horizontal surfaces are able to cool cities during hot summer months. In the process of evapotranspiration, plants use heat energy from their surroundings (approximately 592 kcal per L of water) when evaporating water. One m² (10.76 ft²) of foliage can evaporate over 0.5 litres of water on a hot day and on an annual basis the same area can evaporate up to 700 litres of water.

- This process reduces the 'Urban Heat Island Effect' in the summer. The 'Urban Heat Island Effect' is the difference in temperature between a city and the surrounding countryside. It is mainly due to the expanse of hard and reflective surfaces, such as roofs, which absorb solar radiation and re-radiate it as heat. Reduction of the 'Urban Heat Island Effect' will also reduce the distribution of dust and particulate matter throughout the city and the production of smog. This can play a role in reducing greenhouse gas emissions and adapting urban areas to a future climate with warmer summers.
- Green roofs can play a role in reducing the urban heat island (UHI), augmenting the existing vegetation, but the precise amount of coverage is still uncertain.

Building Insulation:

- Historically, green roofs have been used to insulate buildings. Shading the external surface of the building envelope has been shown to be more effective than internal insulation.
- Green roofs insulate buildings by preventing heat from moving through the roof. Their insulation properties can be maximized by using a growing medium with a low soil density and a high moisture content and by choosing plants with a high leaf area index (i.e. the bigger the leaves, the better). This could play a role in reducing greenhouse gas emissions and adapting urban areas to a future climate with greater incidences of drought and extreme heat.

Creation of Microclimates:

- A green roof will have a noticeable impact on the heat gain and loss of a building, as well as the humidity, air quality and reflected heat in the surrounding neighbourhood. In conjunction with other green installations, green roofs can play a role in altering the climate of the city as a whole.
- On a summer day, the temperature of a gravel roof can increase by as much as 25 °C (77 °F), to between 60-80 °C (140 - 176 F). Covered with grass, the temperature of that roof would not rise above 25 °C (77 °F), thus resulting in energy cost savings.
- 20 cm (7.9 inches) of substrate with a 20-40 cm (7.9 - 15.7 inches) layer of thick grass has the combined insulation value of° 15 cm (5.9 inches) of mineral wool.

- Rooms under a green roof are at least 3 - 4 °C (5.4 - 7.2°F) cooler than the air outside, when outdoor temperatures range between 25-30 °C (77 - 86 °F).

Water

Stormwater Retention:

- Water is stored by the substrate and then taken up by the plants from where it is returned to the atmosphere through transpiration and evaporation.
- In summer, depending on the plants and depth of growing medium, green roofs retain 70-90% of the precipitation that falls on them; in winter they retain between 25-40%. For example, a grass roof with a 4-20 cm (1.6 - 7.9 inches) layer of growing medium can hold 10-15 cm (3.9 - 5.9 inches) of water.

Water Filtration:

- Green roofs not only retain the rainwater, but also moderate the temperature of the water and act as natural filters for any of the water that happens to run off.

Temporal Delay of Stormwater Runoff and Reduced Runoff Volume:

- Green roofs reduce the amount of stormwater runoff and also delay the time at which runoff occurs, resulting in decreased stress on sewer systems at peak flow periods.

Social Benefits

Aesthetics:

- Urban greening has long been promoted as an easy and effective strategy for beautifying the built environment and increasing investment opportunity.

Health & Horticultural Therapy:

- Psychological studies have shown that the restorative effect of a natural view holds the viewers' attention, diverts their awareness away from themselves and from worrisome thoughts thereby improving health.
- People living in high-density developments are known to be less susceptible to illness if they have a balcony or terrace garden. This is

partly due to the additional oxygen, air filtration and humidity control supplied by plants but also from the therapeutic benefits that result from caring for plants. The variety of sounds, smells, colours and movement provided by plants, although not quantifiable, can add significantly to human health and well being.

- Patients in the same hospital, recovering from the same operation, were studied as to the restorative effects of views onto a landscaped courtyard versus a brick wall. The patients with the green view had shorter post-operative stays, took fewer moderate and stronger painkillers and had fewer negative evaluation comments from the nurses.

Improved Safety:

- A garden on the roof is often considered safer than a garden at grade. For example, because access to the roof is often restricted to building tenants or employees, there is less likelihood of assault or vandalism.

Recreation:

- Green roofs can help to address the lack of green space in many urban areas. Studies show that leisure activities in natural settings such as gardens and parks, are important for helping people cope with stress and in meeting other non-stress-related needs.

Preservation of Habitat & Biodiversity

Habitat:

- Rooftop habitats can play one of two roles: a 'stepping stone' habitat connecting natural isolated habitat pockets with each other, or an 'island' habitat remaining isolated from other habitats at grade.
- Green roofs can be specifically designed to mimic endangered ecosystems/habitats.

Flora & Fauna

- Green roofs designed for minimal maintenance are much protected and can become home to plants easily damaged by walking and to birds that nest on the ground. Since the soil on these green roofs is also less likely to be disturbed, it becomes a safer habitat for insects, and the deeper the soil the more diversity the roof can support.
- In Germany, for instance, research has shown that green roofs can support anywhere from 10 to 40 different insect species and have even been found to harbour nesting bird species.

Local Food Production

Green roofs can provide new opportunities for urban agriculture. There are many benefits to growing and distributing food locally including:

- Support of the local economy in growing, processing and distributing;
- Increased access to food by everyone;
- Fresher produce;
- Decreased travel time to market and related environmental costs; and Green Roof

Potential Risks and Considerations

The main environmental issue raised concerning green roofs is their affect on water quality. Although runoff through soil can provide filtration for the water to some extent, growing medium and fertilizers may pollute soil to some extent depending on the composition of the soil or substrate. One study found that green roof runoff had significantly reduced heavy metal presence, specifically copper, zinc, cadmium, and lead. However, several studies have noted an increase in phosphorus release from green roofs compared to normal urban runoff. It is speculated that this release of phosphorous can be controlled by choosing more carefully formulated substrates, but phosphorous release is often a concern with any fertilized area. Green roofs have been shown to act as sinks for nitrates and nitrogen compounds which can act as pollutants in runoff. Overall it seems that green roofs have a somewhat neutral effect on water quality although care should be taken when choosing soil or substrate to avoid release of fertilizers and chemicals. Use of pesticides should also be avoided. The only other major consideration for green roofs is the potential need to upgrade the building structurally to carry the extra load of the soil and plant life. This is less of a concern for extensive green roofs, but with intensive green roofs the added dead load almost always requires that the structure be designed differently to account for the additional weight.

Recommended Site Characteristics

Green roofs can potentially be added to any structure in the world as long as the building has the structural requirements to carry the additional load. However, buildings in certain environments will benefit much more from the application of green roof technology than others. The factors that matter most in determining the suitability of green roof technology for a region are the following:

- Annual rainfall
- Frequency of rain-heavy storms

- Daily and seasonal temperature
- Amount of direct sunlight
- Urban or rural environment

These factors will all affect the performance of a green roof in terms of the benefits that the building owner and the local environment will receive from it. Aesthetic appeal is the only quality that will be unaffected by the location of the site, and some owners may choose to construct a green roof based purely on this factor. Rainfall and storm frequency affect the green roof in terms of stormwater management capability and maintenance. Green roof technology should be more readily applied in areas with frequent heavy rains for two reasons. The first is that green roofs help to mitigate large quantities of storm water runoff in cases of heavy rainfall. The second reason is that in areas of low rainfall green roofs may require watering, which can raise maintenance costs. In this case extensive roofs can be used since they are usually planted with drought resistant species, but even this may not be enough to mitigate the cost of irrigation.

Local temperature and amount of direct sunlight both affect the thermal performance of a green roof. It has been found that green roofs are less effective at preventing heat loss during cold weather. In climates where there is a very long winter or the heating demand of buildings will far outweigh the cooling demand green roofs may not be as practical. On the other hand, green roofs have proven excellent at lowering the buildings temperature on hot days. Additionally, the amount of direct sunlight matters because it is the main factor in determining how much green roofs will lower the cooling demands of a building. In a structure where direct sunlight on the roof is a main cause of cooling load, green roofs will be most effective. Also, the plants on the roof will need a certain amount of sunlight to survive, so a building that spends the majority of the day in partial or complete shade may have problems with keeping shaded plants alive.

Finally, urban environments are the best application for green roofs because they are where most of the environmental problems exist to which green roofs are a solution. Stormwater management and heat island effect are very seldom an issue in more rural environments so the use of a green roof becomes less appealing.

Potential LEED Credits

• SS Credit 6.1: Stormwater Design—Quantity Control

1 Point

To limit disruption of natural hydrology by reducing impervious cover, increasing on-site infiltration, reducing or eliminating pollution from stormwater runoff and eliminating contaminants.

• SS Credit 6.2: Stormwater Design—Quality Control

1 Point

To limit disruption and pollution of natural water flows by managing stormwater runoff.

SS Credit 7.2: Heat Island Effect—Roof

1 Point

To reduce heat islands1 to minimize impacts on microclimates and human and wildlife habitats.

• EA Credit 1: Optimize Energy Performance

1–19 Points

To achieve increasing levels of energy performance beyond the prerequisite standard to reduce environmental and economic impacts associated with excessive energy use.

• IE Q Credit 7.1: Thermal Comfort—Design

1 Point

To provide a comfortable thermal environment that promotes occupant productivity and well-being.

2. 2. GREEN WALLS

Green walls have been used in countries like Germany, Switzerland, and Scandinavia for over three decades. With the recent popularity of the green roofs in North America, green walls have also begun to gain popularity. People use vines and vegetation on the walls of houses for shade from the sun, insulation from the wind and cold and aesthetic purposes. By the year 2030, total energy consumption and greenhouse gas emissions are predicted to both quadruple. Since green walls insulate buildings, which helps reduce energy consumption, and provide natural air filtration, which helps improve air quality, the demand for green walls will continue grow.

Figure 4: Green Walls

- Green walls insulate buildings and provide sound absorption.
- Green walls remove volatile organic compounds from the air and can improve the mental health of nearby persons.
- They require standard plant maintenance with the possible added difficulty of being high in the air and difficult to reach.

Technical Description

Green walls are interior and exterior walls that have vegetative covering and come in a variety of designs and sizes with a wide range of practical decorative vegetation. They utilize almost any type of plant, depending on the region. Orientation, climate, sunlight, wind exposure, and maintenance regimes all influence the palette of plants suitable for any given project. There are two major types of green walls. A green façade, which uses climbing, plants to form a wall covering, and a living wall, which uses modular plants in a panel system. Green walls are also known as bio-walls, vegetated walls, eco-walls, and vertical gardens. No matter what it is called, green walls have made quite an impact. Even Time Magazine recognized its possibilities and named green walls the 31st best invention of 2009.

Although most green walls are relatively low maintenance, five key components have been identified to successfully sustain a green wall. The divisions are location, structural inspections, irrigation, drainage, and plant maintenance. Location is important because it dictates how to access the green wall. Usually a method similar to the installation technique is ideal. Structural inspections are recommended from a preventative standpoint. Check the waterproofing and penetration methods, bracket assembly, structural wall, and water flow. Irrigation must also be inspected for clogged emitters, leaks, filter replacement, and mechanical components. Drainage maintenance is also essential to prevent water collection, whether indoors or outdoors. Materials like leaves, soil, mud and garbage should be cleared out of drains. Lastly, plant maintenance is crucial to have a thriving green wall. Weeding, pruning, dusting, and/or deadheading should be used to help preserve the health of the plants Weeding consists of removing unwanted plant life because it can detract from the water and nutrients needed by the desired vegetation. It is important to prune a green wall by cutting back the plant to prevent overgrowth. Cleaning off dust is only necessary for indoor green walls because dust blocks sunlight from the plant and reduces its ability to photosynthesize. Deadheading simply refers to removing the dying and dead ends of plants by pulling or cutting them off. By eradicating the useless parts, the flora has more chances to bloom and live longer.

Determining the loading for green walls is crucial to a successful design. The weight of the plants, the wind load exerted, the dew and rain amount, the weight of snow, and the weight of the actual structure should all be taken into consideration when determining the loads. The weight for green walls varies greatly, from 1 kg/m2 to 50 kg/m2 of plant area. Wind resistance is minimal on climbers with a shallow profile, while climbers with lots of foliage and branches could produce a lot of stress on its supports. Also, too much growth might damage the support system. Structures with deciduous plants must anticipate supporting double the weight of the plants themselves, to account for dew, rain and snow. Structural systems with evergreen plants must be able to hold triple the weight of the plant to account for dew, rain and snow. The physical structures' weight must be measured with the height above the ground incorporated. If the structure is supported at the top and bottom, then the top should carry the whole load and ½ the wind load while the bottom needs to support only ½ the wind load.

When building a green wall, irrigation needs to be taken into consideration. Most indoor and outdoor systems have built-in irrigation systems. Normally a ¼" drip irrigation tube is installed at the top of each panel with cutouts approximately every 6 inches. The cutouts have to line up with the pressure compensating emitters that allow for free flow of water through each vertical row of cells. Capillary action of the soil and gravity permit water to drip from the top row to the bottom row with special cutouts. Also, infusing liquid nutrients in the plants is recommended through a standard fertilizer loop.

Green Façades

Green façades refer to a guidance structure that provides support for vines or climbing plants to grow up the side of a wall. Most systems use wire fencing, modular trellis systems, or stainless steel cables as support systems. Wall mounted façades are either flush or 7.5-45 cm away for the wall. Green façades are attached with brackets or mounting clips and a waterproof membrane should be installed between the wall and the façade in most arrangements. When using cables or wires, turnbuckles and anchors need to be mounted and attached to each wire for possible adjustments needed as the plants grow and expand. Since green façades contain continuously developing plants, the support systems are essential for directional guidance and load bearing capabilities. There are three main types of support; a trellis of vertical and horizontal elements, just vertical supports, or just horizontal supports. Each system can be made of different materials like wire or wood. Different types of supports are used for different kinds of plants, and there are four main types of climbing plants; self-clinging climbers, vines-climbing plants, leaf-twining climbers & tendril climbers, and ramblers & scrambling plants.

When climbing plants are utilized for high vertical landscaping in green façades, intense weather is a common dilemma; therefore, resilient types of plants should be chosen. Depending on the area, climbers with a high tolerance for frost, wind, or heat should be selected. In addition to planning for the right type of plant, considerations must also be made for a proper schedule. Some climbers may take up to 3-5 years to completely cover the entire area, depending on the height.

Table 1: Types of Climbing Plants

Name	Description	Examples	Considerations
Self-clinging Climbers (Adhesive Pad Climbers and Clinging Wall Climbers)	Both use lateral shoots with glandular discs that adhere to any surface and have strong roots that grow over long distances without any auxiliary support.	Boston Ivy *Parthenocissus tricuspidata* Climbing Hydrangeas Hydrangea petiolaris	May cause harm to buildings by damaging sidings and mortar with their invasive adhesive pads and roots, so they should only be used with a support system and proper maintenance to avoid structural damage
Vine Climbers	A strong affinity to grow upwards by winding around the support with circular movements of their stem tips. Slow to moderate growers need support space of 200-400 mm, and very vigorous species can be up to 800 mm apart.	*Wisteria Sinensis* Honeysuckles *Lonicera* Hops *Humulus Lupulu* Morning glory *Ipomoea Hederacea*	Vertical supports might be needed in most cases, but spacing between vertical supports varies depending on the species.
Leaf-twining and Tendril Climbers	Use their leaves to hold on. Primarily deciduous, but they hold on to the system with their brittle stems in the winter. Slow to moderate climbers need a grid size of 150x200mm, and vigorous climbers need a grid size of 300x500mm.	Clematis and Nasturtiums *Tropaeolum* Passion flowers *Passiflora* Grape vines *Vitis* Ampelopsis *Ampelopsis Brevipedunculata*	Vertical and horizontal supports recommended for leaf-twiners and tendrils.
Ramblers and Scrambling Plants	Holds on to the supports with thorns, bristles, and prickles. Can be used over stretches of horizontal growth with a small vertical range. Horizontal supports are ideal, and optimum vertical spacing is roughly 400mm.	Rosa Constance Spry	Should not be used where people can easily come into contact with them because they are so jagged. Not ideal for vertical growth.

Living Walls

Living walls are walls, indoors and outdoors, composed of individual planting cells attached to a supporting panel system. Panels typically hold 12 to 19 planting cells and are approximately 40 cm high by 40 cm wide. Plants are typically grown horizontally at first. The maturity of the roots increases the soil volume so it pushes against the planting cells, which aids to keep them in place when turned vertically. After a few weeks to a few months, the plants have rooted to the planting cells and are secure in their panels.

Luckily, mounting systems for interior and exterior living walls are generally the same. The panels are usually hung on a bracket system that can attach to most surfaces. A waterproof membrane should be attached behind the mounting brackets and in front of the structural wall, especially on indoor systems. The green wall panels should not touch the structural wall in order to allow adequate air flow that prevents condensation on the back of the panels. Typically, panels are not stacked or interlocked. Instead, each panel is hung individually and can be hung next to each other to cover a wall. When crops are in the planting cells, it is uncommon for the panel to be above six feet high. This allows for easier care by working in an upright standing position.

Fig 5 : Living Walls

A large array of plants can be used for living walls. Proper vegetation is typically selected based upon resilience, site-specific environmental situations, rooting system, color, breeding rate, and texture. Living wall panels can also harvest small shrubs, perennials, edible plants, ferns, and ground covers. Most living walls need to be pre-grown in order to ensure the quality of the product. Pre-grown panels need about 6 to 12 months of lead time before being installed. An automatic drip irrigation system should be put in at least a month before panel installation.

Common Indoor Plants	Common Outdoor Plants
Dracaena Janet Craig	Sedum Reflexum
Dracaena Sanderiana	Sedum Sarmentosum
Button Fern	Black Mondo Grass
Green Prayer Plant	Liriope
Red Prayer Plant	HederaHelix
Croton Petra	Basil
Croton Norma	Thyme
Peperomia Magnoliifolia	Mint
Peperomia Orba	Parsley
Spider Plant	Lettuce
Dracaena Marginata	Onions
African Violet	Radishes

Potential Benefits

- Removes over 80% of Volatile Organic Compounds (VOCs) and can remove other harmful toxins, like Benzene, Formaldehyde and Trichloroethylene, by filtering the air to prevent "Sick Building Syndrome"
- Plant life offsets carbon emissions by respiration: in taking carbon dioxide and emitting oxygen
- Insulates and cools building envelope
- Aids in sound absorption
- Acts as a privacy screen
- Living walls can grow food such as strawberries, carrots, and peppers
- Helps conserve energy by insulating building against heat exchange with the outside air
- Increased greenery reduces canopy level Urban Heat Island (UHI), where manmade surfaces in an urban environment absorb sunlight, raising their temperature and the temperature of the surrounding air.
- Used for marketing by creating a strong visual impact and also by appealing to smell and touch.
- Positive mental health impacts by decreasing in employee stress, ailments, and absenteeism.
- Protects the architectural wall from acid rain, UV light and wind.
- Living walls produce comparable results to green roofs at a depth of 3 inches.
- Supplies nesting habitat and food for birds (Capital Regional District, 2010)
- Aesthetically pleasing.
- Stormwater retention can be designed for using green walls, much like green roofs. The green walls can retain the precipitation by using the soil or a cistern to aid its water supply.

Potential Risks and Considerations

- Needs to be taken care of like normal plants with watering, pruning, deadheading, etc.
- Large areas and heights could pose a problem because of limited access.

- Shoots could penetrate between materials in the building (for example under tiles, cladding or roofs), compromising their structural integrity. This growth must to be reduced to make certain the façade will not interfere with the structural soundness of the building.
- Without proper air and water flow, molding could occur
- Pollen generation should be planned for (especially indoors)
- Some systems require additional energy and money for false light and water pumps, and nutrients.

2.3. STORM WATER RUN-OFF INFILTRATION SYSTEMS

Stormwater run-off infiltration systems such as bioretention areas and vegetated swales are stormwater management tools promoted by Low-Impact Development (LID). LID practices began in the mid 1980s in Prince George's County (PGC), Maryland. They were pioneered to help PGC "address the growing economic and environmental limitations of conventional stormwater management practices". Bioretention technology was the first LID practice introduced and it intended to help control stormwater pollutants, reduce runoff volume, and manage runoff timing.

Stormwater runoff infiltration systems aim to mitigate some of the detrimental consequences of land development, specifically those linked to impervious surface area. Increases in impervious surface area typically lead to increased run-off volume, increased run-off contamination, and decreased ground water recharge. These can then create additional consequences such as erosion, and downstream flooding. The chain of negative impacts can continue as these affect the quality and stability of eco-systems, harming a variety of native vegetation and species. Stormwater run-off infiltration systems are incorporated onto sites in an attempt to reduce and ideally prevent this chain from occurring.

"Under natural and undeveloped conditions, surface runoff can range from 10 to 30 percent of the total annual precipitation. Depending on the level of development and the site planning methods used, the alteration of physical conditions can result in a significant increase of surface runoff to over 50 percent of the overall precipitation".

Therefore, the main goal of stormwater infiltration systems is to reduce imperviousness and restore undeveloped conditions. By creating vegetated areas which replicate pre-development conditions the natural hydrologic cycle can be better maintained thus inhibiting a long list of potential, harmful consequences at the source.

Infiltration systems are designed to capture, store, treat, and transport storm water run-off in a similar manner as the native landscape of an undeveloped lot. By capturing and treating storm-water run-off close to the source, these systems protect both sewage systems and potential water supply sources. Reducing the amount of run-off alleviates the volume handled by a sewerage system. Treating the run-off protects groundwater and surface water supply sources from pollutants commonly found in run-off. The following sections will address two of the most common types of infiltration systems, bioretention areas/basins, also referred to as rain gardens, and vegetated swales. Although both rain gardens and vegetated swales employ the same concepts their overall design, cost and applications vary.

Bioretention Basins/Rain Gardens

Bioretention basins and rain gardens refer to the same type of run-off infiltration systems. The term "bioretention" has a more technical/scientific connotation while rain gardens usually refer to small bioretention areas in residential settings that typically use aesthetically pleasing plants. Both terms are used interchangeably throughout this section.

According to their bioretention design, the name bioretention comes from the ability of the biomass (plants, mulches, soils, etc.) to retain the nutrients and other contaminants commonly found in stormwater run-off (i.e. phosphorus and nitrogen) However, as previously mentioned, volume control and groundwater recharges are also major benefits. These are all accomplished by allowing fifteen different natural processes to occur: interception, infiltration, settling, evaporation, filtration, absorption, transpiration, assimilation, adsorption, nitrification, denitrification, volatilization, thermal attenuation, degradation, and decomposition.

Fig: 6 Bioretention Example

The following natural processes allow bioretention areas to mimic predevelopment ground conditions. Interception refers to the ability of the plants, soils, and mulches to collect and capture rainfall/run-off. This process is crucial because it concentrates the captured water in the basin's ponding area. Settling allows certain solid contaminants in the captured run-off to float to the top of the ponding area. This provides some initial treatment of the water before other processes carry it any closer to sources of groundwater. Once in the ponding area, the run-off then goes through infiltration which is the process of water moving downward from the ponding area, through the planting soil and mulches and into the surrounding and underlying existing soils. As infiltration and settling occur, evaporation at the surface of the ponding area caused by energy from the sun further reduces the volume of water in the shallow ponding area. As an effect of infiltration, particles are filtered through mulches, sands, and soils that are part of the rain garden's design. Filtration accounts for the majority of the removal of particulate matter within run-off. Before water infiltrates enough to be absorbed by plant roots, adsorption takes place in the mulch layer. Here, dissolved metals and nutrients are bound to humus which is created through the breakdown of plants and mulch. Once the plants take up all the water they need, any remaining water is still susceptible to adsorption as the water continues to infiltrate into the deeper soil layers.

During filtration water takes the place of voids and air spaces within the soil, while plant roots and fungi absorb the water. After absorption, over 90% of the water initially absorbed by the plants is released into the air as vapor through transpiration. Assimilation occurs during absorption but refers to plants taking in nutrients instead of water. Further removal of contaminants is accomplished by volatilization, degradation, and decomposition. Volatilization is the process of breaking down a substance into a more unstable form. This occurs in biorentenion areas through denitrification. Denitrification is the process in which microorganisms turn nitrate into other forms such as nitrogen gas and nitrous oxide. These then return into the atmosphere instead of lingering in the run-off or soils. Degradation and decomposition account for the breakdown of chemical and organic compounds respectively. Throughout the cycle of all of these processes, thermal attenuation occurs. This refers to the ability of bioretention areas to lower the temperature of the captured runoff after its infiltration. According to a study discussed in the P.G.C. bioretention manual, a bioretention basin reduced the temperature of run-off by about 11 degrees, 22 degrees Celsius from 33 degrees Celsius.

Bioretention areas are designed to take full advantage of the processes previously mentioned. A layered but holistic and systematic design makes bioretention areas rather simple techniques which promote and encourage very complex natural processes. The typical bioretention areas consist of six different layers: a grass buffer strip, sand bed, ponding area, organic layer, planting soil, and vegetation. Depending on the specifics of the site and project, additional components such as an under-drain and/or overflow system can be incorporated into the bioretention area's design.

The purpose of a buffer strip is to regulate the flow of the run-off by reducing its velocity while acting as the first filtering system for larger particles which may clog the system. Buffer strips have gentle slopes that direct runoff toward a bioretention basin. "To maintain flow towards the basin, slopes should not be less than 0.5% for paved areas and 1% for vegetated areas. In any case, the slopes toward the basin should not be greater than 20%".

A pea-gravel diaphragm (infiltration trench), a layer of small round stones, is optional but recommended in most cases and is typically used as a pretreatment process. A pea-gravel diaphragm distributes run-off flow evenly throughout the basin and filters particulate matter as well. The pretreatment process protects the basin from clogging, thereby potentially reducing maintenance costs.

In a bioretention system pretreated run-off flows into a shallow ponding area. This ponding lies directly above a layer of organic mulch and a designed mix of sand and soil. The ponding area provides for run-off storage, time for particulate settling, time for evaporation of excess run-off, and exposes the run-off to ultraviolet radiation from the sun which aids in the treatment process.

The organic mulch layer helps filter pollutants, prevents soil erosion, and provides a medium for biological growth through the decomposition of organic material. One of the greatest benefits of this layer is that by encouraging the growth of soil microorganisms, bioretention areas have the ability to degrade petroleum-based pollutants which originate from vehicles leaking oils onto impervious surfaces. Under the organic mulch layer lays a layer of mixed sand and soil. This sand and soil is typically designed to maintain the region's native plants and absorb contaminants within a site such as hydrocarbons and heavy metals. Unwanted nutrients, such as nitrogen and phosphorous are also adsorbed to the soil. The final layer of plants/vegetation removes water from the soil through evapotranspiration and pollutants through nutrient cycling this layer also provides the opportunity of making a bioretention area an aesthetically pleasing green space.

Depending on the permeability of the soil and/or the amount of run-off, additional layers may be required. For example, an under-drain system or an overflow system can be incorporated to distribute the excess run-off to nearby receiving waters or a sewerage system. Including either of these two systems creates the distinction between the two types of rain gardens: under-drained and self-contained. Self-contained systems are able to capture, treat, and infiltrate water into the soil without the need of additional draining. The under-drained system is used when infiltration is not suitable due to several possibilities. Infiltration is not suitable or desirable in cases where the groundwater can become contaminated by contaminants in run-off. These include cases where there is less than 4 feet between the seasonal mean high water table and the bottom of the rain garden as well as areas with contaminated soils. Low permeability of existing soils or excessive run-off patterns could also cause the bioretention system to flood. In such cases under-drained systems are also recommended.

Additional differences between under-drained and self-contained rain gardens include drainage time and plant selection. Self-contained areas are designed to be drained within four hours after a 1" rain event. Under-drained rain gardens typically are designed to drain within 2 hours of the design storm event. When an under-drain is used, the run-off is quickly diverted which means that the plants used must be able to withstand both the extremes of flooding and drought. Xeric plants, or those which require very little water, are used on the upper edges and sides of the rain garden while plants which can adapt to floodplain conditions are used in the middle, lower parts. Self-contained rain gardens retain water for a longer period of time but the saturation capacity of the soils throughout the area is comparable to the soil conditions within an under-drained system. Both have low saturation capacity soils along the top and increasing saturation capacity towards the lower parts. However, plants used toward the bottom of self-contained bioretention areas must be able to withstand more inundation. In both the under-drained and self-contained rain gardens, healthy and small plants have proven to adapt more successfully than older, larger plants. Additionally, their rain garden design template explains that "plants with deep fibrous roots tend to have a competitive advantage in a rain garden and provide the most cleaning and filtration benefits to the environment". Therefore, the seeding or early planting of drought resistant plants known to develop deep roots would be ideal.

Potential Benefits

Bioretention areas increase groundwater recharge, enhance the landscape, provide wind breaks, absorb noise, provide wildlife habitat, and reduce the urban heat island effect. In addition, bioretention areas provide the following benefits:

- Conserves or establishes a unique and historical sense of natural identity (i.e. native plants).
- Promotes environmental education and responsibility.
- Increases aesthetic appeal and thus real estate values by up to 20%.
- Lessen storm-water runoff flow
- Improve storm-water quality

Potential Risks and Considerations

- There is very limited data regarding their long-term performance, operation and management.
- Suitability is limited to small drainage areas.

- Their design can become more complex when used in regions with Karst topography (limestone and caves) or in contaminant hot spots, in order to prevent groundwater contamination.

Bioretention areas are susceptible to clogging.

- Bioretention areas require large areas of land; this may conflict with development (i.e. reduce the number of parking spaces)
- Bioretention areas have relatively higher initial costs (construction) compared to conventional stormwater systems.
- Use in cold climates result in costly design modifications.

Since most rain gardens incorporate mulches and plants, they are perceived as part of a site's landscape design and thus are expected to look clean, neat, and well maintained. If these expectations are not met, rain gardens can be rejected from a project or limited to areas out of the general public's site. Therefore the poor aesthetic appeal which rain gardens can develop over time is another major deterrent of many projects. This poor image can be attributed to two possibilities: the improper design and/or improper maintenance of the rain garden. When a rain garden is inadequately designed, the project can look unkempt and/or dead and this can actually discourage proper maintenance. These projects then serve as evidence of failed designs which further discourage the use of bioretention areas. Therefore the proper design of a rain garden, specifically in terms of plant selection is crucial to this technology's overall appeal and reputation.

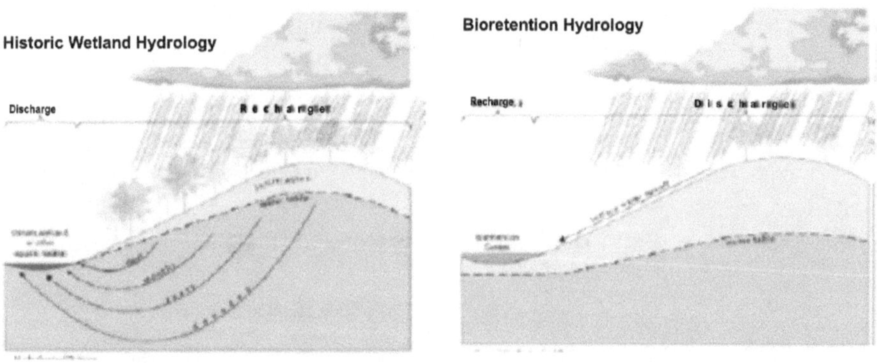

The hydrology of a wetland demonstrates how receiving waters are replenished through infiltrated rainwater. This can range from several days to years and, given adequate rainfall, provides steady and gradual groundwater recharge. On the other hand, the bioretention hydrology diagram shows how a rain garden is only fed by surface water runoff which follows the irregular patterns of rainfall. These differences have lead to the concept of the dry approach which alters the design of the rain garden in several ways including the position of the under drain, the thickness of the soil layer, and the selection of plants.

Conventional systems, shown in Figure 7, are characterized by the low position of the underdrain, a deep soil layer and both xeric (drought resistant) and water-loving plants. However, the dry bioretention design, shown in Figure 8 and Figure 9, show that the high placement of a perforated pipe within a stone trench and a shallow top soil layer allow for better infiltration. Also, diverse drought tolerant grasses and wildflowers are used instead of xeric and water-loving plants. Although it is very difficult to predict the range of conditions which the plants will be exposed to over a long period of time, this dry design approach rightfully assumes that none of the plants (even those in the lower parts of the rain garden) will be exposed to much inundation. While ponding may occur, bioretention areas are designed to infiltrate relatively quickly. By including diverse plants one can experiment with their longevity and performance and alter the overall design later if needed. Approaching bioretention designs in this way can establish a better relationship between vegetation, soil, and performance, ultimately resulting in aesthetically pleasant and functional systems. It should be noted that the conventional designs are more applicable in cases where runoff treatment instead of infiltration is a priority.

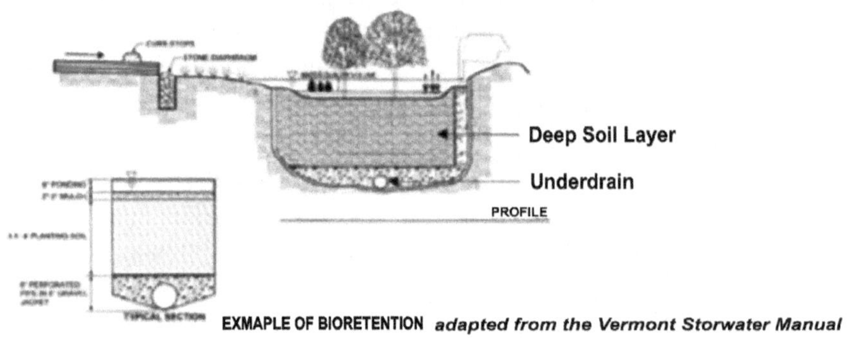

Fig: 7 Conventional Bioretention Design

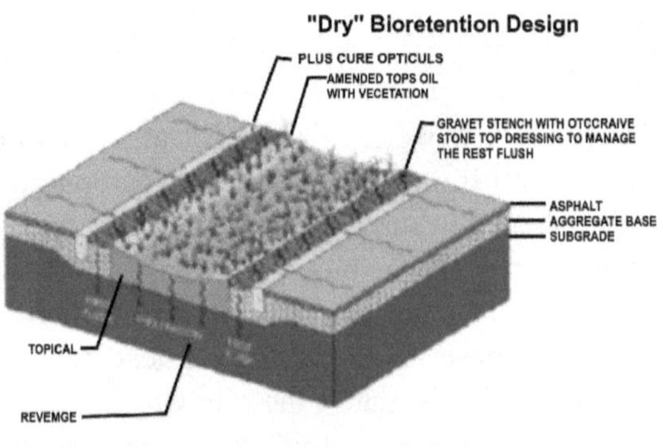

Fig: 8 Dry Bioretention Design

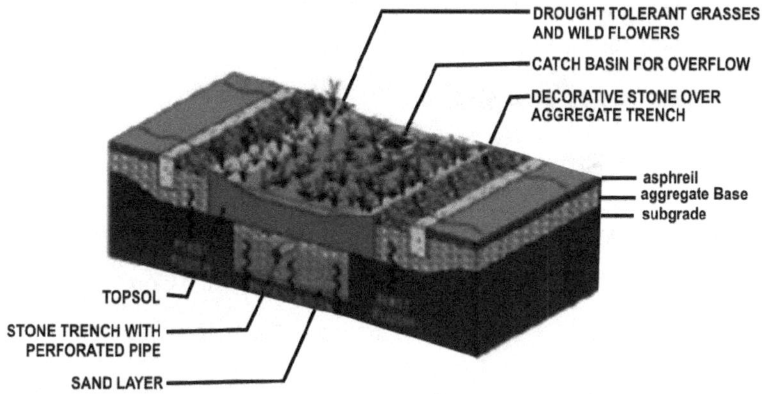

- **Reduce ponding depth and time at planting surface**
- **Appropriate for tight spaces and/or lower infltration rates**

Fig: 9 Subsurface Gravel Retention

Recommended Site Characteristics

Bioretention areas are very flexible in terms of design. Although the types of layers are usually consistent from project to project, the performance of each layer can be altered in order to best suit a specific site. Bioretention basins have been used in residential, commercial, and industrial lots and are very common in run-off source areas of such as parking lots. They are suitable for suburban as well as urban environments and can be easily incorporated into new or existing developments. Factors such as annual rainfall, size of the drainage area, existing soil conditions, existing slopes, and ground water levels will impact the design of rain gardens. Bioretention practices usually perform the best in urbanized spaces and on small lots.

- Bioretention areas work well on sites where little pervious surface exist such as parking lots and large buildings.
- Bioretention areas are suitable on sites where existing developments are required to retrofit stormwater management practices.
- In areas with highly contaminated runoff (such as gas stations), the bottom of a bioretention basin should be lined with impermeable liner to prevent the spread of contamination.
- Size of the drainage area should ideally be less than 1 acre with slopes of less than 20%.
- Size of bioretention basin should be between 5%-7% of drainage area.
- Planting soils should be loamy with a clay content of 10 to 25%.
- The soil should contain 3 to 5% organic material and have a pH of 5.5 to 6.5.

- Bioretention facilities should not be used in areas with shallow aquifers.

Potential LEED Credits

Sustainable Sites:

- Credit 6.1 – "Stormwater Design – Quantity Control" (1 point)
- Credit 6.2 – "Stormwater Design – Quality Control" (1 point)
- Credit 7.1 – "Heat Island Effect – Non-Roof" (1 point)

Water Efficiency:

- Credit 1 – "Water Efficient Landscaping" (2-4 points)

2.4. RAIN WATER HARVESTING

Rainwater harvesting is a water conservation technique that has been used since ancient times. There is evidence that rainwater harvesting systems were used as long far back as 4,000 years ago. However, as people became more urban and more centralized water supply systems became needed rainwater harvesting became used less. Recently pollution and water shortages have made urban planners reevaluate the use of rainwater harvesting, and a number of states and municipalities have passes legislation to encourage the use of rainwater harvesting techniques.

Technical Description

Rainwater harvesting is the process of capturing rainwater and using it instead of potable water. The amount of potable water that is conserved using this method varies greatly depending on various characteristics such as volume and consistency of rainfall, rainwater catchment area, rainwater storage tank size, and the building's potable water usage. These factors impact both capital and operating costs.

Typically rainwater harvesting systems consist of a catchment area, a treatment process, a storage tank, and piping to the intended use, as shown in Figure 10. For most domestic rainwater harvesting systems the catchment areas consists of the building's roof. The treatment, size of the storage tank, and the extensiveness of the rainwater's piping system all depend on the final use of the rainwater.

There are a variety of ways to ensure water quality of rainwater. A very common feature of a treatment system is a first flush device. A schematic of a first flush diagram is shown in Figure 11. The device works by filtering the rainwater to separate debris, and then storing this runoff in a chamber, allowing contaminants to settle and be released through a small hole in the bottom. The cleaner water at the top of the chamber is allowed to flow to the storage tank. This device prevents larger debris from entering the storage tank.

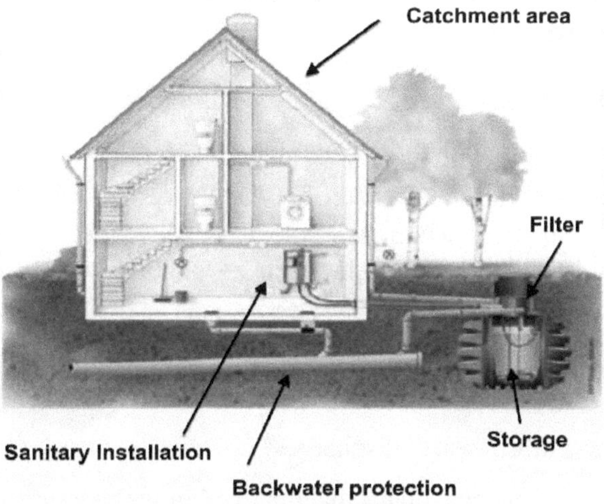

Fig: 10 Rainwater Harvesting

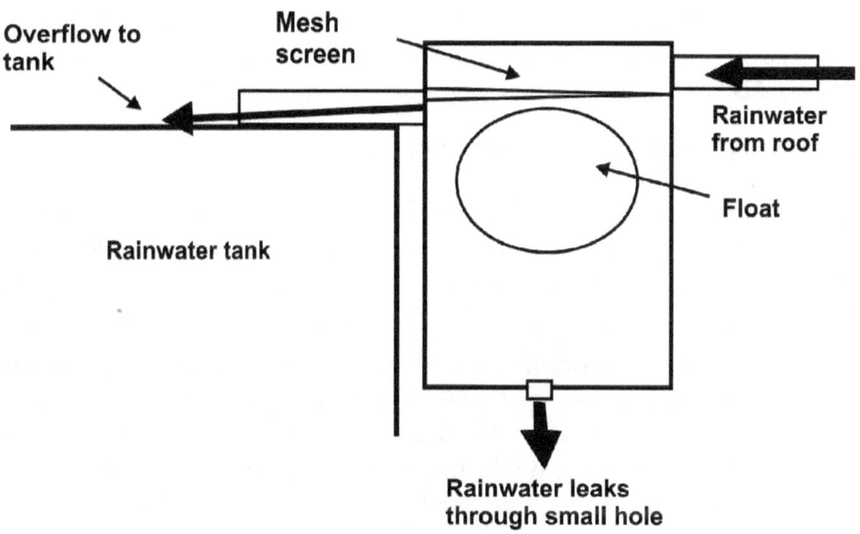

Fig: 11 First Flush Device

After the water is filtered by a first flush device it is stored in a tank. The size of the tank greatly affects the economic feasibility of the system, as the cost of tank installation tends to be the largest component of rainwater harvesting system's cost therefore when designing a rainwater harvesting system it is very important to size the storage tank correctly. The quality of rainwater collected also needs to be monitored if it is to be used for drinking. This is because rainwater can be contaminated with microbes, metals, or chemicals. Also, the physical qualities (such as appearance and odor) of the water must be taken into account. Depending on the quality of rainwater at a site and the intended use, a variety of filtration and/or disinfection methods can be used to improve the quality of rainwater.

Potential Benefits

The potential benefits of using rainwater harvesting include:

- A reduction in potable water use.

When considering a rainwater harvesting system it is useful to note that 1" of rain x 1 sq. ft. = 0.623 gallons. However, between 10% and 25% of rainwater is lost to phenomena such as surface wetting, evaporation, transpiration.

- Potentially lower water bills (see estimated costs below for more information)
- Lower storm water discharges.
- Ability to irrigate plants that might otherwise not receive enough water.
- Ability to fit size, complexity, and cost of system to needs of user.

A small 100-250 L collection bucket can be used for gardening purposes or a large system with over 10,000 L in storage capacity can be installed to supply water for irrigation, toilet flushing, or drinking water.

Potential Risks and Considerations

- Steps must be taken to ensure the water quality of any rainwater harvesting system, especially those that will be used for drinking water. Rainwater systems may have microbial or chemical contamination. The physical qualities of the water must also be taken into account.

Microbial contamination may occur due to fecal material from animals (such as birds) entering the storm water tanks and entry of small animals in the tank. This contamination can lead to bacteria, protozoa, or viruses entering the water and infecting humans. While this risk is low there have been documented cases of Campylobacter and Salmonella outbreaks associated with rainwater collection systems. Upon investigation poor tank design and/or maintenance were found to have contributed to these contaminations. Chemical contamination of rainwater storage tanks is associated with urban traffic, industrial emissions, pesticide over-spraying, or the presence of hazardous chemicals in the roof catchment area (such as lead).

Urban traffic and industrial emissions are unlikely to affect the quality of rainwater in most areas. However, there have been cases when high lead content were associated with large nearby factories. Because of this the residents in that area were advised not to use storm water for drinking or food processing.

Steps should be taken to ensure any rainwater collection system installed is not at risk of this contamination. Steps must be taken to ensure the physical quality of rainwater (appearance, odor, taste) due to possible sediment or organic material that may enter the system. This is usually done through filtering and disinfecting the rainwater.

Because of the unpredictable nature of rainwater, appropriately sized storage tanks need to be installed. These tanks must have an outflow in case the system collects more water than the tank can hold, or else the tank would overflow. Additionally any application of the rainwater should have a back-up water source in case the storage tank runs out of rainwater. The most efficient systems keep the tank as low as possible without running out of water so that the most rainwater is captured when it does rain.

The size of the storage tank installed in a rainwater harvesting system plays a large part in the cost effectiveness of the system. While a larger tank may collect more rainwater over its lifetime, the savings associated with the extra water may not always be worth the extra cost of the tank. For example, in one study the payback period of a rainwater harvesting system could have been reduced from 12 to 4 years if the system had been sized appropriately. Therefore when constructing rainwater harvesting systems it is important to size the storage tank correctly.

Recommended Site Characteristics

- Rainwater harvesting systems can be installed anywhere where rainfall can be captured and used as a source of non-potable water.
- The most effective places for rainwater harvesting systems to be used for everyday use have consistent rainfall, as the rainwater storage tanks then do not have to store as much rainwater and can be smaller which reduces capital costs.
- In arid areas rainwater harvesting can provide a much needed source of water for application such as irrigation by collecting water when it rains during the rainy season and conserving it until the dry season.

Potential LEED Credits

The following is a list of potential LEED points that can be obtained through the use of rainwater harvesting systems.

- LEED Credit SS-C6.1 Stormwater Design - Quantity Control
- LEED Credit SS-C6.2 Stormwater Design – Quality Control
- LEED Credit WE C1.1 Water Efficient Landscaping
- LEED Credit WE C1.2 Innovative Wastewater Technologies
- LEED Credit WE C1.3 Water Use Reduction

2.5. CONSTRUCTED WETLANDS

A constructed wetland is a constructed wetland that is designed to exploit and optimize the natural biological processes that occur in natural wetlands to treat wastewater. The idea of constructed wetlands was developed in Germany in the late 1960s and refined in the 1970s. The first constructed wetland that was installed to treat municipal wastewater was constructed and put into operation in 1974. However, the use of constructed wetlands did not begin to gain popularity until the mid 1980s in Europe and were not introduced to North America and Australia until the late 1980s. Currently as many as 50,000 constructed wetlands have been implemented in Germany, 1,000 in Austria, 800 in the UK, and 8,000 in North America. Due to the lower required capital costs constructed wetlands will likely continue to be an attractive wastewater treatment option for rural municipalities.

Technical Description

Constructed wetlands are wetlands that have been constructed to treat wastewater. This is done by subjecting the water to wetland vegetation, soils, and microbial assemblages, which will treat the wastewater through natural processes such as aerobic and anaerobic digestion.

There are three main types of constructed wetlands. They are surface flow (SF) wetlands (also known as free water surface wetlands), subsurface flow (SSF) wetlands, and vertical flow (VF) wetlands. SF wetlands are when a reed bed is placed into the ground and water is allowed to collect in a shallow body of water in the reed bed. A SSF wetland is when a plant bed is fed water at one end and allowed to percolate through the subsurface to the other side due to a slight incline. A VF wetland is when water is fed to the wetland from the surface and allowed to percolate downward into the soil and is then removed as a deeper depth.

By using constructed wetlands to treat wastewater before it is discharged directly into the natural environment harmful contaminants can be contained. This is to prevent the discharge of harmful pollutants such as pathogens, minerals and dissolved solids, heavy metals, and organic contaminants into the natural habitat. Constructed wetlands also help reduce the need for potable water, as water from a constructed wetland can be used to irrigate plants, flush toilets, or cleaning purposes.

Constructed wetlands are especially attractive for small municipalities that need a low cost alternative to traditional secondary wastewater treatment options. These wetlands can be a lower energy option than other wastewater treatment options. Wetlands are also said to provide social benefits by providing a place for education (for nature study) and recreational activities such as walking, jogging, hunting, and picnicking.

The biggest drawback to using constructed wetlands for wastewater treatment is securing enough land for the wetland. Therefore constructed wetlands are often used as a low cost low energy alternative to mechanical treatment plants in rural areas where the cost of land is less. Constructed wetlands also provide a wildlife habitat that would otherwise not exist and therefore promotes greater biodiversity in a region. Other potential drawbacks that need to be considered are the potential for wetland overflow, the potential for mosquitoes to breed in the wetland, odor control, and the negative effect of lower temperatures on the wetlands effectiveness.

Surface Flow (SF) Wetlands

Surface flow (SF) or free water surface wetlands typically consist of multiple open cells with shallow lagoons that have macrophytes in them. These macrophytes absorb pollutants directly as well as promote chemical and biochemical reactions that help purify the wastewater. A typical layout for a SF wetland is shown in Figure 12.

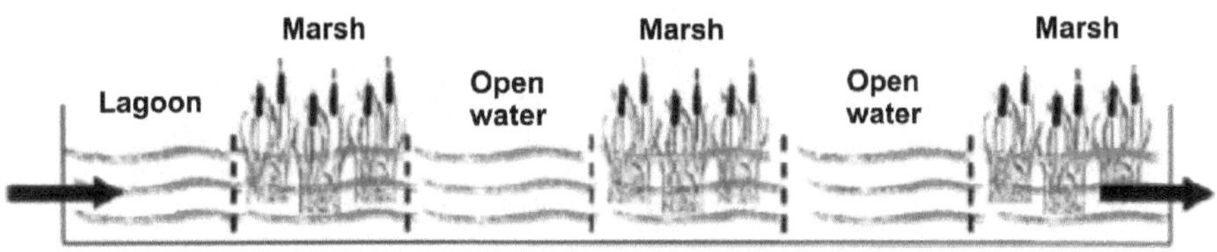

Fig : 12 Example of SF Wetland Layout

Subsurface Flow (SSF) Wetlands

A subsurface flow (SSF) wetland is a wetland that treats wastewater by allowing water to flow through a bed of vegetation, often a reed bed. As wastewater passes through this bed is comes into contact with aerobic, anoxic and anaerobic zones which treat the water. The water in the system is typically contained by some type of waterproof barrier around the edges and bottom of the bed. The bed is typically on an incline to help the water percolate though the system and prevent overflow a typical layout for a SSF system is shown in Figure 13.

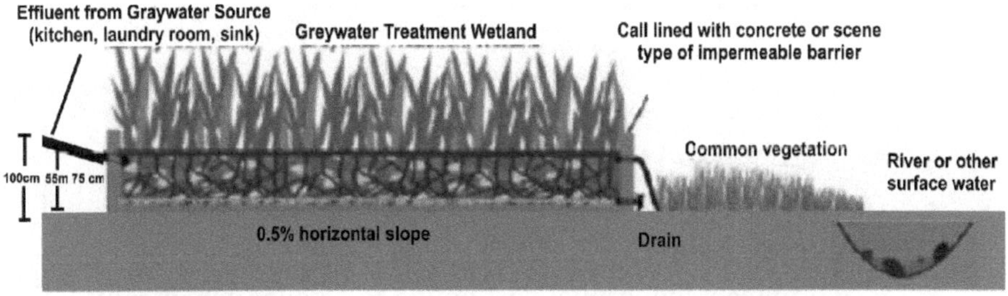

Fig: 13 Typical Layout of a Subsurface Flow Constructed Wetland

Vertical Flow (VF) Wetlands

Vertical flow (VF) wetlands consist of a plant bed that is fed water from the ground surface and treats the water as it percolates though the bed. The water is purified because pollutants are removed by microorganisms present in the beds soil and on the plant roots present in the system. A typical VF wetland setup is shown in Figure 14

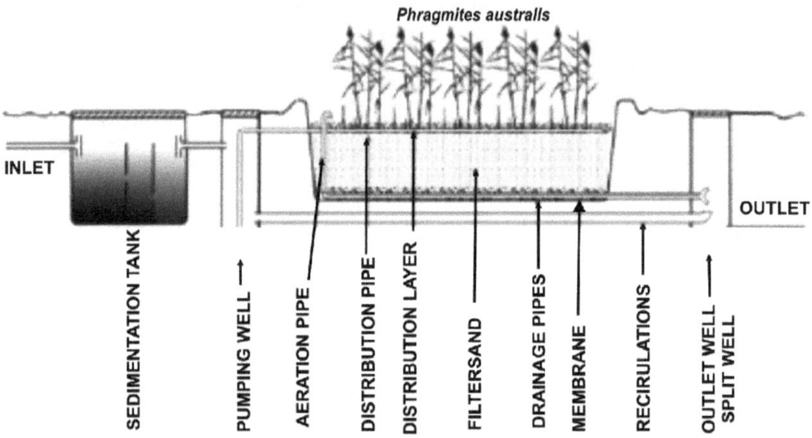

Fig: 14 Example of a VF Wetland Layout

Potential Benefits

1. Can be used to treat wastewater to a high enough quality for discharge or other applications (see below for examples). This can help to reduce pollution and groundwater contamination. The following contaminates can be treated or removed by constructed wetlands:
    - Biochemical oxygen demand (BOD)
    - Chemical oxygen demand (COD)
    - Fecal coliforms
    - E coli
    - Total Suspended Solids (TSS)
    - Total Phosphorus (TP)
    - Total Nitrogen (TN)
    - Heavy metals

- Can be an energy efficient way to treat wastewater compared to traditional methods.
- Can provide a low capital cost option to smaller municipalities that may not be able to afford expensive secondary treatment plants.

- Provides a wildlife habitat where one might not have previously existed.
- Can provide passive recreational benefits for community as well as social benefits by proving a place for activities such as walk or jogging.

Potential Risks and Considerations

- Proper permits are needed in order to construct a constructed wetland.
- When designing it is very important to correctly design the wetlands hydrology, as the wetlands residence time will dictate how effective it is treating the water.
- Wetlands may not operate at consistent purification rates due to factors such as temperature and water pH.
    - Cold months can slow nitrogen cycling due to lower availability of oxygen .
    - If wetland freezes microbial decomposition may decrease.
- The macrophytes that are used in a wetland can make a difference in the effectiveness of the system and multiple varieties should be used for maximum efficiency of the wetland.
- An overflow of a constructed wetland will negatively affect its efficiency due to a washout of solids.
- Constructed wetlands typically require larger areas of land than traditional wastewater treatment plants.
- Constructed wetlands can be a potential breeding ground for mosquitoes if stagnant water is present. Because of this SSF wetlands typically have a lower risk of mosquitoes than SF or VF wetlands.
- The risk of extensive mosquito breeding can be reduced by designing a wetland with at least 30% open water, a wide diversity of plant species, and sections of both deep open water ponds and shallow marshes".
- Odor can become an issue if a wetland is overloaded and anaerobic conditions become prominent. The addition of shallow basins or implementation of cascading outfall structures can help prevent this odor from becoming an issue.
- SSF wetlands are susceptible to clogging if the wetland is not properly maintained.

Recommended Site Characteristics

- SF wetlands have a higher evaporation than SSF or VF wetlands and therefore are suitable for non-discharge wetlands.

- SSF and VF wetlands are more effective at removing solids and organic material in wastewater, and so are more applicable to discharge wetland applications.
- Constructed wetlands are more economical in areas where land is less expensive and more available due to the land requirements of constructed wetlands.
- Constructed wetlands tend to be more effective in warmer climates.
- Constructed wetlands are often attractive to smaller communities due to the prohibitive costs of a traditional wastewater treatment options.

2.6. XERISCAPING

Xeriscaping became popular in the 1980s as a new theory for landscaping and farming during droughts. The term xeriscaping officially means "dry landscaping", originating from Greek "xeros" which means "dry" The overall purpose of xeriscaping is to produce fruitful vegeta tion and beauti ful landscaping with the minimal amount of water consumption. If water usage continues at its current rate, by 2030 the estimated global water demand will be 40% greater than the current supply available. Since the main focus xeriscaping is to reduce water usage, it should be implemented in place of traditional landscaping, in order to help reduce the stain on the water supply.

Figure 15: Xeriscaping Example

- Conserves potable water by reducing usage
- Low impact and flexible to fit a variety of needs
- Xeriscaped areas are very low-maintenance.
- Depending on the intricacy and overall goal, gardens can have large capital costs.

Technical Description

Xeriscaping has seven chief principles that contribute to the overall goal: planning and design, soil improvement, minimizing turf, appropriate plant selection, efficient irrigation, use of mulch, and maintenance. Important aspects of xeriscaping are grouping plants with similar needs together and minimizing the amount of lawn. Although large manicured lawns are popular, they require a great amount of water, and xeriscaping encourages reduction of lawn areas and switching to low maintenance alternative covering. Proper planning and plant selection are also vital to reduce the amount of maintenance and water required to sustain the landscaping. In order to ensure maximum growth, suitable nutrients in the soil must be provided for the plants via mulching and irrigation. Applying these techniques encourages water conservation and improved water quality while maintaining a beautiful garden.

The best type of vegetation to use when building a xeriscaped garden are plants that are drought tolerant. Plants that are appropriate for desert regions are typically hardy, low care, and drought resistant. These particular plants are also inexpensive, easy to locate, and provide attractive colors. Some examples of these types of plants are Bougainvillea, Oleander, Texas/Purple Sage, Lantana, Pampas Grass, Fairy Duster, Red Bird of Paradise, Orange Jubilee, and Yellow Bells. These plants can thrive in dry sunny regions like Phoenix, Arizona.

Planning & Design

Adequate planning is an imperative step to designing an efficient and effective xeriscaped area because the plants and water must work in synch with natural surrounding landscape. Plants with similar water needs should be placed in beds together to allow for optimum growth with minimal water waste. Even though plants that require minimal amounts of water are preferred native plants that require more water can be used. The drought-tolerant plants should be positioned on the side of the prevailing winds so they can shelter the less tolerant plants.

Proper grading of the land also needs to be planned for, in order for the water to soak into the soil and be absorbed by plants rather than becoming runoff. Slopes can be changed or terraced to assist this process. Typically raised beds dry out much quicker than standard flat beds and are not encouraged.

Some environmental considerations that must be taken into account when planning xeriscaped sites are the directional winds and the sunny and shaded areas that may change throughout the day or season. Utilities and obstructions that are underground may be problematic when grading or digging.

Soil Improvement

Soil composition and quality is directly related to the health and fertility of the plants growing in that soil. In order to determine what type of soil is present, it must be tested by collecting a sample. This sample can be analyzed in a lab or with a soil sample kit. Both can determine composition, nutrients, and other characteristics. However, the laboratory results are more accurate.

Most types of soil can be altered to grow various kinds of vegetation. The typical extremes of soil are sand and clay. Sand drains quickly after rain while clay creates a barrier to rain infiltrating the subsurface. The majority of soils fall in between these two categories. Sand can be worked with easily but needs a lot of vegetative covering to shelter it from wind and water erosion. Due to its low moisture and nutrient-holding capacity, sand needs frequent watering and fertilization. Clay, on the other hand, is made up of small particles and can hold so much water that the plants suffer from lack of oxygen. Both types of soil can be improved with generous portions of organic matter such as compost, well-rotted manure, or peat moss. To do this, a layer of organic matter approximately 7.6-10 cm (3-4 in) thick should be spread on the ground and then thoroughly mixed with the existing soil.

Minimizing Turf

Since lawns require water, fertilizer, and gasoline (for typical lawnmowers) in order to keep them looking healthy, xeriscaping focuses on reducing the amount of lawn turf. There are two main ways of accomplishing this; simply minimizing the actual area covered with grass or using alternative lawn coverings in place of grass. No matter what method is used, grass that is suitable for the area should be chosen because different grasses thrive in different locations.

Moss and clover are becoming popular alternatives to the traditional grass lawn Moss is low growing and low maintenance because it derives nutrients and water from the surrounding air. Its ideal conditions are shady, moist areas. Clover is also naturally low maintenance and has the qualities looked for in a lawn. It doesn't discolor, doesn't need to be fertilized, and doesn't grow weeds.

Appropriate Plant Selection

Proper plant selection is significant for xeriscaping in order to conserve water and to ensure thriving vegetation. Choosing plants that require little water and are native to the specific region is preferred. Typically, both types of plants help to ensure optimum growth.

Efficient Irrigation

Since all plants do not need the same amount of water to survive, the prior steps (planning & design, soil improvement, minimizing turf, and appropriate plant selection) help group the plants according to the quantity of water required. By arranging the plants in accordance with those processes the least amount of water will be wasted from over watering and runoff. Typically, drip irrigation systems are the most efficient watering arrangements because it allows for the most control. Drip irrigation provides control over the amount and the time the plants receive water. This type of system is ideal because all plants require slightly more water the first few years before the have become established. After the plant matures, it needs slightly less water.

Drip irrigation is a water conserving alternative to lawn sprinklers and has been called "subsurface drip irrigation". It runs at a low pressure to gradually and precisely deliver water to the plant's roots using plastic tubing. Not only does drip irrigation reduce the amount of water emitted from the irrigation system, but it reduces the amount of water wasted by runoff, evaporation, and overspray. Drip irrigation originated in areas without a large supply of water and has become popular in all types of climates to reduce the cost of irrigation.

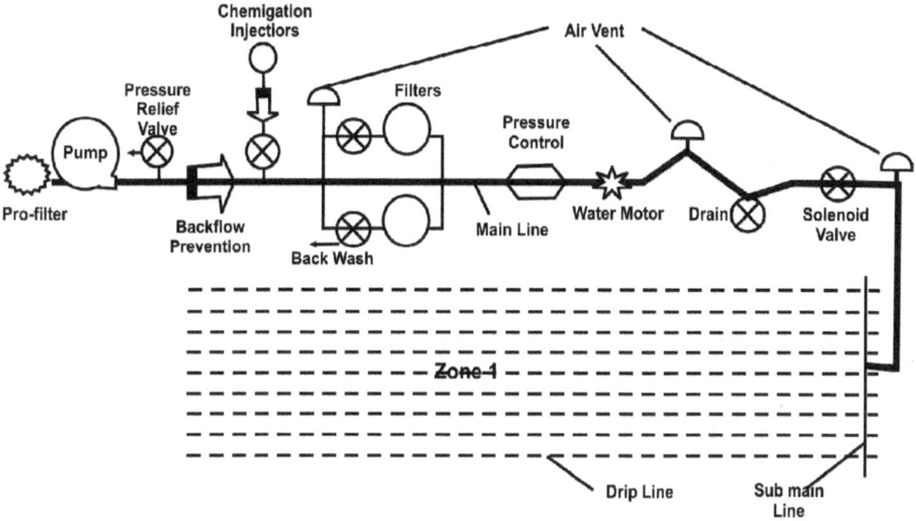

Fig : 16 Diagram for a standard drip irrigation system

Use of Mulch

Mulch can be anything from store-bought shredded bark and compost to naturally occurring leaves and debris. The purpose of mulch is to moderate soil temperature, capture moisture, reduce erosion, and lessen the amount of weeds that could detract from the plants' food and water supply. Since the mulch gradually decomposes, nutrients are slowly added to the soil over time. Typically 2 to 4 inches of mulch are required when first planted and more may be needed as time passes.

In the summer mulch acts as an insulator that decreases the need for water and shields the roots from severe heat. The mulch from the winter typically needs to be replaced in the spring. This allows the plants room to sprout while helping the soil to be warmed and fed. Conditioning compost or manure should be put down in the fall, along with mulch, to guard the plants from winter weather. In the winter, mulch is used to ensure a consistent ground temperature. A steadily frozen ground keeps the plant dormant and thwarts early growth while keeping water inside the garden bed.

Maintenance

Xeriscaped gardens require weeding, pruning, deadheading, and natural pest management Weeding is simply removing an undesired plant from the garden bed because it consumes water, nutrients, and sunlight needed for the desired plants. Pruning involves cutting back parts of a plant in order to allow more room for the growth of that plant and others around it. Deadheading refers to removing the dead parts of plants via cutting or plucking to permit more development throughout the summer and fall. Natural pest management is important because some pests cause harm to plants by eating them or the nutrients they need to survive. By using the correctly selected insects and plants, harmful bugs should not be a problem.

Potential Benefits

- Time and money are saved by having less grass to mow.
- Conserves potable water by reducing usage

Reduces water consumption by up to 50% because water is dispersed directly to the roots.

- Healthy for the local environment
- Reduces the use of fertilizers and pesticides that could contaminate local water supplies.
- Can help reduce water runoff and soil erosion.
- Increased vegetation contributes to reduction of carbon dioxide by using photosynthesis.
- Clover as an alternative lawn covering is drought tolerant, weed resistant, doesn't need fertilizer, soft, requires little mowing, doesn't discolor, and is relatively pest free.
- Aids in plant life development
- Controls the amount of weeds because the water is delivered to the plants deep down in the soil and most weeds have shallower roots.
- Healthier plants result because of the slow constant feed of water which keeps the roots moist.
- Nutrients can be emitted through the drip irrigation system.
- Low impact and flexible to fit a variety of needs
- Drip irrigation is low profile and very quiet.
- Fits uneven and abnormally shaped gardens and fields.
- Drip irrigation doesn't compact the soil like high-pressured sprinklers.
- Timers can be installed on drip irrigation systems to water on a schedule, if desired.

- Drip systems can be buried for a longer service life or left on top of the ground for easy servicing.
- Reduce watering needs by selecting the appropriate type of grass for the local environment.
- Increases home value & curb appeal by heightening the impact of the reduced lawn with surrounding gardens.
- Xeriscaped areas are very low-maintenance.

Potential Risks and Considerations

- Proper maintenance of a drip irrigation system is important because the plastic tubing can leak or become plugged.
- Cultivation and weeding practices need to be taken into consideration when deciding the tube depth.
- Depending on the intricacy and overall goal, gardens can have large capital costs.

❑❑❑

Chapter–3

Solid Waste Management

3.1. SOLID WASTE MANAGEMENT

Solid waste management includes the transportation, processing, recycling and disposal of our waste materials. We live in a disposable world in many ways with the modernization and convenience of our world we have cluttered it with our refuse.

As people begin to become aware of our impact on the Earth we are learning to become less self consumed in our efforts to protect it. India's urban population is about 350 million currently, mostly living in a few large cities and over 30 metropolitan cities and responsible for producing 65 million tons of waste. In India, the amount of waste generated per capita is estimated to increase at a rate of 1-1.33 percent annually. It is estimated that the total waste quantity generated by the year 2047 would be approx-imately 260 million tons per year. It is estimated that if the waste is not disposed off in a more systematic manner more than 1400 sq km of land would be required in the country by the year

2047 for its disposal. Almost 90 percent of the total wastes are managed through land-filled mechanism, requiring around 1200 hectare of land every year with an average depth of 3 m. Though most of these cities have solid waste management (SWM) systems, it isn't a well-developed system yet. The equipment and machin-ery in use are general purpose type or that which have been adopted from other industry. This results in poor utilization of the resources and lowering of the efficiency. Though there have been attempts to adopt the technology developed in other countries like highly mechanized compost plants, incinerator-cum-power plants, and compactor vehi-cles, these attempts have not yielded good results as the solid waste composition in India is much different from the countries where the technol-ogy was developed.

Out of the total expenditure on SWM, around 90 percent is spent on manpower. The SWM system is unplanned and is operated in an unscientific way. Neither the work norms are specified nor the work of collection staff appropri-ately supervised. The vehicles are poorly maintained and no schedule is observed for preventive maintenance. Due to shortage of financial resources, the vehicles are often used beyond their economical life resulting in inefficient operation. Further, there is no coordination of activities between different components of the system. The cumulative effect of all these factors is an inefficient SWM system.

In the current scenario, a given unit of waste takes about 24-36 hours before reaching the large dump yard typically located in the city outskirts. However, the decomposition starts within 8-12 hours that causes spreading of foul smell in the communities. This is non-hygienic, spreads disease caus-ing virus, and importantly indicates losing of an energy source, methane gas, into atmosphere.

Today, SWM system is being conceptualized as a decompo-sition and power generation device that can be installed next to each collection point in a typical community of about 500 families. This unit when operated for 8 hours per day can process expected aver-age daily waste of about 2 tons to generate 200 KWH of electric power and about 1.5 tons of liquid and solid fertilizer. The inorganic waste like glass, metal and plastic is automatically seg-regated by the device before starting to process. The savings are expected to cover the device main-tenance and employ a caretaker. The related benefits are that the underpaid labor needn't spend their days at dump yards in an unhygienic manner and there is saving on fuel as trucks to transport waste to dump yard can be avoided.

Increasing urban population will make waste management a difficult task to handle in the near future if a new approach is not designed and created.

3.2. MUNICIPAL SOLID WASTE

Garbage is generally referred to "Waste" and is also termed as rubbish, trash, junk, unwanted or undesired material. As per the Municipal Solid Waste

(Management &Handling) Rule, 2000 garbage is define as Municipal Solid Waste which includes commercial and residential wastes generated in a municipal or notified areas in either solid or semi-solid form excluding industrial hazardous wastes but including treated bio-medical wastes Municipal solid waste consists of household waste, construction and demolition debris, sanitation residue, and waste from streets. This garbage is generated mainly from residential and commercial complexes.

3.2.1. Main sources of municipal waste –

- House hold waste
- Commercials
- Street sweeping
- Hotels and restaurants
- Clinics and dispensaries
- Construction and demolition
- Horticulture
- Sludge

3.2.2.Composition of municipal solid waste in India

In India the biodegradable portion dominates the bulk of Municipal Solid Waste. Generally the biodegradable portion is mainly due to food and yard waste

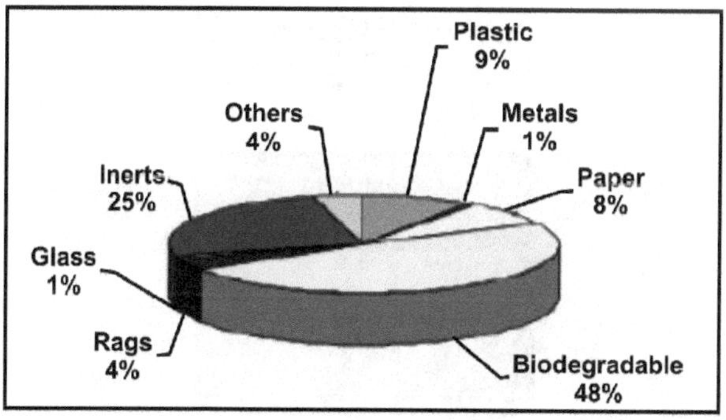

With rising urbanization and change in lifestyle and food habits, the amount of municipal solid waste has been increasing rapidly and its composition changing. There are different categories of waste generated, each take their own time to degenerate (as illustrated in the table below).

The type of litter we generate and the approximate time it takes to degenerate	
Type of litter	Approximate time it takes to degenerate the litter
Organic waste such as vegetable and fruit peels, leftover foodstuff, etc.	A week or two.
Paper	10–30 days
Cotton cloth	2–5 months
Wood	10–15 year
Woolen items	1 year
Tin, aluminium and other metal items such as cans	100–500 years
Plastic bags	One million years ?
Glass bottles	Undetermined

Life Cycle of Municipal Solid Waste

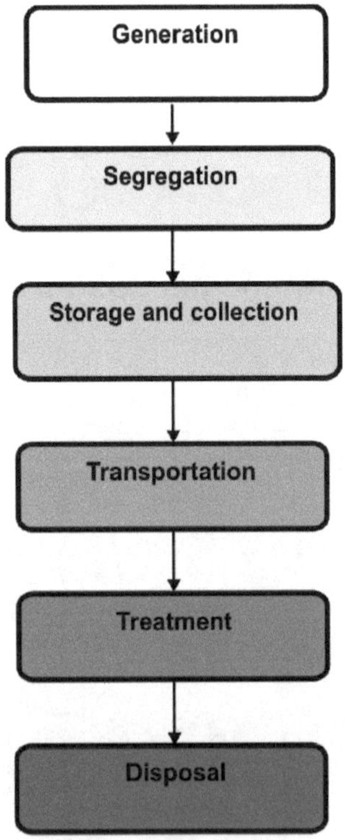

3.2.3. Municipal solid waste management practices in India

The term municipal solid waste refers to solid waste from houses, streets and public places, shops, offices, and hospitals. Management of these types of waste is most often the responsibility of Municipal or other Governmental authorities. Except in the metropolitan cities, SWM is the responsibility of a health officer who is assisted by the engineering department in the transportation work. The activity is mostly labour intensive, and 2-3 workers are provided per 1000 residents served. The municipal agencies spend 5-25% of their budget on SWMA typical waste management system in a low- or middle-income country like India includes the following elements:

- Waste generation and storage
- Segregation, reuse, and recycling at the household level
- Primary waste collection and transport to a transfer station or community bin
- Street sweeping and cleansing of public places
- Management of the transfer station or community bin
- Secondary collection and transport to the waste disposal site
- Waste disposal in landfills

But in most of the Indian cities open dumping is the Common Practices which is adversely affecting on environment and Public health.

3.2.4. Adverse Effect of open dump

An open dumping is defined as a land disposal site at which solid wastes are disposed of in a manner that does not protect the environment, are susceptible to open burning, and are exposed to the elements, vectors, and scavengers.

Open dumping can include solid waste disposal facilities or practices that pose a reasonable probability of adverse effects on health or the environment.

Health Effect

- The health risks associated with illegal dumping are significant. Areas used for open dumping may be easily accessible to people, especially children, who are vulnerable to the physical (protruding nails or sharp edges) and chemical (harmful fluids or dust) hazards posed by wastes.
- Rodents, insects, and other vermin attracted to open dump sites may also pose health risks. Dump sites with scrap tires provide an ideal breeding ground for mosquitoes, which can multiply 100 times faster than normal in the warm stagnant water standing in scrap tire causing several illnesses.

- Poisoning and chemical burns resulting from contact with small amounts of hazardous, chemical waste mixed with general waste during collection & transportation.
- Burns and other injuries can occur resulting from occupational accidents and methane gas exposure at waste disposal sites.

3.2.5. Environment pollution

Air pollution

Dust generated from on-site vehicle movements, and placement of waste and materials.

Water pollution

Runoff from open dump sites containing chemicals may contaminate wells and surface water used as sources of drinking water open dumping can also impact proper drainage of runoff, making areas more susceptible to flooding when wastes block ravines, creeks, culverts, and drainage basins & also contamination of groundwater resources and surface water from leachate emissions.

Soil Contamination

Permanent or temporary loss of productive land

Global Warming and Climate Change

In most of the cities & towns the municipal solid waste is being dumped & burnt in open spaces without understanding the adverse impacts on the environment. The waste in the dumping ground undergoes various anaerobic reactions produces offensive Green House gases such as CO2, CH4 etc. These gases are contributing potentially to Global Warming & Climate Change phenomenon.

Integrated Solid Waste Management

Integrated Solid Waste Management (ISWM) is a tool to determine the most energy-efficient, least-polluting ways to deal with the various components & items of a community's Solid Waste stream.

The twin goals of ISWM are to:

- Retain as much as possible of that energy & those materials in a useful state.
- Avoid releasing that energy or matter into the environment as a pollutant.

3.2.6. Benefits of integrated solid waste management

The concept of ISWM plan derives from the necessity to look at alternative sources of collection, transportation and most importantly, disposal to ensure a healthy living environment in urban cities.Local and regional economies benefit by the continued exchange value of the reclaimed materials and products and the jobs created in reprocessing and reselling them.

National and global resource natural depletion is reduced, contributing to a more sustainable long-term economy. Pollution from landfills is reduced because many toxic or otherwise polluting materials are diverted from the landfills, and because the overall volume of land filled material is reduced.

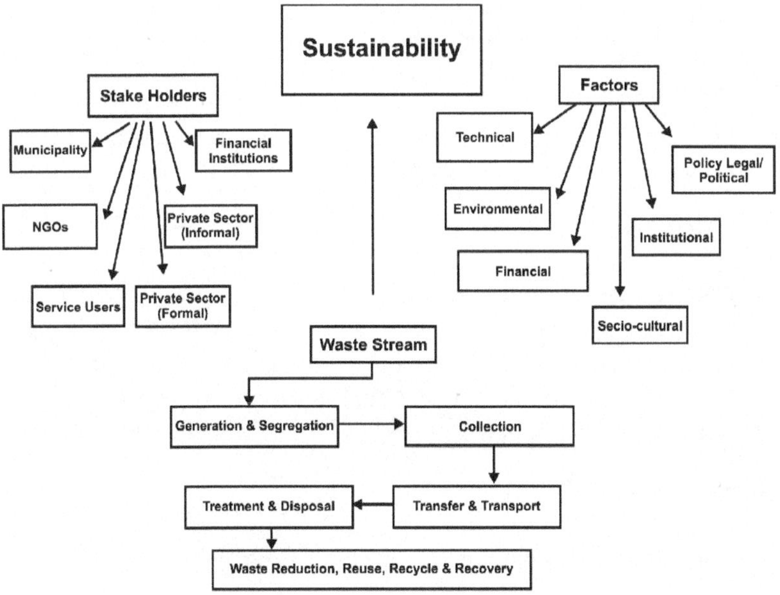

3.2.7. Legal framework for Municipal solid waste in India

Municipal Solid Waste (Management & Handling) Rule was notified by the Ministry of Environment and Forest, Govt. of India [vide No.S.O.908 (B) dated the 25th September 2000]. The objective of these Rules was to make every municipal authority responsible for the implementation of the various provisions of the Rules within its territorial area and also to develop an effective infrastructure for collection, storage, segregation, transportation, processing and disposal of Municipal Solid Wastes. The Civic bodies have the responsibility to enforce these rules.

The major functions of civic body include

- Prohibiting littering of street
- Organizing house to house waste collection.
- Conducting awareness programs to disseminate information to public.
- Providing adequate community storage facilities.
- Use of colour code bins and promotion of waste segregation.
- Transport of wastes in covered vehicles.
- Processing of wastes by adopting an appropriate combination of composting, anaerobic digestion, Pellatisation etc.
- Upgradation of the existing dump sites and Disposal of inert wastes in sanitary landfills.

As per the Rules, the citizens are responsible for

- Segregation of wastes at source.
- Avoid littering of streets.
- Delivery of wastes in accordance with the delivery system notified by the respective Civic body.

3.3. RECYCLING

Recycling turns materials that would otherwise become waste into valuable resources. Collecting used bottles, cans, and newspapers and taking them to the curb or to a collection facility is just the first in a series of steps that generates a host of financial, environmental, and social returns. Some of these benefits accrue locally as well as globally.

Benefits of Recycling

- Recycling reduces the need for land filling and incineration.

- Recycling prevents pollution caused by the manufacturing of products from virgin materials.
- Recycling saves energy.
- Recycling decreases emissions of greenhouse gases that contribute to global climate change.
- Recycling conserves natural resources such as timber, water, and minerals.
- Recycling helps sustain the environment for future generations.

Steps to Recycling a Product

Recycling includes collecting recyclable materials that would otherwise be considered waste, sorting and processing recyclables into raw materials such as fibers, manufacturing raw materials into new products, and purchasing recycled products.

Collecting and processing secondary materials, manufacturing recycled-content products, and then buying recycled products creates a circle or loop that ensures the overall success and value of recycling.

3.4. INCINERATION

The incineration of MSW essentially involves combustion of waste leading to volume reduction and recovery of heat to produce steam that in turn produces power through steam turbines basically, it is a furnace for burning waste and converts MSW into ash, gaseous and particulate emissions and heat energy. The efficiency of the technology is linked to the waste characteristics and their properties such as moisture content and calorific values. When the waste is dry, it may not need any auxiliary fuel except for start-up but when it is rich in inert and moisture content, supplementary fuel may be needed to sustain combustion, adversely affecting net energy recovery. The combustion process involves essentially, drying, volatilization, and ignition and desirably, elimination of odors, and combustion of unburned furnace gases and carbon suspended in the gases. It requires high temperature of the order of 800-1000°C and sufficient air and mixing of gas stream. The minimum temperature for burning carbonaceous wastes to avoid release of smoke and prevent emissions of dioxins and furans is 850°C. In order to ensure proper breakdown of organic toxins, this temperature should be maintained at least for 2 minutes. For steam generation and energy recovery, the combustion temperature should be 1400oC. This will also ensure degradation of all organic compounds. Depending on thc nature of wastes and the operating characteristics of combustion reactor, the gaseous products derived from the combustion of MSW may include carbon dioxide (CO2), water (H2O, flue gas), oxygen (O2), nitrogen oxides (NOx), sulphur dioxide (SO2) and small amounts of hydrogen chloride, mercury, lead, arsenic, cadmium, dioxins and furans, and organic compounds. The combustion residues include bottom ash, fly ash and non-combusted organic and inorganic materials. Modern incinerators include pollution mitigation equipment such as flue gas cleaning and in such versions, sludge from scrubber and waste water adds to the contaminants in lieu of polluted emissions. There are various types of incinerator plant design: moving grate, fixed grate, rotary-kiln, fluidized bed. The typical incineration plant for municipal solid waste is a moving grate incinerator.

3.5. COMPOSTING

Composting is a biological process used for the conversion of organic waste materials into stable humus-like material known as compost. Application of this process includes yard waste, separated and commingled MSW. Most aerobic composting processes (windrow, static pole and in-vessel) involve three steps of preprocessing of waste, aerobic decomposition, and product preparation or marketing. The process offer simple operation however it is a net energy user due to the need of oxygen supply (forced aeration). This process also requires large land area. Other problem associated in this process includes odor, and the quality of compost for marketing. To enhance the economics of compost, it should be of consistent size, free from contaminants such as glass, plastic, and metals, and free of objectionable odor. Composting is an excellent method of recycling biodegradable waste from an ecological point of view. However, many large and small composting schemes have failed because composting is regarded as a disposal process, and not a production process. It is essential to consider the marketing and quality of the product.

The composting process occurs in two major phases. In the first stage, microorganisms decompose the composting feedstock into simpler compounds, producing heat as a result of their metabolic activities. The size of the composting pile is reduced during this stage. In the second stage, the compost product is "cured" or finished. Microorganisms deplete the supply of readily available nutrients in the compost, which, in turn, slows their activity. As a result, heat generation gradually diminishes and the compost becomes dry and crumbly in texture. When the curing stage is complete, the compost is considered "stabilized" or "mature." Any further microbial decomposition will occur very slowly.

The Composting can be classified into two broad Categories

1. Windrow Composting

2. Vermi Composting

It is the end-product of the breakdown of organic matter by some species of earthworm. Vermi compost is a nutrient-rich, natural fertilizer and soil conditioner. The process of producing vermi compost is called vermi composting. The earthworm species most often used are Eudrillus eugineae, Eisenia foetida or Lumbricus rubellus. Small scale vermi composting is done in bins of varying size and style and three different types of practices, such as non-continuous, continuous vertical flow and continuous horizontal flow, are adopted. The methods for large scale vermi composting are windrow and raised bed or flow through systems. Flow-through systems are well suited to indoor facilities, making them the preferred choice for operations in colder climates. Kitchen waste, except oily and spicy items are suitable for worms. But too much kitchen waste leads to putrification before the worms can process it and becomes harmful to the worms. Similarly, material sprayed with pesticides, high-water-content materials like watermelon, woody part of garden waste etc are hindrance to the process. The worms digest proteins and fats in meat scraps, but these materials attract scavengers. Regular removal of composted material, adding holes to the bin, or using a continuous-flow bin etc improve oxygen supply to worms. Insufficient oxygen leads to anaerobic reactions, producing strong odor and creating toxic environment for the worms.

3.6. ANAEROBIC DIGESTION

Anaerobic digestion is define as being the biological decomposition of organic matter of Biological Origin under anaerobic conditions with an accompanying production primarily of Methane (CH4) and secondarily of other gases ,chief of which is Carbon dioxide Anaerobic digestion (AD) is a bacterial fermentation process that operates without free oxygen and results in a biogas containing mostly methane and carbon dioxide. The anaerobic digestion of organic material is accomplished by a consortium of microorganisms working synergistically. Digestion occurs in a four-step process: hydrolysis, acidogenesis, acetogenesis, and methanogenesis. Large protein macromolecules, fats and carbohydrate polymers (such as cellulose and starch) are broken down through hydrolysis to amino acids, long-chain fatty acids, and sugars.

These products are then fermented during acidogenesis to form three, four, and five-carbon volatile fatty acids, such as lactic, butyric, propionic, and valeric acid.

In acetogenesis, bacteria consume these fermentation products and generate acetic acid, carbon dioxide, and hydrogen. Finally, methanogenic organisms consume the acetate, hydrogen, and some of the carbon dioxide to produce methane. Usually the methane content of biogas ranges from 40-70 percent (by volume).

3.7. PRODUCTION OF REFUSE DERIVED FUEL (RDF)

It is basically a processing method for mixed MSW, which can be very effective in preparing an enriched fuel feed for thermal processes like incineration or for use in industrial furnaces. It is a fuel produced by shredding municipal solid waste (MSW) or steam pressure treating in an autoclave. RDF consists largely of organic components of municipal waste such as plastics and biodegradable waste compressed into pellets, bricks, or logs. Noncombustible materials such as glass and metals are removed during the post treatment processing cycle with an air knife or other mechanical separation processing. The production of RDF involves preliminary liberation, size screening, magnetic separation and coarse shredding. The RDF can be used alongside traditional sources of fuel in coal power plants, cement kiln industry, plasma arc gasification modules, pyrolysis plants etc. RDF is capable of being combusted cleanly and can provide a funding source where unused carbon credits are sold on the open market via a carbon exchange. The RDF burning technology includes spreader stroker fired boiler, suspension fired boilers, fluidized bed units, and cyclone furnace units.

3.8. PYROLYSIS & GASIFICATION

It is a process that converts carbonaceous materials, such as biomass, into carbon monoxide and hydrogen by reacting the raw material at high temperatures with a controlled amount of oxygen The resulting gas mixture is called synthesis gas or syngas and is itself a fuel. Gasification is a method for extracting energy from different types of organic materials. The advantage of gasification is that using the syngas is more efficient than direct combustion of the original fuel; as it may be burned directly in internal combustion engines, used to produce methanol and hydrogen, or converted via the Fischer-Tropsch process into synthetic fuel. Gasification can also begin with materials that are not otherwise useful fuels, such as biomass or organic waste.

In addition, the high-temperature combustion refines out corrosive ash elements such as chloride and potassium, allowing clean gas production from otherwise problematic fuels. Thus, it is an important technology for renewable energy. In particular biomass gasification is carbon neutral. Gasification relies on chemical processes at elevated temperatures >700°C, which distinguishes it from biological processes such as anaerobic digestion that produce biogas. In essence, a limited amount of oxygen or air is introduced into the reactor to allow some of the organic material to be "burned" to produce carbon monoxide and energy, which drives a second reaction that converts further organic material to hydrogen and additional carbon dioxide. Several gasification processes for thermal treatment of waste are under development as an alternative to incineration. A major challenge for waste gasification technologies is to reach an acceptable (positive) gross electric efficiency. The high efficiency of converting syngas to electric power is counteracted by significant power consumption in the waste preprocessing, production of large amounts of pure oxygen (which is often used as gasification agent), and gas cleaning. Another challenge in real life is to obtain long service intervals in the plants, so that it is not necessary to close down the plant every few months for cleaning the reactor. Several waste gasification processes have been proposed, but few have yet been built and tested, and only a handful have been implemented as plants processing real waste. Four types of gasifier are currently available for commercial use: counter-current fixed bed; co-current fixed bed, fluidized bed and entrained flow.

3.9. PLASMA PYROLYSIS

Plasma pyrolysis or plasma gasification is a waste treatment technology that gasifies matter in an oxygen-starved environment to decompose waste material into its basic molecular structure. It uses high electrical energy and high temperature created by an electrical arc gasifier and does not combust the waste as incinerators do. This arc breaks down waste primarily into elemental gas and solid waste (slag), in a device called a plasma converter. The process has been intended to be a net generator of electricity, depending upon composition input wastes, and to reduce the volumes of waste being sent to landfill sites. Relatively high voltage, high current electricity is passed between two electrodes, spaced apart, creating an electrical arc where temperatures as high as 13,871°C are reached. The temperature one meter from the arc can reach ~4000°C. At these temperatures most types of waste are broken into basic elemental components in a gaseous form, and complex molecules are atomized - separated into individual atoms.

The reactor operates at a slightly negative pressure, meaning that the feed system is complemented by a gaseous removal system, and later a solid removal system. Depending on the input waste (plastics tend to be high in hydrogen and carbon), gas from the plasma containment can be removed as Syngas, and may be refined into various fuels at a later stage. Dioxin emissions are possible from plasma arcs when chlorine is present although the extremely high temperature at which plasma gasification operates minimizes the possibility. Process gas cleanup can be necessary when gasifying waste streams such as municipal waste streams known to contain heavy metals, chlorine/fluorine, sulfur, etc. The basic thermodynamics indicates that the electricity costs will be unavoidably high when processing wet wastes such as municipal wastes, using plasma power alone. Plasma is considered a 4th state. It may be noted that at this stage, they pose a considerable technological and budgetary challenge to construct a municipal-waste disposal sized plasma arc facility. An issue regarding plasma systems that rely on high temperatures for processing is in the life of their liners. The liner is an important aspect of separating the high interior temperatures of the plasma system from the [metal] shell of the plasma container. Liners are highly susceptible to both chlorine attack and to local variability in [high] temperatures, both of which would be found with typical municipal waste systems, and are not likely to last more than a year in service.

3.10. SANITARY LANDFILL

Sanitary landfill is the controlled disposal of waste on the land, is well suited to the developing countries as a mean of managing the disposal of waste because of the flexibility and relative simplicity of the technology. Sanitary landfilling controls the exposure of the environment and humans to the detrimental effect of solid waste placed on the land. Through Sanitary landfilling, disposal is accomplished in away such that contact between waste and the environment is significantly reduced, and waste are concentrated in a well-defined area. Which result in good control of landfill gas and lechate, and limited access of vector (rodent, flies etc) to the waste. In order to be designated a Sanitary landfill; a disposal site must meet the following three general but basic condition 1) Compaction of Wastes 2) daily covering of the waste (with soil or other material) to remove them from the influence of the outside environment and 3) Control and prevention of negative impact on the public health and on the environment.

3.11. LAND GAS RECOVERY

Methane is a primary constituent of landfill gas (LFG) and a potent greenhouse gas when released to the atmosphere. Reducing emissions by capturing LFG and using it as an energy source can yield substantial energy, economic, and environmental benefits. The implementation of landfill gas energy projects reduces greenhouse gas emission and air pollutants, leading to improved air quality and reduced possible health risks. LFG projects also improve energy independence, produce cost savings, create jobs, and help local economies. Internationally, significant opportunities exist for expanding landfill gas energy.

LFG is extracted from landfills using a series of wells and a vacuum system,. Instead of allowing LFG to escape into the air, it can be captured, converted, and used as an energy source. Using LFGE helps to reduce odors and other hazards associated with LFG emissions, and it helps prevent methane from migrating into the atmosphere and contributing to local smog and global climate change. LFG is extracted from landfills using a series of wells and a blower/flare (or vacuum) system. This system directs the collected gas to a central point where it can be processed and treated depending upon the ultimate use for the gas. From this point, the gas can be simply flared or used to generate electricity, replace fossil fuels in industrial and manufacturing operations, fuel greenhouse operations, or be upgraded to pipeline quality gas.

3.12. BIOREACTOR LANDFILL AS A NEW TECHNOLOGY

A bioreactor landfill operates to rapidly transform and degrade organic waste. The increase in waste degradation and stabilization is accomplished through the addition of liquid and air to enhance microbial processes. This bioreactor concept differs from the traditional "dry tomb" municipal landfill approach.

A bioreactor landfill is not just a single design and will correspond to the operational process invoked. There are three different general types of bioreactor landfill configurations:

Aerobic - In an aerobic bioreactor landfill, leachate is removed from the bottom layer, piped to liquids storage tanks, and re-circulated into the landfill in a controlled manner. Air is injected into the waste mass, using vertical or horizontal wells, to promote aerobic activity and accelerate waste stabilization.

Anaerobic - In an anaerobic bioreactor landfill, moisture is added to the waste mass in the form of re-circulated leachate and other sources to obtain optimal moisture levels. Biodegradation occurs in the absence of oxygen (anaerobically) and due to this primarily methane, can be captured to minimize greenhouse gas emissions and for energy projects. Hybrid (Aerobic-Anaerobic) - The hybrid bioreactor landfill accelerates waste degradation by employing a sequential aerobic-anaerobic treatment to rapidly degrade organics in the upper sections of the landfill and collect gas from lower sections. Operation as a hybrid results in the earlier onset of methanogenesis compared to aerobic landfill.

❑❑❑

Chapter–4

Green Business

Green business, is enterprise that has no negative impact on the global or local environment, community, society, or economy—a business that strives to meet the triple bottom line. Often, sustainable businesses have progressive environmental and human rights policies. In general, business is described as green if it matches the following four criteria:

1. It incorporates principles of sustainability into each of its business decisions.
2. It supplies environmentally friendly products or services that replace demand for non-green products and/or services.
3. It is greener than traditional competition.
4. It has made an enduring commitment to environmental principles in its business operations.

A sustainable business is any organization that participates in environmentally friendly or green activities to ensure that all processes, products, and manufacturing activities adequately address current environmental concerns while maintaining a profit. In other words, it is a business that "meets the needs of the present world without compromising the ability of the future generations to meet their own needs." It is the process of assessing how to design products that will take advantage of the current environmental situation and how well a company's products perform with renewable resources.

Everyone affects the sustainability of the marketplace and the planet in some way. Sustainable development within a business can create value for customers, investors, and the environment. A sustainable business must meet customer needs while, at the same time, treating the environment well. Today, green business is an extremely profitable branch of the business world, and it hosts a range of companies, from prestigious multinational companies to small, locally based companies.

Environmental Sphere

A major initiative of sustainable businesses is to eliminate or decrease the impact made on the environment by harmful chemicals, materials, and waste generated by processes to manufacture products and services. The impact of such human activities in terms of the amount of greenhouse gases produced can be measured in units of carbon dioxide and is referred to as the carbon footprint. The carbon footprint concept branched off from ecological footprint analysis, which examines the ecological capacity required to support the consumption of products.

One of the most common examples of sustainable business initiatives is the act of going paperless. On a higher level, sustainable business practices can include reviewing processes in order to eliminate or recycle waste, making all products recyclable, and eliminating the use of nonrenewable resources via alternatives energies.

Sustainable businesses also look at inputs to determine what products are harmful to the environment and try to find green alternatives that can function at the same or a better level and, preferably, at a lower cost. Company leaders also take into account the life cycle costs for inputs of items purchased. Inputs costs must be considered in regards to regulations, energy use, storage, and disposal.

A business's green initiatives can include conserving materials through remanufacturing, converting harmful gases into clean energy, generating greener power, and improving fuel economy. Designing for the environment (DFE) is also an element of sustainable business. This process enables users to consider the potential environmental impacts of a product and the process used to make that product.

In Korea, rice husks are used as a nontoxic packaging for stereo components and other electronics. The concept of waste is diminished because of inclusive shipping in produce costs the goods would already incur. The same material is later used to make bricks.

The green and sustainability trend has manifested in pressure from consumers, shareholders, employees, partners and governments (regulations) put upon companies to embrace more sustainable and green practices. Many companies resorted to green washing instead of actually creating green innovations by marketing their product in a way that suggests green practices. However, there are many companies that have taken the sustainability trend seriously and are doing so profitably.

Social Sphere

Organizations that give back to the community, whether through employees volunteering their time or through charitable donations are often considered to be socially sustainable. Organizations also can encourage education in their communities by training their employees and offering internships to younger members of the community. Practices such as these increase the education level and quality of life in the community.

In order for a business to be truly sustainable, it must sustain not only the necessary environmental resources, but also its social resources, including employees, customers (the community), and its reputation

Standards

Enormous economic and population growth worldwide in the second half of the twentieth century drove the impacts that threaten health and the world — ozone layer depletion, climate change, fouling of natural resources, and extensive loss of biodiversity and habitat. In the past, the standard approaches to environmental problems generated by business and industry have been regulatory-driven "end-of-the-pipe" remediation efforts. In the 1990s, efforts by governments, NGOs, corporations, and investors began to grow substantially to develop awareness and plans for investment in business sustainability.

One critical milestone was the establishment of the ISO 14000 standards whose development came as a result of the Rio Summit on the Environment held in 1992. ISO 14001 is the cornerstone standard of the ISO 14000 series. It specifies a framework of control for an Environmental Management System against which an organization can be certified by a third party. Other ISO 14000 Series Standards are actually guidelines, many to help you achieve registration to ISO 14001. They include the following:

- ISO 14004 provides guidance on the development and implementation of environmental management systems
- ISO 14010 provides general principles of environmental auditing (now superseded by ISO 19011)
- ISO 14011 provides specific guidance on audit an environmental management system (now superseded by ISO 19011)
- ISO 14012 provides guidance on qualification criteria for environmental auditors and lead auditors (now superseded by ISO 19011)
- ISO 14013/5 provides audit program review and assessment material.
- ISO 14020+ labeling issues
- ISO 14030+ provides guidance on performance targets and monitoring within an Environmental Management System
- ISO 14040+ covers life cycle issues

Six Essential Characteristics

The mature and authentic sustainable business contains these six essentials. These essentials are rooted in many sustainability principals and are very dynamic. There is no reason in the future for essentials not to shift or adjust as we evolve our understanding of a sustainable business.

1. Triple top-line value production

"The TTL Establishes three *simultaneous requirements* of sustainable business activities - financial benefits for the company, natural world betterment, and social advantages for employees and members of the local community—with each of these three components recognized as equal in status." Though this is sometimes called the triple bottom line, triple top line stresses the importance of initial value rather than after the fact effects.

2. Nature-based knowledge and technology

"This biomimicry-based principal involves the conscious emulation of natural-world genius in terms of growing our food, harnessing our energy, constructing things, conducting business healing ourselves, processing information and designing our communities"

3. Products of service to products of consumption

"*Products of service* are durable goods routinely leased by the customer that are made of technical materials and are returned to the manufacturer and re-processed into a new generation of products when they are worn out. (These products are mostly non-toxic to human and environmental health but toxic materials that are used will be kept within a closed loop type system and not be able to escape into the environment). *Products of consumption* are shorter lived items made only of biodegradable materials. They are broken down by the detritus organisms after the products lose their usefulness. (These are also non-hazardous to human or environmental health). This principal requires that we manufacture only these two types of products and necessitates the gradual but continual reductions of products of service and their replacement with products of consumption as technological advancements allow."

4. Solar, wind, geothermal and ocean energy

"This principal advocates employing only sustainable energy technology—solar, wind, ocean and geothermal—that can meet our energy needs indefinitely without negative effects for life on earth."

5. Local-based organizations and economies

"This ingredient includes durable, beautiful and healthy communities with locally owned and operated businesses and locally managed non-profit organizations, along with regional corporations and shareholders working together in a dense web of partnerships and collaborations."

6. Continuous improvement process

"Operational processes inside successful organizations include provisions for constant advancements and upgrade as the company does its business. The continuous process of monitoring, analyzing, redesigning and implementing is used to intensify TTL value production as conditions change and new opportunities emerge."

4.1. GREENING PLASTIC CARDS

Billions of credit, debit, gift and other sorts of plastic cards are manufactured annually - and most will wind up in landfill within a couple of years. It's an environmental problem that can certainly be addressed by the companies involved; but they need to know consumers care about the issue.

Setting the Global Standard for Environmentally Intelligent Plastic Cards

In response to growing consumer and card issuer demand for green transaction and identification cards, the **International Card Manufacturers Association** (ICMA) EcoLabel Standard Program provides a determination of the environmental performance of a manufacturer's cards through a third-party ecolabeling certification program.

ICMA's Green Task Force developed the EcoLabel Standard Program through an open process involving card manufacturers, personalizers, suppliers and issuers internationally. The ICMA EcoLabel Standard Program initiates measurable criteria for assessing the environmental impact of cards for ICMA EcoLabel certification and conforms to global ISO principles for environmental labeling.

Opportunities for a greener bottom line

As businesses seek market advantage by responding to consumer environmental concerns, ecolabeling has evolved as a method of identifying a product's environmental integrity. However, without guiding standards and verification by an independent third-party, manufacturers' environmental claims may be questioned by consumers.

The ICMA EcoLabel Standard Program establishes third-party credibility that a green card product is an environmentally preferable alternative. A comprehensive ICMA EcoLabel Standards Program criteria document titled *Indicators for the Environmental Impact of Cards* is also located on this website, and should be referred to for comprehensive complete criteria and technical information. EcoLabel registration is also available on this website.

EcoLabel criteria

In general, the current ICMA EcoLabel criteria include:

- Reduced materials (minimum of 25%)
- Recycled content (minimum 25% threshold)
- Compostable (municipal and home)
- Biobased content (minimum of 40%)

Assurance levels

- **Declared:** Manufacturer registers and declares the card meets ICMA EcoLabel Standard Program criteria without third-party assessor verification. These cards are "registered."
- **Verified:** Manufacturer registers and provides verification the card meets ICMA EcoLabel Standard Program criteria by a recognized third-party assessor. These cards are "certified."

It is the responsibility of the issuer of an ICMA EcoLabel certified card to conduct any third-party authentication of manufacturer claims, as well as comply with Visa, MasterCard, American Express and other brand issuing organizations' requirements.

ICMA: Greening the marketplace

In addition to licensing member manufacturers, certifying card products and administering ICMA EcoLabel usage, ICMA will:

- Provide best practices to manufacturers contemplating application for EcoLabel licensing and registering/certification of their products
- Disseminate ICMA EcoLabel information to the public and the card industry
- Represent the interests of ecolabeling in international meetings and forums

The card manufacturing industry faces a rapidly changing global marketplace and is looked to for leadership on technological and socio-economic issues such as environmentally friendly card products. This is an industry issue which can build recognition of the card industry as a whole for its environmental intelligence and its commitment to leadership through environmentally responsible manufacturing initiatives.

Benefits of ICMA EcoLabel Standard Program Licensing

- Ability to place approved EcoLabel logo on qualified cards at the issuer's request
- Licensee logo placed on all manufacturer corporate communications conveying a "green" image to customers
- ICMA website listing in a dedicated EcoLabel licensee section
- Manufacturer-driven public relations
- Inclusion in ICMA industry and consumer EcoLabel public relations

4.2. GREEN MEETINGS

Times are changing and business is changing with them. The typical business meeting is no longer held in the office conference room, planned weeks in advance and utilizing lots of resources. Now teleconference calls connect people across great distances. No need to pay employees extra for the costs of traveling. No need to hire a commercial jet to fly to another city. No need to print out enough reports for everyone. Less effort and travel makes life easier for employees too.

Businesses can make use of webcams, email and PDF documents to share vital information with one another during a teleconference. These tools sometimes have a high initial cost, but save money in the long run. They also allow businesses to communicate with each other and with their own employees more frequently, reducing the risk of miscommunication and cutting back on the time involved on projects. Offices can even use alternative energy to provide electricity therefore saving time and money.

The environmental impact of meetings

Aside from the general impact of the fossil fuel industry, think of all the emissions involved with transporting the millions of people who travel to and from meetings each day. Traveling by car to meetings is bad enough, but when it comes to flying; the news is even worse.

So much air travel is business related and according to a recent WWF study, due to the way emissions from airplanes interact with the upper atmosphere their warming effect is thought to be greater than equivalent emissions at ground level - around 2.7 times. The study says that aviation fuel related emissions account for 5% - 10% – of the total impact of carbon dioxide on climate change.

The case for online meetings

While telecommuting full time isn't for everyone, most businesses can take advantage of technology to reduce meeting and conference traveling impact by holding them online. Video conferencing and online meeting services have come a long way in recent years.

The services and software now used include all sorts of amazing features such as video, chat, private audio, application sharing and whiteboards that everyone can interact with.

As long as having a broadband connection, these services work very well and are quite easy to use. Online meeting services are also excellent for webinars - the online version of seminars.

A study on business travel in Europe prepared for ETNO and the WWF in 2006 concluded that by replacing 5 - 30% of current air travel with online meetings and video conferencing, it could reduce carbon dioxide emissions anywhere between 5.59-33.53 million tonnes annually

A 2007 Telstra report found that video conferencing could avoid 2.4 million tonnes of Australian business related carbon dioxide emissions annually, equivalent to 0.43% of Australia's total.

In Europe and Australia, imagine the millions of tonnes of emissions could be saved in the USA each year through increased uptake of online meeting and conferencing. For business, the extensive use of online meeting services is something that can also be used for promotional purposes in terms of the company's environmental commitment.

❑❑❑

Chapter–5

Green Tourism

Tourism is a phenomenon, which has taken off immensely in the past three decades. It concerns us all, be it by allowing us to travel long distances as tourists, or by forcing upon us a mass of visitors to our part of the world. In the past, people did not travel half as much. Financial obstacles and responsibilities to land and animals stopped them from doing so. Only in 1845 did Thomas Cook of Leicester, England, organize the first package tour, making this experience available to people outside of the privileged classes by cutting down on expenses. By 1939, an estimated one million people were traveling abroad each year. Nowadays, the population of the Mediterranean swells to double over the summer, from 130 million resident inhabitants during the winter to 260 million in high season. There were about 698 million international tourist arrivals worldwide in 2000. All regions in the world grew, and the fastest developing region continued to be East Asia and the Pacific. Tourism has become the largest industry in the world. And just like all thriving industries, though it has a lot to give, it also takes a lot in turn. Unfortunately, the toll that we pay for it has been rising steadily. While the prospect of people traveling less in the future seems improbable, to say the least, a new idea has already sprung up: If we cannot stop tourism, let us at least travel sensibly.

The Environmental impact of tourism

Tourism has a large effect on the state of our environment. The three major fields affected are natural resources, the degree of pollution and the physical state of sites and countries visited. The tourist industry generally overuses water resources for hotels, swimming pools, golf courses and personal use. When on holiday, people tend to use more water, especially in hot climates. In Barbados and Hawaii, each tourist uses ten times as much water as the residents. In recent years, golf tourism has increased in popularity. Along with herbicides and pesticides, golf courses require large amounts of water every day, which often results in a lack of water for the local inhabitants. Tourists also create pressure on other resources, such as energy or food. They contribute to deforestation in endangered areas, the loss of wildlife and the depletion of fossil fuels, fertile soil and minerals. The more people travel each year, the higher the degree of pollution there is. Tourism means traveling and this in turn represents a greater demand in fuel. Nowadays, tourism accounts for 60% of all flights worldwide. And one transatlantic return flight produces half the amount of carbon dioxide that a single person does per year by using other resources such as cars or heating. In very hot or very cold countries, bus drivers often leave their engines on while tourists go sightseeing, so that their customers might return to a comfortably air-conditioned bus. All means of transport create noise pollution and, especially in cities with small historic centers, this runs hand in hand with air pollution. Littering is another form of pollution, which has plagued tourist destinations. Apart from environmental pollution, aesthetic pollution is also increasingly becoming a problem, especially in underdeveloped countries. To meet the requirements of western travelers, large modern buildings have been built in tourist hotspots, which look out of place amidst the local architecture and destroy the genuine atmosphere of the place.

The physical impacts of tourism include damage to vegetation and soil, disruption of the natural habitats of animals and the subsequent alteration of ecosystems. Likewise the Oceans are not left unaffected. The running and anchoring of boats and ships, snorkeling, yachting and scuba diving all has its toll. Visitors, lacking discipline, and often-in search of adventure, fish and hunt for species that may be protected or even endangered. At the global level, tourism has a lot to do with the loss of biodiversity. Tourists trample upon vegetation, pollute coastal regions and disturb animals in their natural habitat, which results in the destruction of ecosystems. They also bring new species into the local environment, often unconsciously, which has the same effect. Species that are not native to the environment can cause enormous damage. Mass transportation, especially air travel, contributes to the thinning of the ozone layer, which results in global warming. And global warming has already caused large climate change, which is accompanied by flooding, unusual storms (tornadoes, hurricanes and typhoons) or simply an excessive heat in the summer or a lack of snow in the winter.

Many countries, which represent attractive destination for tourists, have already realized that if they do not try to conserve their natural wealth, the visitors will stop arriving. And as tourism is for many countries an important source of money, then green tourism is their only logical option. The world as such is caught in a vicious circle: growing tourism contributes towards the greenhouse effect and global warming; these cause climate changes; climate changes are accompanied by severe weather and severe weather stops tourists from spending their vacation in the affected areas.

Sustainable Tourism

The United Nations designated the year 2000 as the International Year of Ecotourism. Ecotourists, or green tourists, attempt to travel in a manner not harmful to the environment. But what does this actually involve? Sustainability implies permanence as opposed to impermanence or temporariness. To travel "green" means to travel responsibly while conserving the environment and sustaining the well being of the local people. By optimizing the use of resources and minimizing the social, cultural and ecological impacts, a green tourist enables other people to visit the same region later and still enjoy the same experience. Green tourism is *informative* because travelers learn about their destination and local people learn to appreciate what they have to offer. It *supports the integrity of the place* because conscientious travelers seek out things that are characteristic of the locality in terms of architecture, cuisine, heritage or environment. *The residents benefit from green tourism* because they can offer local supplies and services to foreigners. Environmentally conscious travelers try to *conserve resources* by choosing services that cause minimum pollution. The destination countries try not to spoil what they have to offer, so therefore they do their best to *retain local cultural features*. *Quality, not quantity*, should be the goal of green tourism, therefore permanence and richness of experience is what both parties are striving for.

Tourism as a contribution to Environmental Conservation

If managed wisely, tourism can have many advantages, the predominant one being additional finance for the local budget. Where there is money, there are possibilities. The money tourists spend on entrance fees, parking lots and souvenirs can be used directly for the management and conservation of sensitive areas. Thanks to foreign visitors, Prague has been able to repair many of its historic sites, making the city more beautiful and attractive. Tourism is also a good solution to unemployment, offering jobs to people who would normally engage in illegal activities such as hunting endangered species for markets in Africa. In Uganda, gorillas play a vital role in the local economy. The high price of a gorilla-tracking permit has made the locals realize the importance of this noble animal and this has directly contributed to the preservation of the species.

How Can You Be a Green Tourist?

Before you set off on a journey to your chosen destination, make sure you pack the following things: rechargeable batteries and a recharger; a cloth bag for any local products you buy; a cloth handkerchief instead of bundles of paper napkins; drawing pencils and paper to draw pictures instead of taking photographs which are more toxic. Choose sustainable transportation - arrive by train or bus. If you decide to go by car, offer a ride to friends or advertise on the Internet – autoshare has become an increasingly favored means of transport. When you get there, move around on foot, ride a bike or choose in-line skates.

Use public transport instead of taxis.

Find green accommodation – many cities nowadays offer alternative hotels which provide recycling and composting facilities, chemical-free laundry and dry-cleaning or energy efficient heat and lights. If you cannot find one, you can still make a difference by turning lights out when you do not need them, or disposing of your garbage in nearby recycling bins.

Eat local food and, if possible, choose organic. Not only does this support local farmers and the local economy, but it also saves fuel, which would be used on the transportation of the food to distant regions.

Reduce, reuse, recycle – shop for clothes at second-hand clothes shops; get a used CD of local music; buy second-hand books; have your shoes repaired instead of buying them new.

Promote green tourism among your friends. Tell them about your experiences, advise them on how to travel sustainably, share your Internet links with them.

Eco-tourism is more than a catch phrase for nature loving travel and recreation. Eco-tourism is consecrated for preserving and sustaining the diversity of the world's natural and cultural environments. It accommodates and entertains visitors in a way that is minimally intrusive or destructive to the environment and sustains & supports the native cultures in the locations it is operating in. Responsibility of both travellers and service providers is the genuine meaning for eco-tourism.

Eco-tourism also endeavors to encourage and support the diversity of local economies for which the tourism-related income is important. With support from tourists, local services and producers can compete with larger, foreign companies and local families can support themselves. Besides all these, the revenue produced from tourism helps and encourages governments to fund conservation projects and training programs.

Saving the environment around you and preserving the natural luxuries and forest life, that's what eco-tourism is all about. Whether it's about a nature camp or organizing trekking trips towards the unspoilt and inaccessible regions, one should always keep in mind not to create any mishap or disturbance in the life cycle of nature.

Eco-tourism focuses on local cultures, wilderness adventures, volunteering, personal growth and learning new ways to live on our vulnerable planet. It is typically defined as travel to destinations where the flora, fauna, and cultural heritage are the primary attractions. Responsible Eco-tourism includes programs that minimize the adverse effects of traditional tourism on the natural environment, and enhance the cultural integrity of local people. Therefore, in addition to evaluating environmental and cultural factors, initiatives by hospitality providers to promote recycling, energy efficiency, water reuse, and the creation of economic opportunities for local communities are an integral part of Eco-tourism.

Historical, biological and cultural conservation, preservation, sustainable development etc. are some of the fields closely related to Eco-Tourism. Many professionals have been involved in formulating and developing eco-tourism policies. They come from the fields of Geographic Information Systems, Wildlife Management, Wildlife Photography, Marine Biology and Oceanography, National and State Park Management, Environmental Sciences, Women in Development, Historians and Archaeologists, etc.

Eco-tourism is considered the fastest growing market in the tourism industry, according to the World Tourism Organization with an annual growth rate of 5% worldwide and representing 6% of the world gross domestic product, 11.4% of all consumer spending - not a market to be taken lightly.

What is Eco-tourism?

Fundamentally, eco-tourism means making as little environmental impact as possible and helping to sustain the indigenous populace, thereby encouraging the preservation of wildlife and habitats when visiting a place. This is responsible form of tourism and tourism development, which encourages going back to natural products in every aspect of life. It is also the key to sustainable ecological development.

The International Eco-tourism Society defines eco-tourism as "responsible travel to natural areas that conserves the environment and improves the well-being of local people." This means that those who implement and participate in Eco-tourism activities should follow the following principles:

- Minimize impact
- Build environmental and cultural awareness and respect
- Provide positive experiences for both visitors and hosts
- Provide direct financial benefits for conservation
- Provide financial benefits and empowerment for local people
- Raise sensitivity to host countries' political, environmental, and social climate
- Support international human rights and labour agreements

Aware of the Environment - Today the "Green Laws" of conservation are making people aware of how man and the environment can live symbiotically for more time to come and eco-tourism is the only way to maximize the economic, environmental and social benefits of tourism. Everyone is a stakeholder in the process and we clearly need to avoid our past shortcomings and negative impact that they have had.

In India too the movement is gathering momentum with more and more travel and travel related organization's are addressing the needs of the eco-tourists and promoting eco-tourism in the country. Some basic do's and don'ts of eco-tourism are listed below:

Do's

- Carry back all non-degradable litter such as empty bottles, tins, plastic bags etc. These must not litter the environment or be buried. They must be disposed in municipal dustbins only.
- Observe the sanctity of holy sites, temples and local cultures.
- Cut noise pollution. Do not blare aloud radios, tape recorders or other electronic entertainment equipment in nature resorts, sanctuaries and wildlife parks.
- In case temporary toilets are set-up near campsites, after defecation, cover with mud or sand. Make sure that the spot is at least 30 meters away from the water source.
- Respect people's privacy while taking photographs. Ask for prior permission before taking a photograph.

Don'ts

- Do not take away flora and fauna in the forms of cuttings, seeds or roots. It is illegal, especially inthe Himalayas. The environment is really delicate in this region and the bio-diversity of the region has to be protected at all costs.
- Do not use pollutants such as detergent, in streams or springs while washing and bathing.
- Do not use wood as fuel to cook food at the campsite.
- Do not leave cigarettes butts or make open fires in the forests.
- Do not consume aerated drinks, alcohol, drugs or any other intoxicant and throw bottles in the wild.
- Do not tempt the locals, especially children by offering them foodstuff or sweets. Respect local traditions.
- Polythene and plastics are non biodegradable and unhealthy for the environment and must not be used and littered.

As a traveller, you will have an impact on the environment and culture of the place you are visiting. Here are some rules of thumb to make this impact positive!

Golden Rules When You Travel

- Learn about your destination before you get there. Read guidebooks, travel articles, histories, and/or novels by local authors and pay particular attention to customs such as greetings, appropriate dress, eating behaviours, etc. Being sensitive to these customs will increase local acceptance of you as a tourist and enrich your trip.
- Follow established guidelines. Ask your eco-tour operator, guide and/or the local authorities what their guidelines are for limiting tourism's impact on the environment and local culture. Staying on trails, packing up your trash, and remaining set distances away from wildlife are a few ways to minimize your impact in sensitive areas.
- Seek out and support locally owned businesses. Support local businesses during your eco-travels to ensure maximum community and conservation benefit from your spending.

Eco-Tourism in India is still at a very nascent stage, but there are for sure conscious efforts to save the fragile Himalayan Eco System and culture and heritage of the indigenous people, which is probably the largest concentration in the world.

❑❑❑

Chapter–6

Greenscaping

Landscaping is both science and art and is an aspect of the environmental impact of a hotel that needs to be addressed. Understanding and blending the elements of both nature and construction is effective landscaping. Whether Landscaping is extensive or small consumes a large amount of water, fertilizers and herbicides and generates solid waste.

Ecogreen's Greenscaping Operation provides cost-efficient and environmentally friendly solutions for landscaping. Greenscaping operation deals with two aspects:

1. Solid Waste Management, and
2. Water Conservation

Solid Waste Management

Solid wastes generated by hotel offices are usually in large quantities and toxic those pollute our environment. Stationery, paper and cartridges of copiers and printers are among the normal wastes. To reduce operating expenses, implementing recycling and waste disposal programs are a must for offices. The recycling program should include categorizing the wastes into recyclable and non-recyclable wastes and treating them differently. These programs help to save resources, reduce pollution and protect both the environment and employee health.

Following are some simple solid waste control ideas:

- Avoiding unnecessary paperwork,
- Canceling junk mail,
- Reusing scrap paper for notes,
- Using electronic mail or voice mail over hard copy mail,
- Solid waste management program,

- Recycling all office paper,
- Double- sided photocopying in order to reduce paper use,
- Using refillable cartridge tones,
- Using white paper rather than colored paper for recycling,
- Using fax machines that use both plain and recyclable paper,
- Awareness and involvement of office employees in all stages of Recycling Program.

Water Conservation

An incredible amount of water is used in hotels in Landscaping to keep the plants green and healthy. An efficient irrigation system lets you reduce water use and save money. Given below are some water conservation ideas:

- Checking taps, toilets for leaks frequently,
- Installing leak-detection equipment,
- Minimizing water use in cooling equipment,
- Cleaning corridors with a broom rather than hose,
- Installing water meters for monitoring high consumption equipment and areas,
- Recovering waste water from laundry rinse cycles and dry cleaning cycles for reuse,
- Establishing an employee training program about water conservation.

Greenscaping Operation is all about taking the initiative to examine the impact of resources and learning new ideas to control and manage the flow of resources.

Large-Scale Landscapes

Roads and highways, golf courses and ski resorts, commercial buildings and industrial sites—the widespread use of economically and environmentally costly landscaping is everywhere. By simply changing these large-scale landscapes to "GreenScapes" and focusing on the "4 Rs"—reduce, reuse, recycle, and rebuy, you can help improve both your bottom line and the environment.

GreenScaping encompasses a set of landscaping practices that can improve the health and appearance of your large-scale landscape while protecting and preserving natural resources.

GreenScapes is a program that aims to combine government and industry into a powerful, unified influence over the reduction, reuse, and recycling of waste materials in large land use applications. These land use activities include four million miles of roadside landscaping, Brownfields land revitalization, and the beautification and maintenance of office complexes, golf courses, and parks. More than 100,000 businesses are involved in these land use activities.

GreenScapes that identifies and uses innovative, flexible, and protective ways to conserve natural resources and energy. GreenScapes reinforces these goals by emphasizing a holistic multimedia view of environmental impacts and stewardship. In addition, GreenScapes:

- The cost savings can be achieved from reducing material use and waste, resource conservation, and on the performance and durability of environmentally preferable products such as recycled-content and biobased products.
- The environmentally beneficial landscaping efforts yield water and energy savings, conserves landfill space, and reduces greenhouse gas emissions.

Benefits of Green scaping

Cost Savings

Following the principles of GreenScapes can be a great financial move for your organization. Green landscaping means buying fewer products and switching from the purchase of disposable ones to those that are long-lasting and reusable. Use our online calculators to see how much you can save by comparing costs between environmentally preferable methods and using virgin materials. Buying durable goods might be more expensive at the time of purchase, but over the life of your landscape, maintenance, repurchasing, and tipping costs will go down. These savings can give your business an edge over the competition!

There are also immediate cost savings you can recognize. By composting instead of disposing of your yard waste, for instance, you will save money on disposal costs. Compost adds disease-suppressing properties to soils, reducing your need for pesticides. Even a move as small as leaving grass clippings on your lawn after mowing can save big bucks—lowered disposal costs and, because decomposing grass pieces return valuable nutrients to the soil, lowered fertilizer costs.

Waste Reduction

Millions of tons of waste materials are hauled away, buried, or burned each day from landscaping and grounds keeping operations—trees, shrubs, brush, lumber, asphalt, and concrete, to name only a few. Millions of gallons of excess water, pesticides, fuels, and oils are in use each and every day. Why pay to dispose of this waste when you can avoid it? Following the GreenScapes philosophies of reduce, reuse, recycle, and rebuy can lower your tipping fees and other costs related to disposal.

All of this waste also impacts our environment. By reducing your landscape's consumption, you will be helping prevent greenhouse gases (GHGs), save landfill space, and preserve natural resources.

Water Conservation

Most large-scale landscapes use an incredible amount of water to keep plants green and healthy. There are various GreenScapes activities you can try to reduce your water use and keep your plants beautiful. Just maintaining an efficient irrigation system and adjusting the time of day that you water can save money.

A longer-term adjustment can be made by bringing native plants to your landscapes. Vegetation that is native to your area will be naturally hardier and more tolerant to your weather conditions. Planting native vegetation will reward you with lower water, fertilizer, and pesticide bills.

There are also GreenScapes methods to reduce runoff of storm water and irrigation water that carry top soils, fertilizers, and pesticides into local rivers and lakes. Drawing from storm retention ponds supplies irrigation applications, as does installing rain barrels or cisterns to catch free rain water on and around buildings. These options save water and money while reducing runoff, erosion, and non-point source pollution.

Environmental Impact

The huge amounts of waste generated, water used, and energy consumed to maintain a large landscape have an incredible impact on our environment. Every piece of trash takes up room in a landfill, and produces greenhouse gases not only as it decomposes, but during each step of its production and transportation. Energy is required to treat and transport water—energy that generally comes from nonrenewable, polluting sources. And toxic pesticides and fertilizers abound in a typical large landscape, leading to the pollution of local rivers and lakes. Landscaping by the philosophies of GreenScapes will help you to minimize or avoid these environmental issues, lessening your landscape's impact on the earth.

Energy Savings

Almost every material that you use on your landscape required energy to reach you. Large amounts of energy are used in acquiring materials, manufacturing products, and shipping products to you. Energy is used to produce and ship soil additives, water, tools, machines, paints, and virtually every other material used in landscaping. By purchasing fewer, more durable goods, you are saving an untold amount of energy.

Many green landscaping activities help reduce energy usage. Creating compost on site not only reduces the energy needed to transport organic waste to a landfill, but it eliminates the need for the production and transportation of fertilizers and often pesticides. Compost also absorbs water, reducing the amount of irrigation necessary and the energy required to transport the water. Strategic planting of vegetation around buildings can reduce indoor heating and cooling needs by creating shade.

Climate Impact

Most materials used on landscapes have an impact on our climate. Every product you use emitted GHGs as it was manufactured and transported, and will continue to produce GHGs in a landfill as it decomposes. The constant buying and trashing of products regularly adds GHGs to our atmosphere and impacts the climate.

Additional Benefits

- Reduced exposure of your customers, employees, and yourself to potentially harmful chemicals, solvents, fuels, and pesticides.
- Increased beauty: a natural environment is aesthetically pleasing.
- Improved public perception of your business.
- Knowledge that you are making a difference by helping prevent pollution, curb climate change, and reduce your "environmental footprint" on the earth.

❑❑❑

Chapter–7

Urban Forest

Trees are major capital assets in cities Just as streets, sidewalks, public buildings and recreational facilities are a part of a community's infrastructure, so are publicly owned trees. Trees — and, collectively, the urban forest — are important assets that require care and maintenance the same as other public property. Trees are on the job 24 hours every day working for all of us to improve our environment and quality of life. Urban forest provides many environmental benefits to our community. Aside from the obvious aesthetic benefits, trees within our urban forest improve our air, protect our water, save energy, and improve economic sustainability.

In other words, since most trees have been planted much of the tree cover is in urban areas as opposed to "natural lands". Therefore, estimated pollutant uptake rates are higher for residential compared to natural or unmanaged lands. Possible management implications of these estimates are that air pollutant uptake benefits from tree planting may be optimized by planting in areas where air pollutant concentrations are elevated and where relatively high planting densities can be achieved thereby enhancing the health of urban dwellers.

- Carbon Sequestration
- More income generation through contract landscaping
- Bonsai culture
- Reduction of Other Pollutants
- Urban Forests Protect Our Water
- Urban Forests Save Energy
- Extend the Life of Paved Surfaces
- Increase Traffic Safety
- Improve Economic Sustainability
- Affect Consumer Perceptions and Behaviors

- Increase Real Estate Values
- Increase Sociological Benefits

Carbon Sequestration:

- Heat from Earth is trapped in the atmosphere due to high levels of carbon dioxide (CO_2) and other heat-trapping gases that prohibit it from releasing heat into space — creating a phenomenon known as the "greenhouse effect." Trees remove (sequester) CO_2 from the atmosphere during photosynthesis to form carbohydrates that are used in plant structure/function and return oxygen back to the atmosphere as a byproduct. About half of the greenhouse effect is caused by CO_2. Trees therefore act as a carbon sink by removing the carbon and storing it as cellulose in their trunk, branches, leaves and roots while releasing oxygen back into the air.
- Trees also reduce the greenhouse effect by shading our homes and office buildings. This reduces air conditioning needs up to 30%, thereby reducing the amount of fossil fuels burned to produce electricity. This combination of CO_2 removal from the atmosphere, carbon storage in wood, and the cooling effect makes trees a very efficient tool in fighting the greenhouse effect.
- One tree that shades your home in the city will also save fossil fuel, cutting CO_2 buildup as much as 15 forest trees.
- Approximately 800 million tons of carbons are stored in U.S. urban forests with a $22 billion equivalent in control costs.
- Planting trees remains one of the cheapest, most effective means of drawing excess CO_2 from the atmosphere.
- A single mature tree can absorb carbon dioxide at a rate of 48 lbs./year and release enough oxygen back into the atmosphere to support 2 human beings.
- A healthy tree stores about 13 pounds of carbon annually — or 2.6 tons per acre each year. An acre of trees absorbs enough CO_2 over one year to equal the amount produced by driving a car 26,000 miles. An estimate of carbon emitted per vehicle mile is between 0.88 lb. CO_2/mi. – 1.06 lb. CO_2/mi. (Nowak, 1993). Thus, a car driven 26,000 miles will emit between 22,880 lbs CO_2 and 27,647 lbs. CO_2. Thus, one acre of tree cover in Brooklyn can compensate for automobile fuel use equivalent to driving a car between 7,200 and 8,700 miles.
- If every family planted just one tree, the amount of CO_2 in the atmosphere would be reduced by one billion lbs annually. This is almost 5% of the amount that human activity pumps into the atmosphere each year.

Reduction of Other Air Pollutants:

- Trees also remove other gaseous pollutants by absorbing them with normal air components through the stomatas in the leaf surface.
- Some of the other major air pollutants and their primary sources are:
  - Sulfur Dioxide (SO_2)- Coal burning for electricity/home heating is responsible for about 60 percent of the sulfur dioxide in the air. Refining and combustion of petroleum products produce 21% of the SO_2.
  - Ozone (O_3) - is a naturally occurring oxidant, existing in the upper atmosphere. O_3 may be brought to earth by turbulence during severe storms, and small amounts are formed by lighting. Most O_3 - and another oxidant, peroxyacetylnitrate (PAN) - come from the emissions of automobiles and industries, which mix in the air and undergo photochemical reactions in sunlight. High concentrations of O_3 and PAN often build up where there are many automobiles.
  - Nitrogen oxides - Automotive exhaust is probably the largest producer of NO_x. Oxides of nitrogen are also formed by combustion at high temperatures in the presence of two natural components of the air; nitrogen and oxygen.
  - Particulates are small (<10 microns) particles emitted in smoke from burning fuel, particular diesel, that enters our lungs and cause respiratory problems.
- There is up to a 60% reduction in street level particulates with trees.
- In one urban park (212 ha.) tree cover was found to remove daily 48lbs. particulates, 9 lbs nitrogen dioxide, 6 lbs sulfur dioxide, and 2 lb carbon monoxide ($136/day value based upon pollution control technology) and 100 lbs of carbon.
- One sugar maple (12" DBH) along a roadway removes in one growing season 60mg cadmium, 140 mg chromium, 820 mg nickel, and 5200 mg lead from the environment.
- Planting trees and expanding parklands improves the air quality of our country. A total of 300 trees can counter balance the amount of pollution one person produces in a lifetime.

Urban Forests Protect Our Water

- Trees reduce topsoil erosion, prevent harmful land pollutants contained in the soil from getting into our waterways, slow down water run-off, and ensure that our groundwater supplies are continually being replenished. For every 5% of tree cover added to a community, stormwater runoff is reduced by approximately 2%.

- Research by the USFS shows that in a 1 inch rainstorm over 12 hours, the interception of rain by the canopy of the urban forest in Salt Lake City reduces surface runoff by about 11.3 million gallons, or 17%. These values would increase as the canopy increases.
- Along with breaking the fall of rainwater, tree roots remove nutrients harmful to water ecology and quality.
- Trees act as natural pollution filters. Their canopies, trunks, roots, and associated soil and other natural elements of the landscape filter polluted particulate matter out of the flow toward the storm sewers. Reducing the flow of stormwater reduces the amount of pollution that is washed into a drainage area. Trees use nutrients like nitrogen, phosphorus, and potassium—byproducts of urban living—which can pollute streams.

Urban Forests Save Energy

- Homeowners that properly place trees in their landscape can realize savings up to 58% on daytime air conditioning and as high as 65% for mobile homes. If applied nationwide to buildings not now benefiting from trees, the shade could reduce our nation's consumption of oil by 500,000 barrels of oil/day.
- The maximum potential annual savings from energy conserving landscapes around a typical residence ranged from 13% in Madison up to 38% in Miami. Projections suggest that 100 million additional mature trees in US cities (3 trees for every unshaded single family home) could save over $2 billion in energy costs per year.
- Trees lower local air temperatures by transpiring water and shading surfaces. Because they lower air temperatures, shade buildings in the summer, and block winter winds, they can reduce building energy use and cooling costs.
- Help to cool cities by reducing heat sinks. Heat sinks are 6-19 degrees F° warmer than their surroundings (Global Releaf GA). A tree can be a natural air conditioner. The evaporation from a single large tree can produce the cooling effect of 10 room size air conditioners operating 24 hours/day.
- USFS estimates the annual effect of well-positioned trees on energy use in conventional houses at savings between 20-25% when compared to a house in a wide-open area. (USFS meteorologist Gordon Heisler).

Urban Forests Can Extend the Life of Paved Surfaces

- The asphalt paving on streets contain stone aggregate in an oil binder. Without tree shade, the oil heats up and volatizes, leaving the aggregate unprotected.
- Vehicles then loosen the aggregate and much like sandpaper, the loose aggregate grinds down the pavement. Streets should be overlaid or slurry sealed every 7-10 years over a 30-40 year period, after which reconstruction is required.
- A slurry seal costs approximately $0.27/sq.ft. Or $50,000/linear mile. Because the oil does not dry out as fast on a shaded street as it does on a street with no shade trees, this street maintenance can be deferred. The slurry seal can be deferred from every 10 years to every 20-25 years for older streets with extensive tree canopy cover.

Urban Forests Can Increase Traffic Safety

- Trees can also enhance traffic calming measures, such as narrower streets, extended curbs, roundabouts, etc. Tall trees give the perception of making a street feel narrower, slowing people down. Closely spaced trees give the perception of speed (they go by very quickly) slowing people down. A treeless street enhances the perception of a street being wide and free of hazard, thereby increasing speeds. Increased speed leads to more accidents.
- Trees can serve as a buffer between moving vehicles and pedestrians.
- Street trees also forewarn drivers of upcoming curves. If the driver sees tree trunks curving ahead before seeing the road curve, they will slow down and be more cautious when approaching curves.

Urban Forests Can Improve Economic Sustainability

The scope and condition of a community's trees and, collectively, its urban forest, is usually the first impression a community projects to its visitors. A community's urban forest is an extension of its pride and community spirit.

Studies have shown that:

1. Trees enhance community economic stability by attracting businesses and tourists.
2. People linger and shop longer along tree-lined streets.
3. Apartments and offices in wooded areas rent more quickly and have higher occupancy rates.
4. Businesses leasing office spaces in developments with trees find their workers are more productive and absenteeism is reduced.

Urban Forests Can Increase Real Estate Values

- Property values increase 5-15% when compared to properties without trees (depends on species, maturity, quantity and location)
- A 1976 study that evaluated the effects of several different variables on homes in Manchester, Connecticut, found that street trees added about $2686 or 6% to the sale price of a home.
- A more recent study indicated that trees added $9,500, or more than 18 percent, to the average sale price of a residence in a suburb of Rochester, New York.

Urban Forests Can Increase Sociological Benefits

Two University of Illinois researchers (Kuo and Sullivan) studied how well residents of the Chicago Robert Taylor Housing Project (the largest public housing development in the world) were doing in their daily lives based upon the amount of contact they had with trees, and came to the following conclusions:

- Trees have the potential to reduce social service budgets, decrease police calls for domestic violence, strengthen urban communities, and decrease the incidence of child abuse according to the study. Chicago officials heard that message last year. The city government spent $10 million to plant 20,000 trees, a decision influenced by Kuo's and Sullivan's research, according to the *Chicago Tribune*.
- Residents who live near trees have significantly better relations with and stronger ties to their neighbors.
- Researchers found fewer reports of physical violence in homes that had trees outside the buildings. Of the residents interviewed, 14% of residents living in barren conditions have threatened to use a knife or gun against their children versus 3% for the residents living in green conditions.
- Studies have shown that hospital patients with a view of trees out their windows recover much faster and with fewer complications than similar patients without such views.

❑❑❑

Chapter–8

Mitigation of Pollution – The Plant Way

Pollution is the term used to denote the hindrances caused to living organisms by way of contamination of their physical environment. Pollution to air, water, soil etc. is the major problem faced by the living community. Measures to control the emission of pollution into air, water or soil will certainly reduce the level of pollutants. Mitigation of pollution can be best achieved by combining nature with technology that increases the effectiveness of plants in removing pollution. Use of vegetation is an effective means of pollution control and many researchers have reported their advantages in mitigating pollution.

So far, the main approach has been to dig the polluting chemicals out of the ground and transport them to a landfill. However, after a decade of research, scientists in the early twenty-first century found that hundreds of species of plants, along with the fungi and bacteria that inhabit the ecosystem around their roots, seek out and often break down chemical molecules that can harm most other life.

In the mid-1980s, Dr. B.C. Wolverton and fellow researchers at NASA conducted several studies to determine whether plants could halt indoor pollution and provide a natural way to deal with the problem. It has been suggested by **NASA** and the Associated Landscape Contractors of America (ALCA) that plants are major pollution-absorbing devices: the common indoor plants might provide a natural way of helping combat "SICK BUILDING SYNDROME". Common indoor plants may provide a valuable weapon in the fight against rising levels of indoor air pollution. These plants are not only decorative, but are also surprisingly useful in absorbing potentially harmful gases and cleaning the air inside modern buildings.

In 1989, NASA and the Associated Landscape Contractors of America followed up with a large-scale report, which concluded that "when plants and potting soil are constantly exposed to air containing such toxic chemicals as benzene, their capacity to continuously clean the air improves." Wolverton ultimately concluded that "low-light-requiring houseplants, along with activated carbon plant filters, have demonstrated the potential for improving indoor air quality by removing trace organic pollutants from the air in energy-efficient buildings.

It is true that plants remove carbon dioxide from the air, and the ability of plants to remove certain other pollutants from water is the basis for some pollution control methods. For example, in case of heavy metal pollution, there are sunflowers that capture uranium, ferns that thrive on arsenic, clovers that eat oil, and poplar trees that destroy dry-cleaning solvents. Vegetative strips are one of the means of controlling air pollution. Vegetative filter strips are areas that are planted with vegetation to remove sediments and other run-off from pollutants.

Foliage plants housed in pots containing a commercial, nonsterile potting soil mixture could reduce air concentrations of VOCs like formaldehyde, trichloroethylene and benzene, as well as carbon monoxide. Photosynthesis plays a role in this with the continuous exchange of gaseous substances between plant leaves and the surrounding atmosphere. Philodendrons and aloe vera were the most effective plants for removing formaldehyde; philodendrons and golden pothos were effective in removing benzene and carbon monoxide; and spider plants were effective in removing formaldehyde and carbon monoxide. Flowering plants such as gerbera daisy and chrysanthemums are superior in removing benzene in the atmosphere.

Engineering plants to remove pollution has also gained importance in the recent days. *Arabidopsis plant engineered with the* bacterial RDX pathway could clear a 150 μMolar solution of RDX (a toxic and explosive compound chemically hexa-hydro-1,3,5-trinitro-1,3,5-triazine) in less than a day. Use of plants is thus not only aesthetically pleasing but also serve as natures clean air machine to control pollution.

Introduction

Our earth is undoubtedly warming. This warming is largely the result of emissions of carbon dioxide and other Greenhouse Gases (GHG's) from human activities including industrial processes, fossil fuel combustion, and changes in land use, such as deforestation etc.

Besides outdoor, our indoor atmosphere is also polluted. The overall quality of indoor air in our homes and offices has been declining steadily during the past three decades. Concerns regarding energy conservation during the 1970s led to superior insulation materials, tight-fitting windows and doors, and other construction features which have effectively bottled up our living and work spaces. To protect ourselves, our economy, and our land from the adverse effects of climate change, we must reduce emissions of carbon dioxide and other greenhouse gases.

Indoor Pollution Management

Indoor atmosphere

The life style of the modern people has drastically changed; the food habits or living style of the people has gone very high. People spent their money in decorating houses in gorgeous manner. We see the houses are well furnished and filled with decorative materials; the room walls are shining because most expensive paints are used, the floors are covered with colorful carpets. Furniture like sofa, wooden chair, TV stand, shelves etc are crowded at every room. People spend about 80-90% of out times indoor only.

Health effects

There are various health effects due to these chemicals mostly volatile organic compounds. They are sick building syndromes, nervous problems and mental stress in adult and skin disorders, eye allergies and head ache in children. To have a healthy indoor atmosphere, plants can be effectively used.

Indoor pollutants

Some of the offending pollutants include biological contaminants, such as black mold, and gases like carbon monoxide and radon. However, "off-gassing" is another modern phenomenon which is contributing significantly to indoor air pollution. Off-gassing is the release of various organic compounds by some particularly common sources all around us, ranging from furniture and floor coverings to paper products, printed materials, paint, and simple plastic grocery bags. The off-gassed chemicals are basically used as adhesives and binding agents, solvents, coatings, fire-retardants, insulators, and so forth. Volatile organic compounds and their sources are listed below.

BENZENE found in: Inks, oils, paints, rubber, dyes, detergents, gasoline, pharmaceuticals, cigarette smoke, synthetic fibres.

Potential Health Effects: Skin and eye irritation, may be a contributing factor to chromosomal aberrations and leukemia in humans; chronic exposure to even low levels causes headaches, appetite loss, drowsiness, nervousness, psychological disturbances, anemia, bone marrow disease, carcinogenicity

TRICHLOROETHYLENE found in: Primarily used in the metal degreasing and dry-cleaning industries; also in printing inks, paints, lacquers, varnishes and adhesives.

Potential Health Effects: Irregular heart rhythm, Liver, Kidney and neurotoxicity, cancer. It's on the hazards list of the National Institute of Health list.

FORMALDEHYDE found in: Foam insulation, plywood, particle board, pressed wood products, wrinkle resisters, water repellents, fire retardants, adhesives, binders in floor coverings, carpet backing, permanent press clothing, cigarette smoke, natural gas, kerosene.

Potential Health Effects: Irritates mucous membranes of the eye, nose, and throat; can cause contact dermatitis, irritation of upper respiratory tract and eyes, headaches; can cause asthma and is suspected of causing a rare type of throat cancer.

Indoor Plants as purifiers

The aesthetic value of indoor plants is easily seen, however the unseen ability of Indoor plants to improve indoor air quality. Keeping plants around the home and office purify and renew our stale air by filtering out toxins, pollutants, harmful viruses, mould spores and the carbon dioxide we exhale, replacing these with life sustaining oxygen. In other words they literally suck the toxins out of the air.

Mechanism of pollutants removal by plants

Plants are effective in the adsorption of particulate contaminates (dust, soot, fibers) onto their leaf surface, but only absorb some smaller molecules into their tissues. Once on the leaf, these particulates should be washed off, probably outside. Plants create their own mini- ecosystems, in the air, and in the soil round their roots. Through the processes of photosynthesis, respiration, transpiration, and the activity of microorganisms in the soil, the environment around the plants is changed. Not only is carbon dioxide taken in through the leaves and oxygen produced, but the leaves and soil filter out harmful chemicals in the air. Transpiration produces higher humidity with the release of water vapor from the plants leaves.

Care for Indoor Plants

Light–

When choosing a particular a plant, consider its light requirements. If you can read a book in a room on a foggy day without the aid of artificial light, there is plenty of natural light to suit most plants.

Most plants do not care for bright direct sunlight, especially from south or west windows. Direct sunlight from a warm window will burn the foliage of most plants. Bright diffused light is best. Most house plants can, however, tolerate light from north and east windows.

Watering

The rule of thumb when watering indoor plants is to water only when the top inch of soil becomes dry. Give the plants a good soaking, enough so that water pours from drainage holes. Do not water again until soil surface becomes dry. This watering technique helps to leach fertilizer salts out of the soil. Salt build-up is often responsible for browning leaf tips on many plants, especially palms and spider plants.

Over-watering indoor plants can cause problems. Not only can you kill the plant, you also invite mold to form on the top of the soil. Worse yet, soggy soil attracts fungus gnats, irritating little flies that feed on moist, decaying potting soil. In high humidity climates such as ours it is best to maintain house plants in a potting soil that is not too heavy with peat moss.

Fertilization

Monthly fertilizing with a high nitrogen plant food will keep plants green and growing.

Cleaning the plants

At least once a month give your plants a good hosing down, either outside or in the shower. Be sure to wash the undersides of the leaves as well.

Removing household dust from the foliage allows the plants to "breathe" better. It also helps prevent infestations. Palms especially need their leaves washed regularly to deter spider mite infestation.

Do not use leaf shines of polishes to brighten up plants. These preparations clog the stomata, or leaf pores. Plants need to breathe in order to photosynthesize. If you keep plants well-fed and bathed they will produce their own natural glow.

Do not place indoor plants, especially palms, near drafty doors or windows. Pests like aphids, spider mites and mealy bugs easily blow in with the wind.

Every other week or so take a look at the undersides of leaves and the growing tips of your plants. Spider mites cause mottling or stippling of leaves. Aphids congregate at the growing tips and undersides of leaves.

If plants begin to develop stickiness on the leaves, suspect either aphids or scale, a regular spray of organic pesticides without damaging the plants.

Outdoor pollution

Loss of biodiversity poses one of the greatest challenges to the world community. Out of nearly 2.6 lakhs of flowering plants, above 60,000 taxa are facing extinction or under various degrees of endangerment The problem gets aggravated further due to manifold increase in the level of pollution as a consequence of rapid industrialization and urbanization. The rate of carbon emission has been increasing due to automobile exhaust and smokes from various industries. These industries are also releasing polluted water and effluents into the various water sources

Global warming and carbon emission

There can be no room any more for skepticism on global warming. "The warming of the climate system is unequivocal, as is now evident from increases in global average air and ocean temperatures, widespread melting of snow and ice and rising global mean sea level", says a report of the Intergovernmental Panel on Climate Change (IPCC) released on February, 2002. On the basis of analysis of ice cores spanning thousands of years the report concludes that anthropogenic emissions have resulted in a marked increase in atmospheric concentrations of carbon dioxide, methane and nitrous oxide since 1750 and now far exceed pre-industrialization values. The global increase in carbon dioxide concentrations, points out the report, is primarily because of fossil fuel use and land use change, while the increases in methane and nitrous oxide concentrations are because of agriculture. In particular the incrcease in CO_2 concentration from 280 ppm to 379 ppm in 2005 is far greater than the natural increase (from 180 to 300 ppm) over the last 650,000 years. During 1995 – 2005, there was 1.9 ppm growth rate in CO_2 level. The CO_2 radiative forcing increased by 20 per cent during 1995 – 2005, the largest change for any decade in atleast th last 200 years. According to findings based on improved satellite and in situ tide gauge measurements, the global average sea level rose 1.8 mm a year during 1961- 2003 (Ramachandran, 2007).

Trees and Benefits

- In 50 years one tree recycles more than $37,000 worth of water, provides $31,000 worth of erosion control, $62,000 worth of air pollution control, and produces $37,000 worth of oxygen.
- Two mature trees provide enough oxygen for a family of four.
- Trees help reduce the "greenhouse effect" by absorbing CO^2. One acre of trees removes 2.6 tons of CO^2 per year.
- Forest planting is one of the most cost-effective ways of reducing CO^2. To remove 1 pound of CO^2, planting tree costs less than 1 cent, developing more energy efficient appliances costs about 2 $^{1/2}$ cents, and developing more fuel-efficient cars costs about 10 cents.
- By cooling the air and ground around them, the shade from trees helps cool the Earth's temperature.
- Trees are good noise barriers, making a city and neighborhood quieter.
- Trees help prevent city flooding by catching raindrops and offsetting runoff caused by buildings and parking lots.
- Hospital patients heal faster; require shorter stays and fewer painkillers if room windows face trees.

- A tree-line buffer between fields and streams helps remove farming pollutants before they reach the water.
- Well placed trees help cut energy costs and consumption by decreasing air conditioning costs 10-50% & reducing heating costs as much as 4-22%.
- Trees are the longest living and largest living organisms on Earth.
- People who plant trees become healthier, better looking, richer, and have more friends (well maybe that's stretching it a bit) - plant a tree and find out!
- In deserts, leaves absorb moisture from the dew and frost of the cool nights and release it to cool the air during the warm days.
- Trees enhance the aesthetics of our environment. Their grandeur, tenacity, and beauty are probably the most enjoyable aspect of trees.
- Tree bark and fruit have many medicinal properties, which are still being discovered. In 50 years one tree recycles more than $37,000 worth of water, provides $31,000 worth of erosion control, $62,000 worth of air pollution control, & produces $37,000 worth of oxygen.
- Two mature trees provide enough oxygen for a family of four.
- Birds and animals use trees for their homes and shelter and as a source of food.
- One person causes about 10 tons of carbon dioxide to be emitted a year. One tree removes about 1 ton of CO_2 per year. Planting 30 trees per person will remove each that person's carbon debt for the year.
- Trees increase property values by 5 to 20% due to their landscaping value

Pollution

The chemicals or substances which causes harmful and deleterious effects on living organisms are called pollutants and the process is called pollution. The outdoor pollution may be classified based on the source of pollutants

1. Air pollution
2. Noise pollution
3. Water pollution
4. Soil pollution

Air pollution

In the post independence era as a consequence to rapid industrialization for attaining self sufficiency and random urbanization, the level of pollution has increased manifold causing environmental degradation. According to an estimate, coal based thermal power units in India alone contribute 13 million tonnes of fly ash, 8 million tonnes of particulates, 4,80,ooo tonnes of sulphur dioxide, 2,80,000 tonnes of nitrous oxide, 16,000 tonnes of CO and 5,000 tonnes of hydrocarbons to the atmosphere annually.

In addition, automobiles have further aggravated the problem. Presently there are around 50 million vehicles on the road in India and the number is bound to increase in the times to come (Dhar, 2000). Automobiles contribute 1.8 million tonnes of pollutants in the country annually and the worst affected are the metropolitan cities which receive 80% of the pollutants.

Landscaping with suitable plant species is an effective way for mitigating pollution. Earlier landscaping of urban areas used to be merely for aesthetics but in recent times the concept has changed having ts orientation to achieve duel effect i.e. bioaesthetics and phytoremediation which has considerably helped in ameliorating the environment.

Certain plant species are capable of filtering and absorbing gaseous pollutants. Studies have revealed that a green area of 500 m width surrounding a factory is capable of reducing sulphur dioxide concentration by 70%. Sulphur dioxide and nitrogen dioxide are soluble and get absorbed readily by plant while nitric acid and carbon monoxide are insoluble and absorbed slowly. Damp and wet surfaces of the plants enhance pollutant removal rate by 10% because under such conditions stems, branches, twigs and leaves are engaged in absorption process. Light has also pronounced effect in foliar removal of pollutants by influencing physiological activities and stomatal opening.

The tolerant species of plants function as pollution sink and therefore a number of environmental benefits can be derived by planting tolerant species of plants in polluted areas. For this purpose, evaluation of plant species with respect to their tolerance level to air pollution is essential.

$$\text{Air pollution tolerance index} = \frac{(A(T+P)+P)}{10}$$

A= Ascorbic acid, T = total chlorophyll, P= leaf extract $_pH$, R= relative water content of leaf.

Evergreen trees and their ATPI

Plant Species	PH(P)	RWC(R) (%)	APTI
Ficus glomerata	8.4	71	32
Pithecolobium dulce	6.0	87	28
Polyalthia longifolia	6.0	78	19
Ficus benghalensis	7.9	76	19
Nerium odorum	6.0	84	15
Eucalyptus citriodora	5.2	85	15

Deciduous trees and their ATPI

Plant Species	PH(P)	RWC(R) (%)	APTI
Ficus religiosa	8.2	87	34 * 2
Albizzia lebbek	6.2	47	31 * 2
Cassia fistula	5.9	63	27 * 2
Azadirachta indica	6.2	74	!9 * 2
Sapindus muckorossi	7.0	68	16 * 2
Tamarindus indica	4.0	86	15 * 2

Shrubs and their ATPI

Plant Species	PH(P)	RWC(R) (%)	APTI
Bougainvillea spectabillis	6.0	70	32
Poinsettia pulcherrima	5.9	77	25
Duranta plumieri	5.7	69	15
Murraya exotica	6.1	72	13
Lantana indica	7.5	33	6
Largerstroemia indica	4.3	42	4

Plants for dust pollution

Lot of dust and suspended particular matter are released into the atmosphere from different sources like cement factories, thermal power plants etc. In India dust pollutants comprise around 40% of the total air pollution. Dust particles can lead to allergic asthma, bronchitis and even fibrosis of the lungs.

Many plant species mainly tree and shrubs namely: Alstonia macrophylla,Butea monosperma, Cassia marginata, Cassia siamea,,Dalbergia sissoo, Diospyros embryopeteris, Drypetes roxburghii, Ficus bengalensis, F.infectoria, F.religiosa, Lagerstroemia thorelii, Madhuca longifolia, Peltophorum ferrugineum, Polyalthia longifolia, Shorea robusta, Tecona grandis, Thespesia populnae, Terminalia arjuna, T.muelleri and Thevetia nerifolia have dust trapping ability. The dust trapping ability of the plant species largely depend on on certain morphological characters such as branching habit, arrangement of leaves, better will be the dust trapping ability. It is the upper surface of the leaf which collects most of the dust particle but the lower surface also collects an appreciable amount.

Plants for noise pollution

Any sound having intensity above 65 decible becomes pollutant. People exposed to high level sound may suffer from insominia, cardiac diseases, psychiatric and nervous disorders etc. apart from loss of hearing ability.

For minimizing noise pollution due to vehicular traffic, trees may be planted in single or double row pattern to act as a physical barrier against the horizontal and vertical movement of sound waves. Plant species forming dense canopies are more effective because overlapping branches and leaves offer more resistance in minimizing the intensity of sound.

Designing buffers to reduce noise pollution

To reduce noise of moderate traffic in communities

- Plant belts of trees 7-17m wide along roadsides.
- Plant the nearest edge of the belt within 7-17m of the centre of the nearest 3-7m tall when mature
- Use 2-3m shrubs next to the road and back up tree rows a minimum of 3-7 m tall when mature
- The length of the tree belt should be twice as long as the distance from the road to the recipient of the noise.
- The buffer should also extend equal distance in both directions parallel to the road.

To reduce heavy vehicle noise in suburban or rural areas

- Plant belts of trees 20-35 m wide along roadsides.
- Plant the nearest edge of the belt within 20-35 m of the centre of the nearest 15 m tall when mature
- Use 2-3 m shrubs next to the road and back up tree rows a minimum of 3-7 m tall when mature
- The length of the tree belt should be twice as long as the distance from the road to the recipient of the noise.
- The buffer should also extend equal distance in both directions parallel to the road.

Trees for bio-remediation of urban pollution

Pollutants	**Species**
Gaseous Pollutants	*Pongamia pinnata, Haplophragma adenophyllum, Albizia lebbek, Polyalthia longifolia, Alstonia scholaris, Acacia auriculiformis*
Suspended Particulate matter	*Pongamia pinnata, , Albizia lebbek, Polyalthia longifolia, Alstonia scholaris, Acacia auriculiformis, Terminalia arjuna, Kigelllia pinnata, Cassia siamea,*
Automobile exhaust pollutants/Dust	*Pongamia pinnata, , Albizia lebbek, Polyalthia longifolia, Alstonia scholaris, Acacia auriculiformis, Ficus bengalensis, Peltophorum, Tectona grandis*
Noise Pollution	*Alstonia scholaris, Albizia lebbek, Azadirachta indica, Exythrina variegate, Bauhinia variegate, Cassia nodusa, Butea monosperma, Madhuca indica*

Lawn for pollution management

- 50 x 50 foot lawn releases enough oxygen for a family of four to breathe.
- Reduces air conditioning costs by up to 50 %
- Healthy front lawns of eight houses - cooling effect of about 70 tons of air conditioning - enough to cool 16 homes By reducing energy cost, emission of pollutants from air conditioners would be greatly reduced.

Plants for water pollution

In India, aquatic vascular plants like *Hydrilla verticillata, Spirodela polyrrhiza*, *Bacopa monnierii, Phragmetis karka* and *Scirpus lacustris* have benn found useful to treat chromium contaminated effluent and sludge from leather tanning industries. The aquatic or semi-aquatic vascular plants such as Water Hyacinth(*Eichhornia crassipes*), Pennyworth (*Hydrocotyle umbellata*), Duckweed *(Lemna minor*) and water velvet (*Azolla pinnata*) can take up Pb, Cu, Cd, Fe and HG from contaminated solutions. This ability is being utilized in many wetlands for removing heavy metals as well as organics from water (Raj and Pal,. 1999). Similarly water lilies (Nymphaea) can be used to restore the purity of rivers and water sources polluted with cadmium, mercury, nickel and cobalt by absorbing them.

Morphological and anatomical adaptations for pollutants absorption

There are certain morphological adaptations of the plants for tolerating pollutants in the atmosphere. The rough leaf surface, presence of hairy leaves, large leaf surface area is some of the morphological adaptations. Trichomes are the glandular hairs are present in the epidermis. These hairs protect the epidermis and stomata from pollutants. Damp and wet surfaces of the plants enhance pollutant removal by 10% because under such conditions stems, branches, twigs and leaves are engaged in absorption process. Light has also pronounced effect in foliar removal of pollutants by influencing physiological activities and stomatal opening.

Sulphur dioxide and nitrogen dioxide are soluble and absorbed readily by plant while nitric acid and carbon monoxide are very insoluble and absorbed slowly.

Cells are protected from reactive oxygen species by enzymatic and non enzymatic defense mechanisms. Defense against reactive oxygen species is provided by scavenging properties of molecules, such as ascorbic acid, Ütocopherol, phenolic compounds,and glutathione. Superoxide dismutases catalyze the reduction of superoxide to hydrogen peroxide. Hydrogen peroxide is then converted into water by the action of catalases and peroxidases.

Genetic engineering

The advances in genetic engineering have opened new vistas to en hance the biodegradable and reclamation abilities of the naturally occurring microorganisms and higher plants. Genetically-altered bacteria have become popular in checking oil spills the world over. Now, attempts are on to make plants that can accumulate metals reclaim degraded soil.

The poplar tree, genetically engineered with the bacterial mercuric reductase gene and capable of vaporising mercury from contaminated sites, was reported by a team of Canadian scientists. Trichloroethylene is a heavily used industrial degreaser that's made its way into groundwater because of improper disposal. Both unaltered poplars and the transgenic poplar plants produce the enzymes to break down trichloroethylene, C2HC13, into chloride ions — harmless salt that the plant sheds — and recombines the carbon and hydrogen with oxygen to produce water and carbon dioxide.

The transgenic poplar plants just do it a lot faster. The enzymes used to metabolize the contaminants are from a group called cytochrome P450 found in both plants and animals. Poplars have a lot of P450s and scientists hope to eventually sort them to find ways to manipulate the plant's own genes to ramp up pollution degradation. In the meantime they are conducting experiments inserting a gene that produces cytochrome P450 in mammalian livers, in this case the livers of rabbits. Poplar genes producing cytochrome P450 is expressed in all their cells, but not at the rates acheived by the transgenics.

In Indian mustard, the *E. coli* gene gsh 11, introduced by Yong and co-workers, was reported to have very fast biomass accumulation that led to accumulation of 40-90 per cent higher cadmium concentration in the transformed shoots. Bacterial merA gene, was transferred to yellow poplar trees (University of Georgia, US) to release mercury from the affected sites. In *T. caeruiescens*, work is underway to transfer genes from efficient hyper-accumulators for zinc accumulation by R. Chaney (USDA, Maryland, USA).

Non-degradable toxic chemicals, such as naphthalene, polychlorinated biphenyl, etc., can be degraded into salts, carbon-dioxide and water by some of the altered bacteria.

Bio- and phyto-remediation techniques are gaining importance throughout the world to improve the quality of the environment. In the US, site-specific clean-up of soil and water from toxins has commenced. Also in Europe and Japan, soil and water reclamation through bioremedials has been given high priority.

❑❑❑

FSC
www.fsc.org
MIX
Papier | Fördert gute Waldnutzung
FSC® C083411

Kolibri 360 GmbH
Ferdinand-Jühlke-Straße 7
99095 Erfurt, Deutschland
produktsicherheit@kolibri360.de